A Complete Guide to the Level 5 Diploma in Education and Training

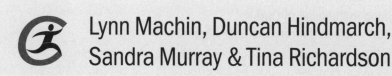

Lynn Machin, Duncan Hindmarch,
Sandra Murray & Tina Richardson

**FURTHER
EDUCATION**

First published in 2014 by Critical Publishing Ltd

British Library Cataloguing in Publication Data
A CIP record for this book is available from the British Library

ISBN: 978-1-909682-53-5

This book is also available in the following e-book formats:

MOBI ISBN: 978-1-909682-54-2
EPUB ISBN: 978-1-909682-55-9
Adobe e-book ISBN: 978-1-909682-56-6

Cover and text design by Greensplash Limited
Project Management by Out of House Publishing
Printed and bound in Great Britain by Bell & Bain, Glasgow

Critical Publishing
152 Chester Road
Northwich
CW8 4AL
www.criticalpublishing.com

MIX
Paper from
responsible sources
FSC® C007785

A Complete Guide to the Level 5 Diploma in Education and Training

FURTHER
EDUCATION

You might also like the following books in our *Further Education* series

A Complete Guide to the Level 4 Certificate in Education and Training
By Lynn Machin, Duncan Hindmarch, Sandra Murray and Tina Richardson
978-1-909330-89-4 Published September 2013

The A–Z Guide to Working in Further Education
By Jonathan Gravells and Susan Wallace
978-1-909330-85-6 Published September 2013

Dial M for Mentor: Critical Reflections on Mentoring for Coaches, Educators and Trainers
By Jonathan Gravells and Susan Wallace
978-1-909330-00-9 Published September 2012

Equality and Diversity in Further Education
By Sheine Peart
978-1-909330-97-9 Published May 2014

Inclusion in Further Education
By Lydia Spenceley
978-1-909682-05-4 Published June 2014

The Professional Teacher in Further Education
By Keith Appleyard and Nancy Appleyard
978-1-909682-01-6 Published April 2014

Teaching and Supporting Adult Learners
By Jackie Scruton and Belinda Ferguson
978-1-909682-13-9 Published June 2014

Understanding the Further Education Sector: A Critical Guide to Policies and Practices
By Susan Wallace
978-1-909330-21-4 Published September 2013

Most of our titles are also available in a range of electronic formats. To order please go to our website www.criticalpublishing.com or contact our distributor, NBN International, 10 Thornbury Road, Plymouth PL6 7PP, telephone 01752 202301 or email orders@nbninternational.com.

Contents

Acknowledgements

We, the authors, would firstly like to acknowledge the use within this text of the Microsoft Office PowerPoint registered trademark.

We would like to thank our families, friends and colleagues for their continued support during the writing of this book.

We also want to thank our publishers, Julia Morris and Di Page, for their professionalism, friendliness, guidance and support.

Finally, thank you for taking the time to read this book. We hope that you enjoy reading it and we wish you all the best with your studies.

Lynn, Duncan, Sandra and Tina

Meet the authors

 **Lynn Machin** is an Award Leader, Senior Lecturer and an MA, Ed.D, PhD Supervisor within the School of Education at Staffordshire University. Lynn has a variety of roles within initial teacher training in further education including developing the modules that make up the Diploma in Education award. Her particular research interest is the exploration of how students can learn to learn and develop as self-directed and autonomous learners. She has written and co-authored several books for teachers within FE, including *A Complete Guide to the Level 4 Certificate in Education and Training*.

 **Duncan Hindmarch** is Award Leader for and Senior Lecturer within the School of Education at Staffordshire University. With a background in teaching English for Speakers of Other Languages (ESOL), he has over 15 years of teaching experience. Duncan is a Senior Fellow of the Higher Education Academy and Fellow of the Institute for Learning and has led development and implementation of ESOL, Initial Teacher Training (ITE) and education programmes. Duncan has co-authored several books, including *A Complete Guide to the Level 4 Certificate in Education and Training*.

 **Sandra Murray** is an Advanced Practitioner and Curriculum Leader in the Department of Teacher Training at Newcastle-under-Lyme College. Sandra has a wide range of experience supporting and teaching practitioners in the lifelong learning sector and has been teaching on Initial Teacher Education (ITE) programmes since 2006. Her particular research interest is inspirational and outstanding teaching. She has written and co-authored several books for teachers within FE, including *A Complete Guide to the Level 4 Certificate in Education and Training*.

Tina Richardson is an Award Leader and Senior

Lecturer within the School of Education at Staffordshire University. Tina has taught in compulsory education, further education and higher education. For the last 15 years she has been involved in teacher training for FE, in particular the subject specialist qualifications for teachers. Her particular research interest is the use of meta-cognitive reading strategies in the Functional Skills classroom. As well as teacher training books, including *A Complete Guide to the Level 4 Certificate in Education and Training*, Tina has also co-authored a book on using e-readers in the classroom.

About this book

Welcome to this book, which has been written with you, the learner, in mind. If you are about to embark (or even if you are already enrolled) onto a level 5 Diploma in Education and Training (DET) qualification then this book is for you. The intention of this book is to support you in your studies as you work towards achieving your DET qualification. It does this through:

o coverage of the LSIS (2013) mandatory content in the level 5 DET qualification;

o alignment of chapters to the new 2014 Standards underpinning the level 5 DET qualification and as provided by the Education and Training Foundation;

o encouraging you to critically reflect upon your practice;

o incorporating information and tasks that can help you with your referencing and study skills;

o providing case study scenarios and examples;

o indicating sources of information for further in-depth study;

o being research informed and written by teacher educators with learners' needs in mind;

o providing critical questions and critical tasks throughout and at the end of each chapter;

o providing information regarding optional units;

o providing information about possible progression routes following achievement of the level 5 DET qualification.

The topics, questions and tasks within this book have been tailored to the demands of the level 5 DET qualification and other, similar, teacher training qualifications designed for trainees working within the further education and skills sector.

Each chapter begins by providing a visual concept map of the topics to be covered, professional links (for example to the new 2014 Standards) and definitions of some of the key terms within the chapter. Following a list of each chapter's objectives are points for reflection. The detailed text is accompanied by critical questions and tasks to encourage you to think more deeply about the issues or examine your practice, and a final section in each chapter provides you with an opportunity to check your understanding and assess your learning. Case studies are included throughout to bring the text to life and show how the theory can be applied to practice.

The penultimate chapter of the book provides information about possible progression from the level 5 DET qualification. It includes information about recognition of prior learning (RPL) which is a possible pathway for you to use credits gained from your DET qualification, or similar, towards other qualifications, including a BA or MA degree. The final chapter provides coverage of key study skills, including advice about reading critically, note taking, presenting your work and using Harvard referencing correctly.

Suggested answers for some of the questions within the *Check your understanding* sections can be found at the back of the book. There is also a helpful glossary of terms and acronyms (see Appendix 2) as well as appendices providing useful templates for key documents that are mentioned within some of the chapters.

Introduction

INTRODUCTION

All of the chapters within this book provide you with specific information about teaching and learning. However, it is important that you also have some background information about the sector and an understanding of the reasons for the seemingly constant change to teacher training within further education. This introductory chapter provides you with:

o   an understanding and appreciation of the historical background that led to the introduction of the level 5 Diploma in Education and Training (DET) qualification;

o   an outline of the purpose of the level 5 DET qualification;

o   an appreciation of the requirements of the level 5 DET qualification.

Terminology

The further education and skills sector refers to all education undertaken by learners aged 16 and over. Terms like post-compulsory education and the lifelong learning sector (LLS) encompass all post-compulsory education regardless of where it occurs, whereas further education (FE) generally refers to post-compulsory education that takes place within a college environment. These terms continually interchange with each other and the use of them is often dependent upon the shifting political landscape as well as when associated reports and literature were written. You are likely to hear all of these terms used by your colleagues and tutors; however, as the sector is now known as the further education and skills sector, for ease and brevity this book will use the term FE throughout.

Similarly, differences in the names given to teacher training provision within FE also exist. Variations in the terms used for this within literature, policy and reports include initial teacher training (ITT), initial teacher education (ITE) and post-compulsory education and training (PCET). Again for ease of brevity, this book will use the term ITE throughout. You will find a list of some of the abbreviations that are used in the further education sector at the back of this book (Appendix 2).

A SHIFTING LANDSCAPE

The further education and skills sector includes:

o   colleges (FE, sixth form and Special Educational Needs);

o   community learning and development;

o   higher education (HE);

o   work-based learning;

o   careers guidance.

Within these environments there exists an extensive range of subjects (Crawley, 2012) and learners are taught across a range of abilities from pre-entry (below level 1) to HE (level 7) according to the Qualifications Credit Framework (QCF). In order to teach such diverse groups of learners it is necessary to have an equally diverse teaching workforce and, due to continual political influences, this workforce has been, and continues to be, subject to constant change. A report, published by the 2020 Public Services Hub (PSH) in conjunction with the Learning and Skills Improvement Services (LSIS) in 2011, suggested that the future of the further education and skills sector sits between two long-term futures, ie

One future in which liberalisation and spending cuts create a culture of retrench-ment and policy incoherence; where market mechanisms create winners and losers without engaging citizens; where further education is pushed and pulled by more powerful local players.

Another future that is fundamentally more collaborative, networked, and socially productive; where colleges are incubators of social value and hubs for service integration; where further education serves the needs of learners through being a creative partner in local growth and service reform agendas.

(PSH and LSIS, 2011, p 7)

The report, initiated by Sir Andrew Foster in 2010, focuses on the second of the two futures illustrated above. It posits that a focus on social productivity can provide '*a fresh approach to policy and practice that can give practitioners and policymakers the means to make sense of the change around them, and begin shaping new realities on the ground*' (PSH/LSIS, 2011, p 8). This report, like many of its predecessors, focuses on ways in which changes in government ideologies and policies can influence changes in FE. As Table 1 illustrates, these changes, certainly during the last two decades, have focused on the government's vision for high quality teaching that results in learners being equipped with the skills to work in an increasingly competitive national and global marketplace.

Table 1 Key documents and reports (continued on pages 4 and 5)

Date	Title	Comments
1944	Butler Act	This Act introduced a tripartite system of secondary education, ie grammar, secondary modern and technical schools.
1944	McNair Report	This report followed the Butler Act and raised concerns about deficiencies in the system of recruiting and training teachers, particularly those involved in teaching post-compulsory education.
1957	Willis Jackson Report (1957)	Promoted the concept of a qualified post-compulsory workforce.
1966	Russell Report (1966)	Continued to build on the concept of a qualified post-compulsory workforce.
1972	James Report (National Archives Cabinet Papers, 1971–72)	Promoted post-compulsory teacher training being accredited by universities.
1992	Further and Higher Education Act (National Archives Cabinet Papers, 1992)	Transferred responsibility of funding and governing post-compulsory education from LEAs to the FEFC, leading to a more economic and cost-efficient approach.

Date	Title	Comments
1998	FENTO Standards (Lingfield, 2012)	FENTO implemented a set of post-compulsory teacher training Standards. Awarding bodies and universities reviewed their provision in line with these Standards. Although sporadic, training of teaching staff increased. These Standards were rolled out nationally in 2001.
2002	Success for All Report (DfES, 2002)	The first of several reports suggesting that post-compulsory teacher training be reviewed and that properly trained teachers could improve the UK's workforce and economic prospects.
2003	Initial Teacher Training of Further Education Teachers (HMI 1762) (Ofsted, 2003)	The report concluded that FENTO provided a good baseline of what was required of teachers but lacked any ethos of professional development.
2004	Equipping our Teachers for the Future (DfES, 2004)	Pivotal in the implementation of the LLUK and the introduction of a new suite of ITE qualifications. This report also noted that training beyond qualified teaching status was necessary in order for teachers to be up to date with learners' needs.
2005	Foster Report, Realising the Potential (Foster, 2005)	Stressed the need to address the issues of an ageing workforce and the need to improve vocational and pedagogic skills through comprehensive workforce planning.
2006	Raising Skills, Improving Life Chances (DfES, 2006)	Considered that the UK's economic future depended on productivity as a nation and that FE providers were central to achieving this, but was not currently achieving its full potential as the powerhouse of a high skills economy.
2006	Prosperity for All in a Global Economy – World Class Skills (Leitch, 2006)	Prosperity for all could be achieved through a national training programme for those teaching in the LLS.
2007	LLUK Standards (LLUK, 2007)	These replaced the FENTO Standards.
2007	Further Education Teachers' Qualifications (England, No 2264)	These regulations stipulated that all teachers working in the LLS needed to be registered with the IfL and submit evidence of qualification and annual continual professional development. All lecturers joining the sector after 2001 needed to become qualified within their identified role.

Date	Title	Comments
2009	Enquiry into Teacher Training in Vocational Education (Skills Commission, 2009)	Specifically the enquiry set out to examine whether teachers in the LLS were being trained in the skills to deliver the emerging 14–19 vocational curricula – and proposed the merger of the General Teaching Council and the IfL in order for those working within the LLS to have parity of qualifications with teachers in schools.
2009	Workforce Strategy Report (LLUK, 2009)	Set out priorities for training teachers including the need to employ a diverse range of teachers with backgrounds and vocational skills that align with the learners that they teach.
2009	Skills for Growth (BIS, 2009)	This document proposed phasing out funding for the IfL and the membership fee payable by trainees and teachers.
2011	Wolf Report (Wolf, 2011)	This report considered how vocational education for 14–19 year-olds could be improved and promoted the concept of FE teaching in schools to ensure that young people are taught by those best suited to do so.
2011	Education Strategy 2020 (World Bank, 2011)	Impacted on the future of teacher training in order to meet its global strategic objectives as the UK would benchmark learners' performance against a variety of comparator countries.
2011	The Further Education and Skills Sector in 2020 (PSH and LSIS, 2011)	This report focuses on the future of the further education and skills sector, specifically in relation to its social productivity approach to education.
2012	Lingfield Review (Lingfield, 2012)	This report recommended the deregulation of ITE and suggested that the regulations had not made the intended impact.
2012	Consultation on the Revocation of the Further Education Workforce Regulations (BIS, 2012)	A response in relation to the proposed revocation of regulatory teacher training.
2013	Qualifications Guidance for Awarding Organisations: Level Five Diploma in Education and Training (LSIS, 2013c)	A new framework of units and credits for initial teacher education was introduced.
2014	The Education and Training Foundation	A new set of Standards was rolled out.

> ### *Critical question*
>
> Why have all of these policies and reports been necessary?

> ### *Comment*
>
> You will find some reasons provided below as well as by looking at some of the readings suggested at the end of the chapter and by doing some research.

Background and reasons for some of the changes in FE

Although attempts at educating the working classes, albeit to a limited extent, can be traced back for several centuries it was not until the 1940s that any real concerns were raised about the quality of the teaching within further education. Both the Butler Act (1944) and the McNair Report (1944) identified inadequacies within further education. Both also presented the notion of appropriate training for teachers within FE and were pivotal in the subsequent provision of short training courses. These courses focused on developing teachers' subject specialisms (IfL, 2006) rather than developing their pedagogical skills (Orr and Simmons, 2010).

Further reports, for example the Willis Jackson Report (1957) and the Russell Report (1966) continued to emphasise the need for robust further education teacher training courses; the courses that were available were mainly focused on subject specialisms and were voluntary rather than mandatory. A pivotal change came about in April 1992 when, in order to give FE colleges more autonomy and responsibility for growth in student numbers, the implementation of the Further and Higher Education Act resulted in the incorporation of FE colleges. Responsibility for FE colleges transferred from Local Education Authorities (LEAs) to the Further Education Funding Council (FEFC), which in 2000 became the Learning and Skills Council (LSC) (Armitage et al., 2003). In April 2010 this was replaced by the Skills Funding Agency. It was the function of the LSC to ensure that high quality post-16 provision was available to *meet the needs of employers, individuals and communities'* (DfES, 1999, p 23). With this mandate and with post-compulsory education being increasingly profiled by the Labour government's (1997–2010) belief that improvement to the teaching and learning provision within FE was necessary for the development of a *'world leading education system that would be at the heart of national priorities for economy and society'* (DIUS, 2007, p 2), the gaining of qualified FE teacher status became increasingly important to those spearheading these initiatives.

Changes to Standards and qualifications

The Labour government's belief that raising the quality of teaching would lead to a better qualified national and global workforce was instrumental in the implementation of the Further Education National Training Organisation (FENTO) which swiftly rolled out a set of Standards. These Standards provided a good baseline of what was required of teachers but lacked any ethos of professional development (Ofsted, 2003). Following a series of yet more government reports (DfES, 2006; Leitch, 2006; Foster, 2005; DfES, 2004; see Table 1) FENTO was replaced by Lifelong Learning UK (LLUK) which, in 2007, rolled out a new set of Standards to replace those implemented by FENTO.

The LLUK (2007) Standards contained core units of assessment and learning outcomes that were designed with the intention of providing a benchmark of the skills and attributes required by trainees in order for them to become qualified (DfES, 2004). As reported by the Skills Commission (2009, p 4), education within FE could only be as good as those teaching within it and a qualified workforce would improve the retention and achievement of learners and enable them to work and to compete in a globalised economy and working environment. The LLUK (2007) Standards and associated units of assessment and learning outcomes were nested within the following generic teaching qualifications:

o   Preparing to Teach in the Lifelong Learning Sector (PTLLS) – level 3 or 4;

o   Certificate in Teaching in the Lifelong Learning Sector (CTLLS) – level 3 or 4;

o   Diploma in Teaching in the Lifelong Learning Sector (DTLLS) – level 5.

Trainees needed to achieve a PTLLS qualification which provided them with an initial licence to practise. Then, dependent on whether they were in an associate or full teaching role as defined by LLUK (2007), trainees needed to achieve either a CTLLS or DTLLS qualification. Trainees who achieved a CTLLS qualification could apply for Associate Teacher of Learning and Skills (ATLS) status and trainees who achieved a DTLLS qualification could apply for Qualified Teacher of Learning and Skills (QTLS) status. As part of the application process for either ATLS or QTLS trainee (now qualified) teachers needed to evidence 30 hours (pro rata if they were part time) of professional development and be registered with the Institute for Learning (IfL).

However, although the impetus for the LLUK (2007) Standards was to develop and ensure the quality of the teaching provision within FE and was seen by many to have, at least in part, begun to achieve this aim (Crawley, 2012) they, like the FENTO Standards, were, just a few years after their inception, deemed to be *'inadequate'* (Lingfield, 2012, p 24) and in September 2012, amended workforce regulations meant that FE teachers did not have to be members of the IfL (LSIS, 2013a, p 4). From March 2013, LLUK was replaced by LSIS, which, later in 2013, was replaced by the Education and Training Foundation (ETF).

The new approach to ITE *'did not need to rely upon government regulation but rather gave the sector some autonomy to decide for itself the best way to raise, and to maintain, standards'* (LSIS, 2013a, p 4). LSIS were tasked with *'simplifying and renaming the teaching qualifications'* (LSIS, 2013a, p 4) and from this, and within the QCF, emerged several new qualifications:

o   Award in Education and Training – level 3 (12 credits);

o   Certificate in Education and Training (CET) – level 4 (36 credits);

o   Diploma in Education and Training (DET) – level 5 (120 credits).

This book covers the mandatory requirements of the DET qualification. Links to further information about the Award and the Certificate qualifications can be found at the end of this introduction.

WHAT IS THE LEVEL 5 DIPLOMA IN EDUCATION AND TRAINING QUALIFICATION?

The purpose of the DET qualification is to equip trainee teachers with the skills necessary to work in a range of contexts within FE. It might be that the qualification you are taking has a different title than a level 5 DET. Although awarding organisations will use the level 5 DET title (as determined by the QCF), higher education institutions (HEIs) can accredit and validate their own teacher training qualifications which are then quality assured by the Framework for Higher Education Qualifications (FHEQ). These qualifications are mapped to the same Standards and learning outcomes as those presented in the level 5 DET qualification. A common title, and one that is recognised by LSIS as being equivalent to the level 5 DET qualification, is Certificate of Education in Post Compulsory Education and Training. Furthermore, many HEIs also map the Standards and learning outcomes to higher level teacher training qualifications such as:

○ Professional Graduate Certificate in Teaching in the Lifelong Learning Sector (PGCE) – level 6;

○ Post Graduate Certificate in Teaching in the Lifelong Learning Sector (PGCE) – level 7.

The level 5 DET qualification is suitable for both in-service and pre-service delivery modes:

○ pre-service: this route is for trainees who are not employed in the sector but do have access to teaching hours and a range of learning encounters. These teaching hours are often through a placement being provided for them by their award tutor;

○ in-service: this route is for trainees who are currently employed as teachers, ie trainees who are receiving on-the-job training and are work-based learners.

Level and size of the DET qualification

In order to be accredited with a DET qualification you will need to achieve:

○ 120 credits at levels 4 and 5, with a '*minimum of 20 credits and a maximum of 60 credits at level 4*' (according to the guidance for HEIs; LSIS, 2013b, p 7).

One unit of credit is equal to 10 notional hours of learning (Ofqual, 2013).

The level of the DET qualification has been determined using the QCF. The QCF ranges from '*entry level to level 8*' (Ofqual, 2013, p 1). Each of these levels is categorised according to the level of '*difficulty and the standards of knowledge, skills and competence*' (Ofqual, 2013, p 1) that are required in order to achieve the learning outcomes and requirements for any qualification. The level 5 DET qualification is made up of (see Figure 1):

○ 75 credits from Group A. Within Group A are the mandatory units that you must pass to achieve your level 5 DET qualification;

○ 45 credits from Group B. Within Group B is a selection of optional units that you (or maybe your tutor) can choose from. Whichever units you (or your tutor) choose they must add up to at least 45 credits. More information about the optional units can be found in Appendix 1.

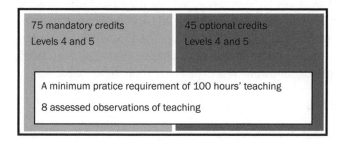

Figure 1 Level 5 Diploma in Education and Training (QCF) – 120 credits
Source: LSIS (2013b, p 23)

The topics contained within the mandatory units (Table 2), are covered in this book. There are similarities between some of the topics in the mandatory units and those in some of the optional units, for example those relating to behaviour, inclusive practice, quality assurance and action research, so this book can also help you in your understanding and study of these.

Table 2 Mandatory units of the DET

Mandatory units – Group A *75 credits must be achieved from this group*	Credit value	Level
Teaching, learning and assessment in education and training	20	4
Developing teaching, learning and assessment in education and training	20	5
Theories, principles and models in education and training (Note that achievement of this unit is a pre-requisite unit *Developing teaching, learning and assessment in education and training*)	20	5
Wider professional practice in education and training	15	5

Source: LSIS (2013c, pp 14–15)

It is possible that only certain optional units will be available from your initial teacher training institution. Your tutor will advise you about the optional units that are available to you as well as those which are the most appropriate for you in relation to the context in which you teach. In time it is possible that more optional units will become available, and again your tutor will advise you about these. You will find a link to LSIS and the mandatory and optional units available in the reference section at the end of this introduction.

All of the units are underpinned by a set of Standards that, as noted in Table 1, were introduced by the Education and Training Foundation in May 2014. You will need to demonstrate your ability to apply these Standards to your practice. The topics covered within this book can help you to do this. You will also find that each chapter maps the Standards to the learning outcomes being discussed within it and as is appropriate to do so.

Required teaching hours

The level 5 DET qualification is about developing and improving your practical skills and therefore you will need to have access to at least 100 hours of teaching practice. This teaching should be sufficiently varied as to provide you with opportunities to experience a range of teaching encounters. LSIS (2013b, p 8) suggests that practice should be with groups and individual learners and should encompass:

○   different teaching practice locations/settings/contexts;

○   teaching across more than one level;

○   teaching a variety of learners;

○   teaching individuals and groups;

○   experience of non-teaching roles; and

○   gaining subject-specialist knowledge through workplace mentoring.

Observation of your practice

In order to monitor your progress a minimum of eight observations, totalling a minimum of eight hours, need to take place throughout the whole of your course of learning and, although developmental, you will need to demonstrate that you have met a required standard of practice. Each observation must be a minimum of '*30 minutes' duration*' (LSIS, 2013b, p 9). Specifically, Chapter 8 offers guidance about how you can prepare for your observations and what you can expect to happen during and after the observation process.

SUMMARY

You can see from the information provided in this introduction that, as trainee FE teachers, you belong to a sector that is constantly reshaping itself in line with government ideologies and policies. It is continually striving to make a difference and to train and to produce qualified and skilled teachers who can provide their learners with a quality education that will equip them with the skills, attitudes and attributes to live and work in modern society. By embarking on the DET or equivalent qualification you are taking an important step to becoming one of these teachers. This book will support you in your studies and as you progress in your teaching career.

 TAKING IT FURTHER

In addition to the literature already commented upon in this chapter you may find the following of interest.

Excellence Gateway, *Addressing Literacy, Language, Numeracy and ICT Needs in Education and Training. Defining the Minimum Core of Teachers' Knowledge, Understanding and Personal Skills*. [Online]. Available at: www.excellencegateway. org.uk/node/12019 (accessed May 2014).

IfL (2009) *Review of CPD, Making a Difference for Teachers, Trainers and Learners*. London: Institute for Learning.

LSIS (2013) *Qualifications Guidance for Awarding Organisations: Level Four Certificate in Education and Training*. Coventry: LSIS.

LSIS (2013) *Qualifications Guidance for Awarding Organisations: Optional Units for QCF Education and Training Qualifications*. [Online]. Available at: www. excellencegateway.org.uk/node/65 (accessed May 2014).

Lucas, N, Nasta, T and Rogers, L (2009) *Evaluating How the LLUK/SVUK Assessment Regime Is Shaping ITT Curricula and the Professional Development of Trainees*. London: UCET.

Machin, L (2009) *Language and Literacy, Minimum Core, Audit and Test*. Exeter: Learning Matters.

Machin, L, Hindmarch, D, Richardson, T and Murray, S (2013) *A Complete Guide to the Level 4 Certificate in Education and Training*. Northwich: Critical Publishing.

Murray, S (2009) *Information, Communication, Technology, Minimum Core, Audit and Test*. Exeter: Learning Matters.

Smithers, A and Robinson, P (2000) *Further Education Re-formed, Microsoft Reader*. London: Routledge.

REFERENCES

Armitage, A, Bryant, R, Dunnill, R, Flannagan, K, Hayes, D, Hudson, A and Kent, J (2003) *Working in Post-Compulsory Education*. Buckingham: Open University Press.

BIS (2009) *Skills for Growth, The National Skills Strategy*. [Online]. Available at: http:// webarchive.nationalarchives.gov.uk/+/http:/www.cabinetoffice.gov.uk/media/310446/ skills_strategy.pdf (accessed 30 June 2014).

BIS (2012) *Consultation on the Revocation of the Further Education Workforce Regulations*. London: Department of Business, Innovation and Skills.

Butler Act (1944) *The Cabinet Papers 1915–1982*. [Online]. Available at: www. nationalarchives.gov.uk/cabinetpap (accessed May 2014).

Crawley, J (2012) 'On the brink' or 'designing the future'? Where next for Lifelong Learning Initial Teacher Education? *Journal to Inform and Improve Practice*, 4(1): 2–12.

DfES (1999) *Learning to Succeed: A New Framework for Post-16 Learning*. London: HMSO.

DfES (2002) *Success for All, Reforming Further Education and Training*. London: DfES.

DfES (2004) *Equipping Our Teachers for the Future*. London: DfES.

DfES (2006) *Raising Skills, Improving Life Chances*. London: DfES.

DIUS (2007) *The Further Education Teachers' Qualifications (England)*. London: HMSO.

Foster, A (2005) *Realising the Potential: A Review of the Future Role of Further Education Colleges, Report Summary*. Nottingham: DfES.

IfL (2006) *Towards a New Professionalism*, IfL Annual Conference. London: Institute for Learning.

Leitch, S (2006) *Leitch Review, Prosperity for All in the Global Economy: World Class Skills*. www.hm-treasury.gov.uk/leitch (accessed May 2014).

Lingfield, R (2012) *Professionalism in Further Education, Interim Report*. London: Department for Business, Innovation and Skills.

LLUK (2007) *New Overarching Professional Standards for Teachers, Trainers and Tutors*. London: LLUK.

LLUK (2009) *The Workforce Strategy Report for the Further Education Sector in England, 2007–2012 (revised)*. London: LLUK.

LSIS (2013a) *Teaching and Training Qualifications for the Further Education and Skills Sector in England: Guidance for Employees and Practitioners*. Coventry: Learning Skills Improvement Services.

LSIS (2013b) *Teaching and Training Qualifications for the Further Education and Skills Sector in England, Guidance for Higher Education Institutions*. Coventry: Learning Skills Improvement Services.

LSIS (2013c) *Qualifications Guidance for Awarding Organisations: Level Five Diploma in Education and Training*. Coventry: Learning Skills Improvement Services.

McNair Report (1944) *Report of the Committee Appointed by the President of the Board of Education to Consider the Supply, Recruitment and Training of Teachers and Youth Leaders*. London: HSMO.

National Archives Cabinet Papers (1971–72) *Committee of Inquiry into Teacher Training (James Committee): Minutes, Papers and Report*. [Online]. Available at: http://discovery. nationalarchives.gov.uk/SearchUI/Details?uri=C6944 (accessed 11 June 2014).

National Archives Cabinet Papers (1992) *Further and Higher Education Act*. [Online]. Available at: www.legislation.gov.uk/ukpga/1992/13/introduction (accessed 11 June 2014).

Ofqual (2013) *Qualifications and Credit Framework*. [Online]. Available at: www.ofqual.gov. uk/qualifications-and-assessments/qualification-frameworks/ (accessed May 2014).

Ofsted (2003) *The Initial Training of Further Education*. [Online]. Available at: www.ofsted.gov.uk/Ofsted-home/Publications-and-research/Browse-all-by/Education/Teachers-and-teacher-training/Phases/Post-compulsory/The-initial-training-of-further-education-teachers-2003 (accessed 27 April 2014).

Orr, K and Simmons, R (2010) Dual identities: the in-service teacher trainee experience in the English further education sector. *Journal of Vocational Education and Training*, 62(1): 75–88.

PSH and LSIS (2011) *The Further Education and Skills Sector in 2020: A Social Productivity Approach*. London: RSA.

Russell Report (1966) *The Supply and Training of Teachers for Further Education*. London: Department of Education and Science.

Skills Commission (2009) *Skills Commission Inquiry into Teacher Training in Vocational Education*. London: Skills Commission.

Willis Jackson Report (1957) *The Supply and Training of Teachers in Technical Colleges*. London: HMSO.

Wolf, A (2011) *Review of Vocational Education, the Wolf Report*. London: Department for Education.

World Bank (2011) *Learning for All: Investing in People's Knowledge and Skills*. Washington, DC: World Bank Group Education Strategy 2020.

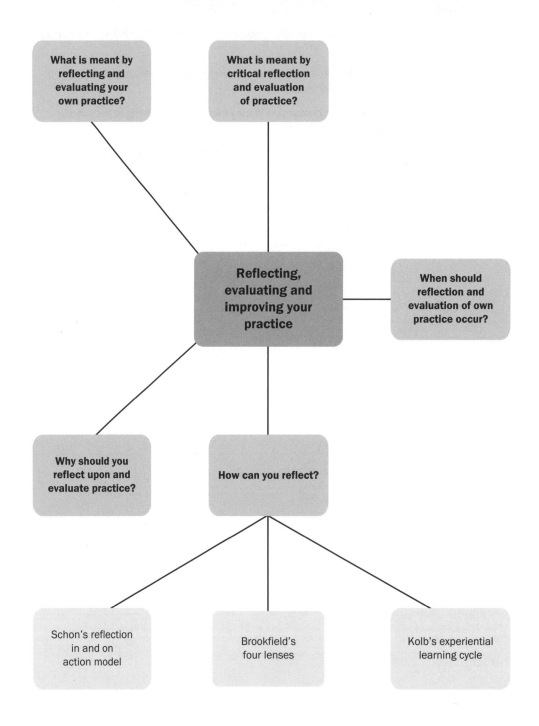

1 Reflecting, evaluating and improving your practice

What is meant by reflecting and evaluating your own practice?

What is meant by critical reflection and evaluation of practice?

Reflecting, evaluating and improving your practice

When should reflection and evaluation of own practice occur?

Why should you reflect upon and evaluate practice?

How can you reflect?

Schon's reflection in and on action model

Brookfield's four lenses

Kolb's experiential learning cycle

PROFESSIONAL LINKS

This chapter assists with your understanding of the following LSIS (2013, p 28) mandatory content:

○ theories and models of reflection;

○ theories and models of evaluation;

○ methods of evaluation;

○ using feedback from learners and others;

○ identifying areas for improvement in own practice.

This chapter also contributes to the following Professional Standards as provided by the ETF (2014):

Professional values and attributes

Develop your own judgement of what works and does not work in your teaching and training.

1   *Reflect on what works best in your teaching and learning to meet the diverse needs of learners*

2   *Evaluate and challenge your practice, values and beliefs*

10   *Evaluate your practice with others and assess its impact on learning*

A list of all of the Standards can be found at the back of this book (Appendix 7).

KEY DEFINITIONS

Cognition	The acquisition of knowledge through reasoning.
Critical reflection	Challenging assumptions and deliberating on an event or action and giving consideration to how well it went and what could be done differently next time.
Critical thinking	Thinking that is informed by evidence and that has a purpose in mind.

→

Groupthink	The practice of thinking or making decisions as a group, resulting typically in unchallenged, poor-quality decision making.
Meta-cognition	Thinking about your thinking.
Theories in use	The incorporation and use of prior learning and learned theories in order to make informed or in-action decisions.

INTRODUCTION

Reflection and evaluation may be something that you don't engage in as much as you would like to or as much as you should in your role as a teacher. This chapter, through its alignment to literature, asking questions and providing activities, is designed to support you in your understanding of how to apply reflection and evaluation to develop your practice. It therefore aims to support you in:

○ identifying, exploring and critiquing some of the key theories and models of reflection;

○ identifying, exploring and critiquing some of the key theories and models of evaluation;

○ considering approaches to evaluation;

○ developing your use of feedback from learners and others effectively;

○ identifying and developing your skills of critical reflection and evaluation of your practice.

STARTING POINT

What do you already know about reflecting and evaluating your own practice?

○ What do you currently understand by the term *reflection of practice*?

○ What do you currently understand by the term *evaluation of practice*?

○ In relation to your role as a teacher what issues do you normally reflect on?

○ What models of reflective practice are you already aware of?

○ Is reflection the same as thinking?

WHAT IS MEANT BY REFLECTING AND EVALUATING YOUR OWN PRACTICE?

There is a wealth of literature and information available regarding what is meant by reflecting and evaluating practice. For example, Donald Schön (2002) describes reflective practice as a process in which teachers engage in order for them to consider an issue. Some theorists (eg Argyris and Schön, 1978; Kolb, 1984; Brookfield,1995; Moon, 2006) suggest that reflecting and evaluating own practice relates to a continuous cycle of self-observation and self-evaluation in order for teachers to understand their own actions and the reactions they prompt in themselves and in learners. These views, along with others (discussed later in this chapter), encapsulate the notion of reflection being a process of analysis and evaluation through the use of a variety of strategies. In the context of teaching and learning these strategies include those that support your ability to *critically reflect* upon your practice.

Critical task

Carry out your own research to see what other definitions of reflective practice you can discover. How are they similar to and different from the ones you have just read?

WHAT IS MEANT BY CRITICAL REFLECTION AND EVALUATION OF PRACTICE?

Critical reflection requires you to develop and to use your meta-cognition (thinking about thinking) skills. Evaluation requires you to use available evidence, facts and views in order to make a judgement about something. So you need to reflect on your actions, issues and/or situations and also evaluate the outcomes and any impact of your actions, issues and/or situations. You can do this by asking more questions and also by being more questioning; that is developing your ability to enquire and to use analytical and evaluative skills in relation to your cognitive (thinking) and affective (feeling) domains (Chapter 7 has more details about these domains). Being critically reflective and exploring your practice and experiences through the use of your cognitive and affective domains is important because they can help you to identify assumptions, analyse arguments, aid your ability to ask yourself questions and identify how you can improve your performance as a learner and as a teacher (Anderson et al., 2001, p 2). For example, as a teacher you will regularly ask yourself the following question: *How well did today's lessons go and what evidence am I using to make an informed judgement about this?* Thinking about the lesson is important. However, for reflection to be critical and to serve a purpose your thinking needs to go beyond superficiality and needs to be a deep and intense process whereby probing questions are asked and pre-held assumptions are challenged (Brookfield, 1995). Reflecting critically about experiences that have occurred in your practice as well as acknowledging the feelings that you have in relation to them enable *new* thinking and *new* ideas to be formed and it is these *new* concepts that allow *new* experiences to occur (Gibbs, 1988).

HOW CAN YOU REFLECT?

Developing your skills to critically reflect and your ability to evaluate actions and situations more effectively involves your capacity to ask yourself and others, as Brookfield (1995) suggests, probing questions and to challenge pre-held assumptions. This capacity can be developed through building your own learning power and aptitude to know what it is that you actually need to learn (Claxton, 2006). This can be achieved through thinking about the knowledge and skills that you currently have and what skills and knowledge you might need to have in order to develop as a reflection practitioner. You then need to develop strategies to gain these skills and knowledge. One useful strategy is to use one or more of the many models that exist to help you to reflect and evaluate your practice. For example, the models presented by Schön (2002), Brookfield (1995) and Kolb (1984) are just three models, amongst others, that can assist you in this process.

Schön's reflection *in* and *on* action model

Schön (2002) contends that the ability to reflect is one of the defining characteristics of professional practice. He considers that the capacity to reflect *in* action (ie while you are actually doing something) together with *on* action (ie reflecting after an activity or event) is an important combination. Reflecting *in* action may be related to the actual mechanics of teaching (for example, managing a question and answer activity that is not going as well as anticipated) and reflecting *on* action may be related to post-lesson consideration about what went well and what could have been done better.

It can be difficult to reflect when you are actually doing something as, due to your involvement in the experience, you are unable to stand back from it, de-personalise it and give yourself time to stop and think. Reflection is not an automatic process and is made more difficult by the fact that you might need to challenge some deeply held beliefs and views. Therefore, Schön (2002) suggests that effective reflection needs the involvement of another person who is able to ask you appropriate questions so that your thoughts are not continually driven by espoused theories or theories in use. Espoused theories are the ones that you think you use while theories in use are the ones that actually align with what it is you actually do.

According to Argyris and Schön (1978) through your lifetime you will have developed mental maps. These mental maps are influenced, and have been influenced, by your attitudes and beliefs. It is these mental maps (even those that you may have forgotten about) rather than any theories that you espouse to use, that influence your actions regarding given situations. For example, you might consider yourself to use an adult–adult style of communication with your learners whereas, actually, you use a parent–child approach. Or, you may consider yourself to be a democratic leader but in reality your actions are those of an autocratic leader. Theories in use inform your actions and might, when you reflect *on* action, not necessarily be the best or only action you could take (Schön, 2002).

Critical reflection involves what Argyris and Schön (1978) describe as double-loop learning rather than single-loop learning. With single-loop learning your thinking centres around the attitudes, beliefs and values that you currently hold and these govern the variables which inform your actions (Argyris and Schön, 1978). When you question these variables you are reflecting using a double-loop learning approach and doing this can result in a change of thinking and subsequently in your actions.

 Case study

Susan, who teaches functional skills, was finding the new term difficult. In one particular class several of her learners were displaying consistently poor behaviour and causing disruptions in the class. She was unsure why this was happening as she had prepared well for the class and had included group tasks and scheduled time for questions and answers. She explains her concerns about the disruptive behaviour to her line manager who, although demonstrably sympathetic, provides no guidance beyond asking to remain informed about the situation.

Critical questions

What might the views of learners and other teachers be about the situation outlined in the case study above?

What could Susan do to improve the learners' behaviour and to stop the disruptions in the class?

Comment

Critical reflection involves being aware of the differences between your beliefs and actions and between your actions and the intended outcome. Susan was doing the right thing through planning and preparing well for her lessons. However, through seeking the views of others and looking at her own actions critically she could become more questioning about the purpose and intended outcomes of her actions. She could have thought about whether the activities were the best for the type (eg age, abilities) of learners and if they could be managed differently to promote better behaviour and improved learning.

Brookfield's four lenses

Brookfield (1995) contends that reflection and evaluation of practice requires a four-lens approach:

o   autobiographical as both learner and teacher;

o   seeing yourself through your colleagues' eyes;

o   seeing yourself through your learners' eyes;

o   theoretical literature.

Autobiographical lens as a learner and teacher

Self-reflection is a crucial component of self-development and improvement of practice. Focusing on your own experiences as a teacher can reveal features of your teaching that may require further development and, as Hillier remarks,

> *without critical reflection, teaching will remain at best uninformed, and at worst ineffective, prejudiced and constraining ... reflection really makes a difference to what we do as teachers ... we can question our routine, convenient, everyday practices and ask ourselves about what really does and doesn't work and we can challenge some of our deeper, social and cultural thoughts, feelings and reactions.*
>
> (Hillier, 2002, pp 5–11)

Brookfield (1995), with similarity to Argyris and Schön (1978), contends that during any process of self-reflection it is important that you consider your reasons behind your thoughts, ie what assumptions might you be making and how might your views differ if these assumptions were not present. Critically reflective teachers challenge their assumptions and reframe their thinking and, consequently, their actions. Challenging your assumptions can be a really difficult thing to do as you may not be aware of what these are and even if you do you may not want to let go of views that you have held true for most of your life. Critical reflection involves looking at the practices and views that you have taken for granted, and the reasons behind these views, and considering possible alternatives. It could be that what you considered to be truisms are, in fact, unquestioned and unexamined assumptions.

Examples of some assumptions include:

o   critical thinking is an intellectual function of adult life;

o   teachers working in the further education and skills sector don't have as many negative issues to address as teachers within the compulsory sector regarding their learners' engagement in learning;

o   it's easy to teach self-motivated and able learners.

The above examples might be true in some circumstances but not all adults engage in critical reflection; teachers working in FE will have some negative issues to deal with although these might differ to those that are present in compulsory education and, as Argyris (2008) purports, teaching self-motivated and able learners can be difficult because they are adept at deflecting blame and protecting established practices. One way of developing your ability to reflect and evaluate your practice and to become more aware of any assumptions can be through keeping a diary, journal or log of critical incidents. These accounts become reflective when, rather than simply describing an event or action, you think more deeply about a critical incident and learn from it.

Critical question

What key factors do you need to consider when writing about a critical incident?

Comment

Your answer should include:

- why the incident was significant;
- the context of the incident;
- why you acted in the way that you did;
- what skills you used and what theories you applied;
- what you would do differently next time. ·

Your colleagues' eyes

Due to pre-held views and assumptions about yourself you may not always see yourself or aspects of your practice in the same way as your peers or colleagues do. Discussing your practice with your colleagues and observing others' practice are two ways that can help you see your practice through different lenses and to identify some elements of your own practice that you may want to change.

However, discussions (or learning conversations) need to be purposeful and held within trusted relationships so that honesty and confidentiality are assured. Examples of purposeful learning conversations might include issues relating to classroom practice but they might also include issues relating to institutional compliance or learners' expectations.

Critical question

What can you do to support your colleagues in reflection and evaluation of their practice and how might any steps you take to do this develop your own practice?

Comment

By engaging in peer observations and learning conversations with your colleagues you move beyond your own thoughts, ie your own lens, thereby providing opportunities for you to challenge your assumptions as well as providing you with a range of different views and ideas about possible teaching and learning strategies.

 Case study

Jason has been teaching for three months and has just had his first observation. Jason considered that his lessons normally went well with the learners mostly remaining on task and with very few behavioural issues and therefore he had kept to the same teaching and learning format during the observation as he would normally adopt. Alongside setting clear objectives and pre- and post-lesson recap questioning techniques this format included group work. Jason spent time with each group in order to help and support them. He was therefore surprised when the observer suggested that it seemed that his planning and strategies seemed to be related to his concern for maintaining order in the class rather than for providing a flexible and innovative learning environment.

Critical questions

What assumptions might Jason have made regarding his view of the lesson?

Do you think that the longer you do a job the better you become because you learn through experience?

Comment

If you look at the case study above it is possible to see that Jason, albeit with good intent, was planning his lessons more from a teacher perspective than he was from a learner perspective. Perhaps, as research suggests can happen with new teachers (Orr, 2013), Jason may have assumed his lessons to be good because the behaviour of the learners was good and they were meeting the objectives that he had set for the lesson. However, the observer might have thought that Jason hadn't taken sufficient account of the impact on the learners that his intrusion into the groups while they were working on task might have. His observer might also have thought that Jason's objectives were not sufficient to stretch and challenge some learners and that he needed to encourage all learners to be more questioning. Although length of experience does not automatically confer insight and wisdom it can provide opportunities for you to reflect on experiences and for you to consider what should, or could, be done differently to improve future experiences.

Your learners' eyes

Reflecting and evaluating your practice through your learners' eyes is important as it provides useful information about their learning needs.

Brookfield (1995) suggests that it is not always good practice for a teacher to enter a group as they immediately change the power dynamics of the group and learners' behaviours may change as a result of this. From their perspective (their lens) learners may see your presence as an interruption to their task, or as a form of assessment of their abilities to do the task. Furthermore, some learners may become self-conscious about what it is they were saying, or had intended to say whereas other learners might want to impress you and stifle opportunities for others to speak.

As well as reflecting and evaluating your practice by considering teaching and learning situations from the learners' perspectives there are other approaches that you could adopt that would help you to do this. For example, you could collect post-lesson feedback from your learners. This can be done by the use of sticky notes, with comments, placed on your desk, or a very brief evaluation sheet that learners complete at the end of each lesson. Other approaches include end-of-module and end-of-course evaluations, attendance and achievement records and observations of your learners' motivation and engagement in learning.

Looking at your practice through your learners' eyes can help you see more clearly the learning encounters that you have prepared for them through their eyes. Doing this can help you to see if 'learners take the meanings that you intend them to do from your teaching lessons' (Brookfield, 1995, p 30) as variations in learners' prior knowledge, characteristics and backgrounds influence how they construct knowledge as well as any pre-disposed assumptions they hold of how they should learn and what good teaching looks like.

Critical task

Prepare a list of possible teaching and learning strategies and ask your learners to put in order the ones that they would prefer you to use in the teaching lessons. Once this is done discuss with them the reasons for their choices. Explain to them your reasons for using different approaches.

Theoretical literature

Literature can help you to understand your experiences by naming them in different ways and by providing you with some tools to change your approach (Brookfield, 1995). While, as Brookfield notes, discussions with your peers are useful, an appreciation of theoretical frameworks can provide you with information that enables you to challenge and present an argument to others when appropriate and can also help to reduce *group-think*. Groupthink is when individuals within a group, perhaps due to collective thinking or a desire to maintain harmonious relationships, make decisions that are not as individually reflective or evaluative as they could be.

Importantly, applying some of the theories that you read about to your practice can help you to become a better teacher through increasing your knowledge, which can also help you to improve your decision making.

Critical questions

What literature have you read recently that has informed your practice or which has challenged any pre-held assumptions?

How could Brookfield's four lenses be applied to your professional practice?

Comment

Others' viewpoints can help you to consider:

o   how else you could do something;

o   how and why other people do things;

o   what you might be able to do to make teaching and learning experiences better for you and your learners.

Kolb's experiential learning cycle

Kolb (1984), whose work was influenced by Lewin (1890–1947), Dewey (1859–1952) and Piaget (1896–1980), outlines four significant stages of reflection:

o   *concrete experience*: this relates to actually doing something and/or having an experience;

o   *reflecting*: this relates to reviewing and reflecting upon the concrete experience and considering what happened, why it happened and what you might do differently next time;

○ *abstract conceptualisation*: this relates to the learning and conclusions that you arrive at following the reflective process about the original experience. You formulate ideas more fully so that you can have a different type of experience than you did at the start of this process (ie the concrete experience);

○ *active experimentation*: this refers to testing out your newly formed ideas when the opportunity presents itself to do so.

Kolb asserts that it is not necessary to commence this cyclical approach at the beginning (concrete experience). It may be that you observe an experience before you try it out or that you test out an idea which then provides you with the concrete experience. You work your way through the cycle from the point at which you started. Using this cyclical approach does require you to stop, think and reflect before and following your teaching lesson. It also requires you to develop a plan or strategy to improve future lessons.

Critical question

Can you think of a time/s when you have used Kolb's model as part of your professional practice?

Comment

If you have undertaken any action research you may have used Kolb's model. Action research requires you to consider your purpose of the research and to try out some form of intervention, following which you consider the impact of the intervention.

WHY SHOULD YOU REFLECT AND EVALUATE YOUR PRACTICE?

Critical reflection is necessary in order to be aware of your behaviour and so effect change (Osterman and Kottkamp, 2004). As noted by the ETF, reflective and enquiring practitioners should: '*think critically about their own educational assumptions, values and practice in the context of a changing contemporary and educational world*' (ETF, 2014, p 1). Reflecting on your practice supports your improvement of it. Your role as a teacher is to raise learners' aspirations such that each and every learner meets or exceeds their potential. A good teacher provides an environment in which learners can learn, an outstanding teacher provides an environment in which learners '*learn exceptionally well and, as a result, acquire knowledge quickly and develop a thorough understanding of a wide range of different aspects of their learning programmes*' (Ofsted, 2013, p 46).

Reflecting and evaluating can provide you with the skills and tools to continually develop and improve your own practice so that your learners '*develop high levels of resilience, confidence and independence when they tackle challenging activities'* (Ofsted, 2013, p 53). Therefore, reflecting on and evaluating your practice is a vital factor of professional development. It can be used to inform action and to make judgements and it is the ability to reflect critically that distinguishes between deep and surface learning and enables changes or transformation to occur in practice. Importantly, a lack of reflection and evaluation of practice can lead to *'anxiety, frustration, and often failure'* (Knowles, 1975, p 15). Reflecting and evaluating can lead to improvement of your practice and can also help you to manage or alleviate stress.

If you do not reflect upon your experiences (and of course take appropriate actions following your reflections) you are likely to continue having the same type of experiences. Reflecting on your experiences can help you to make new meanings from your new learning. Mezirow (1991, p 5) terms this *'transformative learning'* and this informs what and how changes can be made to your practice in order to more fully develop and to be equipped with the skills to offer a quality learning experience to your learners.

Critical questions

What can you do to develop your skills as a critically reflective practitioner?

What barriers to reflection are there?

Comment

You can gather as much information as possible from a variety of sources to inform and to shape your thinking. Doing this can help you to challenge any pre-held assumptions, biases and beliefs.

So that you can effectively develop new meanings from your thinking you need to consider what theories and factors influence your thinking. Like Schön (2002), Argyris (2008) and Moon (2006), Claxton (2006) and Huddleston and Unwin (2002) consider that it is a person's use of mental models to explore and examine theories in use that influence their responses during their process and application of reflection, that can ultimately lead to changes in attitudes and outcomes. Action in the sense of reflection does not relate purely to physical activity. It also applies to how you adapt your mental models when some new thinking occurs (perhaps through reading literature or conversations with your colleagues). This action relates to your shift in thinking and this shift will influence your behaviour and how you experience and approach future incidents. Continually reviewing and developing your mental models is important in order for you to make informed decisions that lead to improved outcomes and strategies.

Critical question

Identify five reasons why reflecting and evaluating your own practice is important.

Comment

Reflecting and evaluating your own practice is important so that you can take account of an event that has occurred or action that you have taken. Doing this helps you to consider your reactions to the event as well as the consequences of your actions. Reflecting and evaluating your practice also gives you the opportunity to consider your theories in use, to challenge any pre-held assumptions and can also support your thinking about how you would act if a similar event occurred in the future. Following reflection you may want to consider your personal and professional development needs and then develop a plan of action so that you can achieve any goals, which can include strategies for changes in your behaviour, which you have set.

Critical question

You deliver lessons on a back-to-back basis for the first three days of the week and the last two days are usually taken up with meetings with colleagues and tutorials with your learners. How could you incorporate opportunities for regular reflection and evaluation into this busy schedule?

Comment

When you are busy it is important that you work as effectively and efficiently as possible and adopting behaviours and processes that allow you to reflect and evaluate without consuming too much of your time is important. As noted earlier in this chapter it is important to ask learners for feedback and to set aside regular time for discussions with colleagues. You may also find keeping a journal, making notes and/or recording your thoughts useful although as these are often a discursive account of events and are seen through just one (your) lens they may not be useful for challenging assumptions.

Case study

As part of her DET course Ribya's teacher has asked her to keep a reflective journal. At first Ribya does this diligently but after a while she begins to see this as a tiresome task that consumes her time. Any attempt at reflection becomes descriptive, superficial and repetitive.

Critical task

Thinking about the case study above consider what strategies Ribya could use to retain her motivation in maintaining a useful and purposeful journal.

WHEN SHOULD YOU REFLECT AND EVALUATE YOUR OWN PRACTICE?

Reflection and evaluation can take place at any time but you need to consider when, for you, it is likely to be the most effective. For example, you should reflect and evaluate your practice at the end of a module or programme in order for you to make informed decisions about any necessary changes required to improve the module or programme. Reflection is also necessary following a critical incident (which could be either a positive or negative incident). However, the ability to critically reflect and evaluate practice can be improved by gathering together as much information as possible. Doing this will help you to make informed decisions that are as devoid of espoused theories and assumptions as possible as well as being grounded in whatever data is available.

However, there will be times when you reflect in action, when you make an instant decision to amend or change your plans or to perhaps intervene in an incident. The consistent application of reflection to practice will develop your ability to make appropriate decisions and to take appropriate actions.

Critical question

When and where do you currently reflect and might a change in either of these improve your current experiences of reflection? If so, how?

Comment

Some people need a quiet room, a relaxing chair and a cup of tea or coffee before they can truly engage in reflection about their practice. Others might need to hear music playing or have some other form of background noise. The time of day as well as your emotional state of mind can also make a difference to the optimal environment for your engagement in reflection.

SUMMARY

In order to provide an excellent learning environment for your learners it is important that you critically reflect and evaluate your practice. Being able to make informed decisions and to challenge any pre-held assumptions is crucial to your ability to do this well. Developing your ability to critically reflect through self-assessment, learning conversations with colleagues and peers and through reading literature not only enhances your potential to become, or remain, an outstanding teacher but can also enhance your ability to engage in debate and discussion at the different levels that are often expected of you as a teacher (with parents, governors, management and at conferences and events).

 Check your understanding

You will find suggested answers to some of these questions at the back of this book.

Question 1: What does the phrase *critically reflecting and evaluating own practice* mean?

Question 2: What approaches could you use to critically reflect and evaluate your practice?

Question 3: What strategies can you use to check out any espoused theories that you may hold?

Question 4: Choose three models of reflection, either from those discussed in this chapter or from those you discovered for yourself and analyse their similarities and differences.

Question 5: Think about the following situations and for each one consider a) what impact it might have had on the lesson and b) what action could have been taken to sort the issue out.

○ Having prepared a PowerPoint presentation you were unable to log on to the computer in the classroom that you had been allocated.

→

    ○   You delivered a lesson on equality and diversity and what started off as an interesting discussion about bullying and harassment turned into an opportunity for two people to air their views about each other.

Question 6: List three things that you might do to develop your ability to reflect and evaluate your own practice.

Question 7: What strategies could you use to ensure that you learn to recognise, acknowledge and, where possible, avoid making assumptions or using espoused theories?

Question 8: Consider one significant incident that has occurred recently in your teaching practice. Ask yourself:

    ○   What happened?

    ○   Why did it happen?

    ○   What have I done about it (and why)?

Question 9: In order to enhance your skills as a learner and teacher think about the following:

    ○   What areas of your practice do you want to develop, ie what are your aims?

    ○   What is your purpose for having these aims?

    ○   What strategies could you develop and use in order to meet these aims?

    ○   How will you be able to review and evaluate how successful you have been in achieving these aims?

Question 10: Read the case study on page 31 and then answer the following questions.

    ○   What are the issues that Den should be reflecting about?

    ○   Why does Den need to reflect on these issues?

    ○   What approaches could Den use to help him to reflect on these issues?

    ○   What action/s following his reflections could Den take?

    ○   What could Den do in order to see if any action that he had taken following his reflections had the required result?

Case study

Den is halfway through his level 5 DET qualification. He's enjoying the taught class lessons and gets on well socially in the class with his peers. However, he is finding it difficult to find the time to write his assignments as well as managing his hours in an FE placement as a trainee teacher delivering functional skills to four groups of learners who are enrolled onto a motor vehicle technician course.

So far, Den has passed all his assignments. He knows that he doesn't always complete them as well as he could do if he spent more time on them. Although his tutor and mentor both said that his lessons were satisfactory there were quite a few areas for development and Den thinks that his practice might improve more, or more quickly, if he could concentrate more fully on the DET course, for example if he could spend more time reading the recommended literature and trying out some of the ideas suggested in the literature and by his tutors and peers.

Having given up his job as a senior administrator in a bank Den had been excited at the prospect of teaching learners who he thought would be motivated due to studying for a qualification that they knew would help them to gain their chosen employment. However, he is now feeling that the job is harder than he first envisaged. The learners, mostly boys aged around 16–18, were not as attentive as he thought they should be, most had limited levels of concentration and easily became disengaged from any task given to them. They were not badly behaved but were passive rather than active learners and, at times, some of them were too chatty or had been caught playing games on the computer instead of focusing on the task given to them.

He had spoken to the learners and they had said that when they enrolled onto the course they hadn't known that they would have to attend classes for mathematics and literacy and that this made them feel like they were still at school. Particularly the few girls in his classes (six in total) said that although they got on well with the boys in their class they didn't feel that they had a group of class buddies. The learners emphasised that it was the topics they disliked and not Den and that they found the classes boring. Following his conversations with his learners Den spoke with two other teachers who taught the same groups as him but for practical course-related topics, and they said that generally the learners worked well.

Adding to the stress and demotivation that Den was encountering was a growing concern that many of the learners were not going to submit work of a good enough standard for them to pass the functional skills elements of the qualification and Den was very aware that this could result in them not passing their motor technician qualification.

End-of-chapter reflections

○ Only learners themselves can learn and only they can reflect on their own experiences.

○ Reflection should be pursued with intent.

○ In order to reflect critically you need to consider experiences using both cognitive and affective domains.

○ Is there any point in reflecting if you don't act upon it?

○ How do you think you will be able to use your learning from this chapter to develop your practice?

 TAKING IT FURTHER

In addition to the literature already commented upon in this chapter you may find the following of interest.

Boud, D and Falchikov, N (2007) *Rethinking Assessment in Higher Education: Learning for the Longer Term.* Oxon: Routledge.

Boud, D, Keogh, R and Walker, D (eds) (1985) *Reflection: Turning Experience into Learning.* London: Kogan Page.

Brookfield, S (2012) *Teaching for Critical Thinking: Tools and Techniques to Help Learners Question Their Assumptions.* San Francisco, CA: Jossey-Bass.

Further Education and Training Foundation (2014) *Professional Standards. Review of the Professional Standards for Teachers and Trainers in England.* Harrogate: Pye Tait Consulting.

Ghaye, T (2011) *Teaching and Learning through Reflective Practice: A Practical Guide for Positive Action.* Oxon: Routledge.

Hatton, N and Smith, D (2005) Reflection in teacher education: towards definition and implementation. *Teaching and Teacher Education*, 11(1): 33–49.

Hillier, Y (2005) *Reflective Teaching in Further and Adult Education.* 2nd edn. London: Continuum International Publishing Group.

McGregor, D and Cartwright, L (eds) (2011) *Developing Reflective Practice: A Guide for Beginning Teachers.* Maidenhead: McGraw-Hill Education.

Marcus, J, Miguel, E and Tellima, H (2009) Teacher reflection on action: what is said (in research) and is done (in teaching). *Reflective Practice*, 10(2): 191–204.

Roffey-Barentsen, J and Malthouse, R (2009) *Reflective Practice in the Lifelong Learning Sector.* Exeter: Learning Matters.

REFERENCES

Anderson, L W, Krathwohl, D R, Airasia, P W, Cruikshank, K A, Mayer, R E, Pintrich, P R, Raths, J and Wittrock, M C (eds) (2001) *A Taxonomy for Learning, Teaching, and Assessing: A Revision of Bloom's Taxonomy of Educational Objectives*. New York: Longman.

Argyris, C (2008) *Teaching Smart People How to Learn*. Boston: Harvard Business School Press.

Argyris, C and Schön, D (1978) Organizational Learning: A Theory of Action Perspective. Reading, MA: Addison Wesley.

Brookfield, S (1995) *Becoming a Critically Reflective Teacher*. San Francisco, CA: Jossey-Bass.

Claxton, G (2006) Expanding the Capacity to Learn: A New End for Education? (Opening Keynote Address, British Educational Research Association Annual Conference, 6 September, Warwick University). [Online]. Available at: www.guyclaxton.com/documents/New/BERA%20Keynote%20Final.pdf (accessed May 2014).

ETF (2014) *Professional Standards for Teachers and Trainers in Education and Training, England*. [Online]. Available at: www.et-foundation.co.uk (accessed May 2014).

Gibbs, G (1988) *Learning by Doing: A Guide to Teaching and Learning Methods*. Oxford: Further Educational Unit: Oxford Polytechnic.

Hillier, Y (2002) *Reflective Teaching in Further and Adult Education*. London: Continuum.

Huddleston, P and Unwin, L (2002) *Teaching and Learning in Further Education: Diversity and Change*. London: Routledge Falmer.

Knowles, M (1975) *Self-Directed Learning: A Guide for Learners and Teachers*. San Francisco, CA: Jossey-Bass.

Kolb, D (1984) *Experiential Learning: Experience as the Source of Learning and Development*. Upper Saddle River, NJ: Prentice-Hall.

LSIS (2013) *Teaching and Training Qualifications for the Further Education and Skills Sector in England: Guidance for Higher Education Institutions*. Coventry: Learning Skills Improvement Service.

Mezirow, J (1991) *Transformative Dimensions of Adult Learning*. San Francisco, CA: Jossey-Bass.

Moon, J (2006) *Reflection in Learning and Professional Development*. Oxon: Routledge.

Ofsted (2013) *Handbook for the Inspection of Further Education and Skills*. Manchester: Ofsted.

Orr, K (2013) Cultures, colleges and the development of ideas about teaching in English. *Further Education. Research in Post-Compulsory Education*, 18(4): 377–88.

Osterman, K and Kottkamp, R (2004) *Reflective Practice for Educators: Professional Development to Improve Student Learning*. 2nd edn. London: Corwin Publishers.

Schön, D (2002) *The Reflective Practitioner*. Aldershot: Ashgate Publishing.

2 Roles, responsibilities and professional relationships in education and training

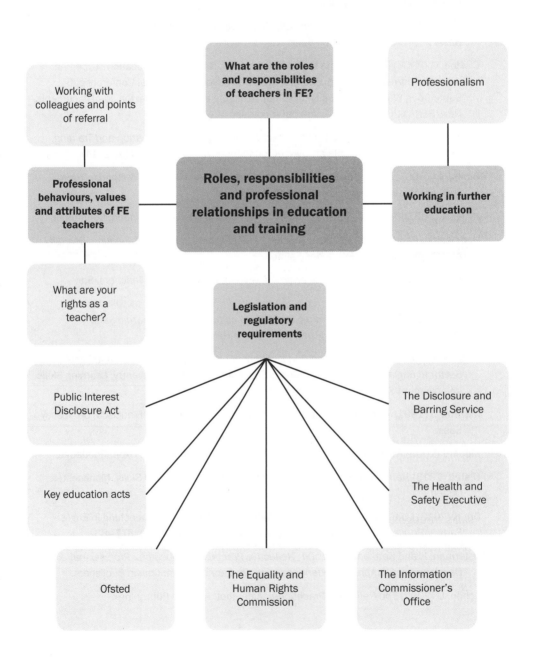

Working with colleagues and points of referral

What are the roles and responsibilities of teachers in FE?

Professionalism

Professional behaviours, values and attributes of FE teachers

Roles, responsibilities and professional relationships in education and training

Working in further education

What are your rights as a teacher?

Legislation and regulatory requirements

Public Interest Disclosure Act

The Disclosure and Barring Service

Key education acts

The Health and Safety Executive

Ofsted

The Equality and Human Rights Commission

The Information Commissioner's Office

PROFESSIONAL LINKS

This chapter assists with your understanding of the following LSIS (2013, p 28) mandatory content:

- legislation, regulatory requirements and codes of practice;
- teacher-related roles;
- own role and responsibilities;
- relationships between teachers and other professionals;
- role boundaries;
- points of referral.

It also contributes to the following Professional Standards as provided by the ETF (2014):

Professional values and attributes

Develop your own judgement of what works and does not work in your teaching and training.

3 *Inspire, motivate and raise aspirations of learners through your enthusiasm and knowledge*

6 *Build positive and collaborative relationships with colleagues and learners*

Professional knowledge and understanding

Develop deep and critically informed knowledge and understanding in theory and practice.

7 *Maintain and update knowledge of your subject and/or vocational area*

8 *Maintain and update your knowledge of educational research to develop evidence-based practice*

12 *Understand the teaching and professional role and your responsibilities*

Professional skills

Develop your expertise and skills to ensure the best outcomes for learners.

19 *Maintain and update your teaching and training expertise and vocational skills through collaboration with employers*

A list of all of the Standards can be found at the back of this book (Appendix 7).

KEY DEFINITIONS

Code of practice	An agreement of appropriate behaviour for practitioners within a profession.
Dual professionalism	Gaining and maintaining professional standing as a teacher and in your area of expertise.
Employment rights	Your employer's legal responsibilities towards you.
Inclusion	Universal education participation to the best of the learner's ability.
Points of referral	Specialist learner support beyond your professional practice toward which you have a responsibility for directing learners.
Practice	Your teaching role and professional responsibilities.
Professional attributes	The application of the role's skills and qualities.
Professional values	The moral views underpinning the profession.
Statutory responsibilities	Legal requirements of education professionals.
Support services	Institutions responsible for protecting learners and supporting specific needs.

INTRODUCTION

This chapter is designed to support you in your understanding of your role and responsibilities to your learners and to others with whom you may come into contact. It therefore aims to support you in:

o   identifying legislation, regulatory requirements and codes of practice relevant to your practice;

o   examining your role and responsibilities as a teacher;

○   exploring relationships between teachers and other professionals;

○   identifying role boundaries;

○   considering points of referral.

STARTING POINT

What do you already know about your role and responsibilities as a teacher?

○   What is your current understanding of your role as a teacher?

○   What is your current understanding of your responsibilities as a teacher?

WHAT ARE THE ROLES AND RESPONSIBILITIES OF TEACHERS IN FE?

At the heart of effective teaching is your responsibility to learners, colleagues and other stakeholders to provide a positive role model in every aspect of your work as a teacher, and as Fazaeli contends, *'Every learner deserves to have professional teachers and trainers, who have the confidence, up-to-date knowledge, understanding and personalised approach to ensure the best outcomes for their learners'* (Fazaeli, in IfL, 2010, p 4). One of your main goals is to motivate learners to develop their ability and aspiration to learn. Your focus is therefore to inspire them to develop their personal, social and professional skills to the best of their ability, including how to take responsibility for their own academic and social development.

As part of your DET qualification, LSIS recommends that you have a breadth of teaching and learning experiences as well as experience of the wider professional roles associated with teaching in FE (see Chapter 10). Look at Table 2.1 and consider your current role and experiences in relation to the LSIS recommendations.

Table 2.1 Roles and responsibilities (continued overleaf)

LSIS recommendation	To what extent does my current role meet this expectation?	How could I develop my role further?
different teaching practice locations/ settings/contexts		
teaching across more than one level		

LSIS recommendation	To what extent does my current role meet this expectation?	How could I develop my role further?
teaching a variety of learners		
teaching individuals and groups		
experience of non-teaching roles		
gaining subject-specialist knowledge through workplace mentoring		

The list in Table 2.1 is not exhaustive and it may be that you already or will have a broader range of experience and role responsibilities than those mentioned. There is further discussion about your roles and responsibilities throughout this chapter.

Critical question

What is your view of an ideal teacher?

Comment

Coffield's (2008, p 39) small-scale research discussed FE learners' perceptions of teachers, finding that as well as subject expertise and enthusiasm:

The good tutor is: punctual, prepared and organised; reliable and trustworthy; helpful and encouraging; checks that all students have understood before moving on; provides clear explanations and uses a variety of methods; marks work appropriately and on time; and cares for all students and respects their views.

Coffield (2008) also found that learners value humanity in a teacher – the personal interest in each learner. Do not underestimate the value of listening to learners or being afraid to discuss learning with them. Coffield and Higgins and Byrne (2008) recommend regular feedback from learners arguing that this is more often insightful than spiteful, with learners valuing opportunities to contribute and reflect on how to improve personal behaviour for learning (see Chapter 6).

WORKING IN FURTHER EDUCATION

FE encompasses a huge variety of subjects, levels and learners and as noted by the IfL:

> *at the heart of the further education and skills sector is diversity. Education and training practitioners are drawn from as diverse communities as their learners, both in terms of background and experiences as well as their subject or vocational areas.*
>
> (IfL, 2012, p 9)

Providing an optimum learning environment for a diverse range of learners is key to your role as a teacher. The DET qualification supports you in your development as a teacher. There have been four major restructurings between 2010 and 2014 relating to teacher training; each has been underpinned by a set of professional Standards setting out what is expected of teachers working within an FE environment. Currently, legislation and your roles and responsibilities as a teacher are shaped by the requirements of LSIS (2013), the ETF (2014) Standards and government legislation (see the introduction at the beginning of this book for further information).

Professionalism

The drive towards achieving professionalism from 2007 focused on attaining mandatory qualifications in terms of the concept of dual-professionalism, defined by the IfL as '*deep knowledge, conceptual understanding and expertise in teaching and learning processes and contexts, matched with expert subject knowledge and skills*' (IfL, 2012, p 4). The changes made from 2007 incorporated a requirement for all teachers to have a minimum core competence in literacy, numeracy and ICT; to have a minimum level 3 qualification (such as A levels) in or related to the subject they taught, and to gain a generic teaching qualification equivalent to their role. Slater's (2013) summary of international education research found that teachers in high performing systems have high literacy and numeracy levels and the Wolf Review (2011) emphasised the need for these subjects to be at the core of all learning due to their fundamental importance in every subject and career. As a teacher, along with advice and support from your tutor, it is your responsibility to ensure competency in these skills.

Although since the deregulation of ITE in September 2013 (BIS, 2012a) there is no longer a mandatory requirement to become teacher qualified, employers and other stakeholders (eg learners, parents) still want their staff to be well trained and qualified. Research has found that teachers, learners and employers reported positively about the benefits of ITE with 89 per cent of respondents supporting a need for ITE (IfL, 2012, p 6). On a broader scale this aligns with Slater's (2013) international research which finds that a consistent factor of high-performing education systems is having teachers who are pedagogical experts to complement their subject expertise.

The IfL (2012) suggests that effective teaching moves beyond a requirement for subject knowledge, arguing that effective teachers also need to have specific skills and qualities to facilitate learning and motivate learners: '*Professional teachers and trainers have deep knowledge, conceptual understanding and expertise in teaching and learning processes which they can apply in a diverse range of contexts for a diverse population of learners'* (IfL, 2012, p 4). Slater (2013) found that the best performing systems internationally have clear guidance on how to evidence achievement and, as a teacher, you are provided with this by LSIS as well as by the professional Standards introduced by the ETF.

LEGISLATION AND REGULATORY REQUIREMENTS

Legislation is defined by an act of parliament. You probably will not need to read the original documents, but it is essential to understand how legal changes affect your practice. Do not assume that someone else has already done this in your organisation – you may need to inform your management where changes are necessary. Therefore, it is useful to sign up to regular updates from organisations related to education to help you understand such developments. Remember, as with any source, these organisations may have a political stance which could prejudice the objectivity of their findings. Therefore, you should research the organisation's credentials and consider a variety of sources to evaluate the validity of differing viewpoints.

The following summarises some of the key legislation and regulatory bodies which directly relate to your role as a teacher. This is not an exhaustive list so it is important that you are aware of changes in government policy, how this affects your institution's policies and your own professional practice.

Key education acts

There have been several acts of parliament relating to education, many of which are outlined in the introduction at the beginning of this book. Key acts include the 1944 Education Act, which raised the compulsory education age initially to 14 (Jones, 2003) and the Education Reform Act 1988, which opened the way for a national curriculum and accountability practices such as Ofsted and league tables (Whitty, 2008). The Education Act 2011 has made widespread changes such as school organisation and partial deregulation of teachers' qualification requirements.

> ### Comment
>
> This will help you to understand the context of current and future developments as will looking at some of the literature recommended in the Taking it further section at the end of this chapter.

The Equality and Human Rights Commission: Equality Act 2010

The Equality and Human Rights Commission (EHRC) is a statutory body that incorporates many of the essential acts and legislative requirements that, as a teacher, you will need to adhere to and be aware of. For example, the Equality Act 2010, which is in place to protect human rights (DfE, 2013), replaces all previous equality legislation such as the Special Educational Needs and Disability Act 2001. A specific Code of Practice (DfE, 2013) for Special Educational Needs learners is currently under development for schools and FE (see Chapter 3).

The Health and Safety Executive: Health and Safety at Work Act 1974

The Health and Safety Executive (HSE) is the national independent regulator for work-related health, safety and illness (HSE, 2014). A major part of your professional practice is to take health and safety concerns seriously in terms of the learners for whom you are responsible, your colleagues and of course yourself (see Chapter 3). The HSE is responsible for the Health and Safety at Work Act 1974, amended 2013.

Public Interest Disclosure Act 1998

This aims to enable workers to raise concerns about professional practice, commonly known as *whistleblowing*. ATL (2014) gives examples of serious professional issues which an employee may raise, for example:

o   a criminal offence by the employer;

o   failing to comply with any legal obligation (such as failure to carry out Disclosure and Barring Service enhanced checks);

o   miscarriage of justice;

o   danger to the health and safety of any individual;

o   damage to the environment;

o   the covering up of any of the above.

Your institution should have a policy on how you can raise such concerns without suffering workplace victimisation.

The Office for Standards in Education, Children's Services and Skills

The Office for Standards in Education, Children's Services and Skills (Ofsted) is responsible for regulating education provision, including FE, so they will inspect your institution and your practice, using their framework. As explained in the *Handbook for Inspection of Further Education and Skills* (Ofsted, 2014a), your institution is judged to be:

o   Grade 1: Outstanding;

o   Grade 2: Good;

o   Grade 3: Requires improvement;

o   Grade 4: Inadequate.

(For further information relating to Ofsted and grades see Chapter 8.)

Critical questions

What Ofsted grade does your institution currently hold? Can you explain why?

What specific remarks were made about the subject area in which you teach?

How do you contribute to your subject area's self-evaluation and action plan to improve practice?

Should your institution gain a grade 3 or 4, it will be re-inspected and may face special measures (see Chapters 7 and 8), so it is important that you are aware of your responsibilities as a teacher and ensure that these are carried out. Although Ofsted is sometimes criticised for its approach to inspections in terms of potentially negative effects on teachers and learning (Park, 2013) as well as the validity of their findings (O'Leary, 2012; Waldegrave and Simons, 2014) it is the main adjudicator of quality provision in education so it is essential that you keep up to date with changes in its approach.

Critical task

Look on Ofsted's *Good Practice* database for examples relating to your teaching practice. What can you learn from these to inform, change and improve your practice?

The Information Commissioner's Office: Data Protection Act 1998

The use and storage of data by organisations is controlled by the Data Protection Act (DPA) (ICO, 2014), meaning that ensuring appropriate information usage is a legal responsibility for the organisation and its employees. You may have to use potentially sensitive data such as information relating to disability to inform your planning, teaching and assessment strategies.

The DPA 1998, amended 2011, is guided by eight fundamental principles relating to how information is distributed, used and stored. Information must be:

1. used fairly and lawfully;

2. used for limited, specifically stated purposes;

3. used in a way that is adequate, relevant and not excessive;

4. accurate;

5. kept for no longer than is absolutely necessary;

6. handled according to people's data protection rights;

7. kept safe and secure;

8. not transferred outside the UK without adequate protection.

Critical questions

Investigate your institution's data protection policy.

What processes are in place at your organisation to ensure legal compliance with the above principles?

What are your professional responsibilities regarding data distribution, use and storage?

What role boundaries might exist in relation to the supply of information?

Comment

You need to make sure that you and your organisation adhere to all of the principles within the DPA. For the most part you are likely to find that adherence to the DPA principles is unproblematic but at times you may be asked to provide information to another professional (perhaps a colleague, parent or someone senior to you) whereby you need to stop and think about the appropriateness and legality of disclosing the information requested. Remember, regardless of a person's role or hierarchal position boundaries exist in relation to whom you supply information. Seek guidance from your organisation, the Information Commissioner's Office and the Equality and Human Rights Commission if necessary.

Disclosure and Barring Service

The Disclosure and Barring Service (DBS) replaced the Criminal Records Bureau (CRB) and Independent Safeguarding Authority (ISA) in 2012. The purpose of the DBS is to help employers make safe recruitment decisions by preventing unsuitable people from working with vulnerable groups (DBS, 2014). Before you started your teaching practice your employer should have ensured that you had a DBS criminal record check. Your employer will request further checks throughout your career. Additionally, you are legally obliged to immediately inform your employer of any changes to your record, or any issues which may bring about a change.

Critical question

Do you think a DBS check is sufficient to verify the suitability of a teacher to practice?

PROFESSIONAL BEHAVIOURS, VALUES AND ATTRIBUTES OF FE TEACHERS

When developing relationships with learners, teachers, other professionals and stake-holders your behaviour, values and attributes should take account of those stipulated within the ETF (2014) Standards and should inform all aspects of your professional practice. Behaviours and values relate to the underlying moral and ethical principles of your role, such as honesty, whereas attributes relate to the skills you are able to apply, such as communication (see Chapter 5 for more information about communication).

Critical question

List the core professional values that a teacher should have. Why are these important to your learners?

Comment

Your role as a teacher is much more than one of delivering information to learners; core values should underpin every aspect of your professional practice. The IfL's Code of Practice considers that teachers should have:

○   integrity;

○   respect;

○   a duty of care to learners.

The IfL's Code of Practice and the ETF (2014) Standards value ongoing engagement with reflective practice (see Chapter 1) for continuous professional development. Similarly, they strongly advocate collaboration with colleagues and promoting inclusion within your practice. The ETF Standards also emphasise the concept of education having a broader social and economic value.

Critical question

What attributes should a teacher have and why are these important for learners?

Comment

The ETF (2014) Standards outline key attributes relating to the ability to apply reflection, good communication skills, enthusiasm, creativity and innovation within your practice. You need to be able to apply learning processes that motivate and engage your learners and which also promote the economic, emotional and intellectual well-being of learners. Echoing Ofsted's Common Inspection Framework (2014a), the Standards also make behaviour management central to promoting equality and inclusion (see Chapter 3). The Standards stress the importance of developing assessment practice to support learner progress and achievement (see Chapter 4) as well as developing and maintaining subject/vocational expertise, which concurs with the IfL's concept of *dual professionalism* (see Chapter 10).

Working with colleagues and points of referral

Your primary aim as a teacher is to enable each of your learners to achieve to the best of their ability through working in a safe and supportive environment. However, this does not mean that you can solve all of their problems – you are not a social worker, lawyer, bank manager, counsellor or doctor. You are probably not qualified for these roles so must not attempt to take them on in the misguided belief that you are helping your learners. This does not mean that you ignore the issues that your learners may have and only deal with academic issues. If a learner informs you about an issue or you have reason to consider that there may be one, it is your legal responsibility to *signpost* (direct) learners to the appropriate support service and contact the service directly yourself. Therefore, find out who provides specialist support for issues such as finance, health, counselling and so on. Learners may request that you do not tell anyone before or after disclosing an issue. However, it is your legal duty to report concerns to the relevant authorities, so never agree to such a promise.

What are your rights as a teacher?

Your employment contract explains your rights and responsibilities as a teacher, according to organisational requirements and national legislation; for example your right to belong to a recognised union such as ATL or UCU. UCU (2013) advises that you should request clarification on any issues you have with your contract prior to formal acceptance and regardless of which sort of contract you are on (fixed, zero hours, permanent) your employer will also be subject to the Equality Act 2010, meaning that they must not treat you less favourably and you must not be subject to discrimination, harassment or victimisation. Furthermore, Massey (2013) contends that a teachers' authority has been clarified and strengthened in the Education Act 2011, including a reinforcement of disciplinary powers and a right to anonymity in cases of misconduct allegations until a case hearing, with the intention of reducing the number of unfounded allegations against staff.

While points of referral generally relate to other bodies or people who are in a position to support and advise you and your learners from a teaching perspective a valuable point of referral is the learners themselves. Gathering feedback from your learners whenever possible can help you to reflect and develop your mental models (see Chapter 1 for further information), as noted by Coffield:

> Students are seasoned observers of teachers and have become adept at spotting the differences between them as well as the strengths and weaknesses of individuals. As such, they could become valued, perceptive, knowledgeable and constructive allies in the quest for continuous improvement.
>
> (Coffield, 2008, p 56)

SUMMARY

Both the IfL's (2010) Code of Practice and the ETF (2014) Standards provide useful guidance regarding your roles, responsibilities and your professional and ethical development as a teacher. Importantly, listen to, value and act on the feedback from your learners in order to help your continual improvement of your teaching.

 Check your understanding

You will find suggested answers to some of these questions at the back of this book.

Question 1:   What are your responsibilities as a teacher?

Question 2:   What document/s might you refer to if you wanted to know the definitions of direct and indirect discrimination, victimisation and harassment?

Question 3: Investigate your institution's health and safety policy and note down any specific health and safety policy/code/guidelines for your subject.

- How are learners taught about health and safety/emergency procedures at the beginning of the course?

- How is their *understanding* of these checked throughout the course?

Question 4: What support services does your organisation provide?

Question 5: What are the procedures for signposting learners towards appropriate support at your institution?

Question 6: What opportunities does your institution provide for professional appraisal, development and career progression?

Question 7: Is your contract zero hour, part time, full time, permanent or temporary? What are the advantages and disadvantages of this in relation to other contracts available at your institution and others?

End-of-chapter reflections

- Ensure you are fully aware of the points of referral for different student issues at your organisation.

- Carefully check your contract so that you are fully aware of your rights, roles and responsibilities.

- Investigate the different professional bodies representing the sector and consider joining any which meet your needs as a professional education practitioner.

- Reflect on your ongoing development as a teacher, using the ETF Standards (2014) and IfL Code (2008) to guide you.

 TAKING IT FURTHER

In addition to the literature already commented upon in this chapter you may find the following of interest.

Association of Teachers and Lecturers. [Online]. Available at: www.atl.org.uk/ (accessed April 2014).

→

Business Innovation and Skills (BIS) (FE and skills section). [Online]. Available at: www.gov.uk/government/topics/further-education-and-skills (accessed April 2014).

Centre for British Teachers. [Online]. Available at: www.cfbt.com/ (accessed 30 July 2014).

Control of Substances Hazardous to Health (COSHH). [Online]. Available at: www.hse.gov.uk/coshh/ (accessed April 2014).

DfE (2010) *Overview of the Equality Act 2010.* [Online]. Available at: www.gov.uk/government/publications/equality-act-2010-advice-for-schools (accessed April 2014).

Education and Training Foundation. [Online]. Available at: www.et-foundation.co.uk/ (accessed April 2014), including free online training courses: www.foundationonline.org.uk/ (accessed 30 July 2014).

Equality and Human Rights Commission (EHRC). [Online]. Available at: www.equalityhumanrights.com/ (accessed April 2014).

Ofsted. *Good Practice.* [Online]. Available at: www.ofsted.gov.uk/resources/goodpractice (accessed April 2013).

REFERENCES

ATL (2014) *ATL Advice: Whistleblowing.* [Online]. Available at: www.atl.org.uk/publications-and-resources/factsheets/whistleblowing.asp (accessed May 2014).

BIS (2012a) *Consultation on the Revocation of the Further Education Workforce Regulations: Government Response.* London: BIS, www.gov.uk/government/uploads/system/uploads/attachment_data/file/85883/12-970-revocation-further-education-workforce-consultation-response.pdf (accessed April 2014).

Coffield, F (2008) *All You Wanted to Know about Teaching and Learning but Were Too Cool to Ask.* London: LSN.

DBS (2014) *Disclosure and Barring Service.* [Online]. Available at: www.gov.uk/government/organisations/disclosure-and-barring-service (accessed April 2014).

DfE (2013) *Special Education Needs Code of Practice and Regulations (Consultation).* [Online]. Available at: www.gov.uk/government/consultations/special-educational-needs-sen-code-of-practice-and-regulations (accessed April 2014).

ETF (2014) *Professional Standards for Teachers and Trainers in Education and Training: England.* London: Education and Training Foundation, www.et-foundation.co.uk/our-priorities/professional-standards-2014/ (accessed 30 July 2014).

Higgins, J and Byrne, M (2008) *Behaviour Management: A Whole Organisation Approach.* Belfast: LSDA NI.

HSE (2014) *About HSE*. [Online]. Available at: www.hse.gov.uk/aboutus/index.htm (accessed May 2014).

ICO (2014) *Guide to Data Protection*. [Online]. Available at: http://ico.org.uk/for_ organisations/data_protection/the_guide (accessed April 2014).

IfL (2008) *Code of Professional Practice*. London: Institute for Learning, www.ifl.ac.uk/ membership/ifl-code-of-professional-practice/ (accessed April 2014).

IfL (2010) *Brilliant Teaching and Training in FE and Skills*. London: Institute for Learning.

IfL (2012) *Professionalism: Education and Training Practitioners across Further Education and Skills*. London: IfL.

Jones, K (2003) *Education in Britain: 1944 to the Present*. Cambridge: Polity Press.

LSIS (2013) *Qualification Guidance for the Level 5 Diploma in Education and Training*. Coventry: LSIS.

Massey, A (2013) *Best Behaviour: School Discipline, Intervention and Exclusion*. London: Policy Exchange, www.policyexchange.org.uk/publications/category/item/best-behaviour-school-discipline-intervention-and-exclusion (accessed May 2014).

Ofsted (2014a) *Handbook for the Inspection of Further Education and Skills (revised 25 April 2014)*. Manchester: Ofsted, www.ofsted.gov.uk/resources/handbook-for-inspection-of-further-education-and-skills-september-2012 (accessed April 2014).

O'Leary, M (2012) Exploring the role of lesson observation in the English education system: a review of methods, models and meanings. *Professional Development in Education*, 38(5): 791–810, www.wlv.ac.uk/default.aspx?page=13219 (accessed April 2014).

Park, J (2013) *Detoxifying School Accountability: the Case for a Multi-Perspective Inspection*. London: Demos, www.demos.co.uk/publications/detox (accessed May 2014).

Slater, L (2013) *Building High Performing and Improving Education Systems: Teachers*. London: CfBT, www.cfbt.com/en-GB/Research/Research-library/2013/r-hpes-2013 (accessed April 2014).

UCU (2013) *Contracts of Employment*. Birmingham: UCU.

Waldergrave, H and Simons, J (2014) *Watching the Watchmen: the Future of School Inspections in England*. London: Policy Exchange, www.policyexchange.org.uk/ publications/category/item/watching-the-watchmen-the-future-of-school-inspections-in-england (accessed May 2014).

Whitty, G (2008) Twenty years of progress? English education policy 1988 to the present. *Education Management Administration Leadership*, 36(2): 165–84.

3 Learners and their individual needs

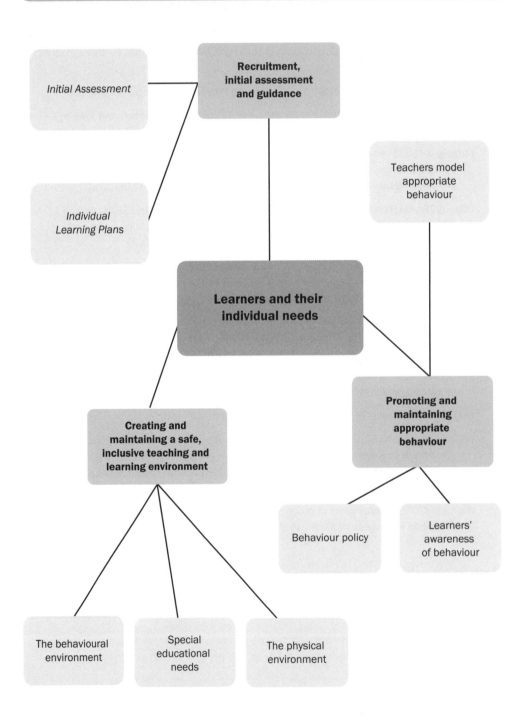

Initial Assessment

Recruitment, initial assessment and guidance

Teachers model appropriate behaviour

Individual Learning Plans

Learners and their individual needs

Promoting and maintaining appropriate behaviour

Creating and maintaining a safe, inclusive teaching and learning environment

Behaviour policy

Learners' awareness of behaviour

The behavioural environment

Special educational needs

The physical environment

PROFESSIONAL LINKS

This chapter assists with your understanding of the following LSIS (2013, p 28) mandatory content:

○ learning preferences;

○ inclusion and inclusive teaching;

○ learner support needs;

○ involving learners in learning and assessment;

○ agreeing learning targets/goals/outcomes;

○ safe, supportive and motivating learning environment;

○ promoting and maintaining appropriate behaviour.

This chapter contributes to an understanding of the following Professional Standards as available from the ETF (2014).

Professional values and attributes

Develop your own judgement of what works and does not work in your teaching and training.

5   *value and promote social and cultural diversity, equality of opportunity and inclusion*

6   *build positive and collaborative relationships with colleagues and learners*

Professional knowledge and understanding

Develop deep and critically informed knowledge and understanding in theory and practice.

11   *manage and promote positive learner behaviour*

Professional skills

Develop your expertise and skills to ensure the best outcomes for learners.

13   *motivate and inspire learners to promote achievement and develop their skills to enable progression*

A list of all of the Standards can be found at the back of this book (Appendix 7).

KEY DEFINITIONS

Advancing equality of opportunity	Actively supporting the individual needs and capabilities of each student enabling achievement to the best of their abilities.
Diversity	Promoting progress and achievement in learners of all backgrounds, heritages and abilities.
Initial assessment and guidance	Test to direct learners onto the most suitable learning opportunities.
Learner aspirations	The overall goal of your learners beyond successful completion of your course.
Learning environment	Wherever learning takes place: classroom, workshop or employment placement.
Prior learning experiences	The knowledge, skills, experiences and attitudes (positive or negative) which learners bring to the course.

INTRODUCTION

As a teacher almost everything you do will be in consideration of learners and their individual needs. This chapter, through its alignment to literature, asking questions and providing activities, is designed to support you in your understanding of how you can prepare and deliver teaching and learning to a diverse range of learners. In this way this chapter aims to support you in:

○ understanding your learners' learning preferences;

○ developing approaches for inclusive teaching;

○ exploring how you can meet learners' learning needs;

○ involving learners in learning and assessment;

○ agreeing learning targets/goals/outcomes;

○ developing a safe, supportive and motivating learning environment;

○ promoting and maintaining appropriate behaviour.

STARTING POINT

What do you already know about reflecting and evaluating your own practice?

o Why do you think meeting individual learner's needs is important?

o Are you already aware of any theories, models and principles for learning?

RECRUITMENT, INITIAL ASSESSMENT AND GUIDANCE

Learners possess a range of differing experiences, aptitudes and qualifications and through engaging in initial assessment (IA) both you and your learners can become more aware of what their individual needs are in relation to their current ability and future potential (DfES, 2006). IA therefore:

> *makes judgements about previous learning and achievements whilst at the same time attempting to give indications, or measures, of the learner's capacity to progress along one of a number of pathways. The outcomes of the process shape the learning and support that can best secure achievement and progression for the individual learner.*
>
> (Green, 2003, p 7)

Initial assessment

IA aims to:

1. identify learner motivations, aspirations and skills to guide the learner onto an appropriate course;

2. identify reasonable adjustments for supporting identified Special Educational Needs (SEN);

3. inform learners of their current ability, development needs and pathway to achieving their aspirations;

4. inform planning in terms of the group and individual ability.

Aim 1: To identify learner motivations, aspirations and skills to guide the learner onto an appropriate course

Effective recruitment processes ensure that learners have the right skills and qualifications to meet the entry requirements of the course. Most likely you went through a recruitment process prior to enrolling on your DET qualification. Similarly, your learners will need to go through a recruitment process and the awarding organisation (AO) that accredits the qualification that they are taking along with any organisational requirements should provide clear guidance of entry criteria onto the course. This may include specific English and mathematics qualifications and/or a Disclosure and Barring Service (DBS) check (see Chapter 2). For any potential learner that does not meet the necessary requirements you should provide them with advice and development targets so that they can reapply at some future date. If the course is inappropriate for their needs, provide clear guidance on alternative learning opportunities. Avoid enrolling learners onto a course if they do not meet the entry criteria; they may have had previous negative education experiences, so allowing them onto a course which they are not (yet) academically or socially equipped for may repeat this cycle of failure. Therefore, it is in the learner's best interest to enrol on a course which they have the capability to achieve, as if they are not achieving they can become demotivated and this may lead to behaviour issues disrupting other learners' opportunities.

An inclusive learning environment is important so (amongst other reasons) no learner considers that they are being treated less favourably than any other learners. It is your organisation's legal duty to ensure that entry criteria are not prejudicial. As noted by the Equality and Human Rights Commission (EHRC):

> Terms of admission should not discriminate against a person with a protected characteristic. Terms which indirectly discriminate against people with a protected characteristic or in the case of a disabled applicant, result in discrimination arising from disability, will be unlawful unless you can show they are a proportionate means of achieving a legitimate aim.
>
> (EHRC, 2014)

The EHRC warn that any decision not to recruit a learner needs to be clearly justified in terms of the learner being unable to meet the overarching aims of the course, even with *reasonable adjustments* in place (see Chapter 2 for more information). Do not make assumptions about what a learner can or cannot achieve and ensure that your planning and use of resources promote an inclusive and supportive learning environment and take consideration of theories and principles of learning (see Chapter 6 for more information). When necessary ensure that you consult the learner, the AO guidelines and the relevant support services in your organisation to find the best course of action. It is also important that you keep records of any reasons for not recruiting learners.

Critical questions

What are the entry requirements for the courses that you teach?

How do you record and evidence that the entry criteria are being met?

Aim 2: To identify reasonable adjustments for supporting identified Special Educational Needs (SEN)

The recruitment process and subsequent IA represent key opportunities for learners to disclose any known Special Educational Needs. Learners may not be comfortable disclosing information on the first day of their course to someone they have just met. Therefore, provide regular opportunities for disclosure during the course, such as during tutorials. It is important that you record necessary information and that you, in line with your organisation's requirements, store information about learners in compliance with the Data Protection Act (DPA) (ICO, 2014; see Chapter 2). Following disclosure, the DPA assumes the organisation as a whole is aware and that processes are in place to inform, for example, anyone covering classes in which the learner is present.

Aim 3: To inform learners of their current ability and development needs

IA results need to be shared with learners as soon as possible, as they provide a starting point for their studies (Knasel et al., 2006). Results need to be clearly explained and the learners' understanding checked (Green, 2003). Regardless of the subject qualification, IA should include assessment of English and mathematics. The Wolf Review (2011) contends that these skills are crucial to further academic and employability develop-ment; therefore IA can highlight individual learner's needs and you, as their tutor, can encourage learners to address broader developmental needs through enrolment onto supplementary courses.

Aim 4: To inform whole group and individual planning

IA is essential for developing resources and planning teaching and learning activities, enabling consideration of the overall group ability to adjust your scheme-of-work accord-ingly. It also informs group profiles, enabling other teachers working with your class to quickly access relevant learner information. IA therefore enables you to start planning necessary teaching practice adjustments, assessment strategies and support arrange-ments, highlighting which individuals need extra support, how this can be achieved and how all learners can be stretched and challenged. Each learner's IA therefore forms the basis of their individual learning plan (ILP) – see Chapter 7 for further information.

ILPs to record and support changing learner needs

Information gained from IA forms the first stage of creating ILPs. These serve sev-eral purposes within your organisation, negotiating goals, planning learning, recording achievements and tracking learner progress (QIA, 2008). Martinez (2001) argues that when developed through negotiation between teacher and learner, they are a powerful tool for ongoing self-assessment (see Chapter 4) and motivation. For younger learners, Martinez also advises ILP discussions with parents to promote parental engagement with education – a factor known to increase achievement.

Problems with ILPs

QIA (2008) argues that when effectively implemented, ILPs empower and motivate learners by developing their ownership of learning and progress. Martinez (2001), while supporting this, acknowledges potential problems. Though targets should be achiev-able, if set too easy they could demotivate the learner by reinforcing low expectations. Furthermore, ILPs can develop into box-ticking exercises to inform quality systems, forgetting about learner development in the process. Therefore, ensure that ILPs are recorded in a language level appropriate to the learner and give them a copy to aid their personal reflection. ILPs should not be used to encourage a view of learning being a solitary process, but be part of raising aspirations for every learner (Jones, 2006). This means giving them as much ownership as possible, acknowledging achievement, setting new targets, and most importantly engaging in a productive discussion about their motivations and approaches to learning.

CREATING AND MAINTAINING A SAFE, INCLUSIVE TEACHING AND LEARNING ENVIRONMENT

The primary responsibility of an organisation, teachers and other staff is to ensure that learners are supported within a safe (physical and behavioural) environment.

The physical environment

Your organisation is responsible for providing learners with a physically safe environment such as well-maintained buildings and equipment. Equipment must be used safely and under appropriate supervision, with risk assessments in place following HSE guidelines (2014). HSE consider that health and safety is everyone's responsibility. Always model the latest industry/trade-specific health and safety guidance when teaching vocational subjects. When an issue occurs, follow organisational procedures which probably include ceasing to use the equipment, removing learners from the area and immediately reporting the problem. Your organisation must also make reasonable adjustments to enable access around the campus and resources for learners with disabilities. The Equality Act 2010 and the Public Sector Equality Duty 2011 legislate that education providers are legally obliged to make reasonable adjustments to help learners with disabilities participate and achieve in education (see Chapters 2 and 8 for more information).

The behavioural environment

There are *protected characteristics* which you must be aware of to help ensure that discrimination (direct or indirect), victimisation and harassment of learners and staff are prevented (Equality Act 2010, cited in EHRC, 2014). The *protected characteristics* for the further and higher education organisations are:

o   age;

o   disability;

o   gender reassignment;

o   pregnancy or maternity;

o   race;

o   religion or belief;

o   sex;

o   sexual orientation.

You and your organisation should actively promote positive relations between learners with differing characteristics. Where there is low participation and/or achievement of learners with different characteristics, you will need to demonstrate how you are addressing such issues (ATL, 2013) (see Chapters 2 and 8 for further information).

Special educational needs

ATL (2013) categorises disabilities as cognition/learning, sensory/physical and communication/interaction. Specific disabilities such as dyslexia, visual impairment and autism are examples of each category. There are also behavioural/emotional issues such as Attention Deficit Hyperactivity Disorder (ADHD). All learners have multiple-characteristics, so no one should be solely defined by a single aspect such as disability, race or gender (Barnard and Turner, 2011). For learner support, the SEN Code of Practice has been a requirement in all schools since 2001 and an updated version will be released in 2014 (DfE 2013). For the first time, FE learners will be included up to the age of 25, and learner statements will be replaced with an overarching Education, Health and Care Plan (ATL, 2013), so it is essential that you and your organisation are aware of this and have an implementation strategy. The SEN Code of Practice aims to promote closer working between local authorities and health care providers as well as enabling parents/carers and, where appropriate, the individual, to manage their own support budget as they see fit.

Critical question

What policy changes and staff training is your organisation planning in preparation for the new SEN Code of Practice?

PROMOTING AND MAINTAINING APPROPRIATE BEHAVIOUR

Critical task

Using Table 3.1 as a guide, list the various learner behaviours that occur in your class.

Divide these into those supporting learning and those disrupting it.

Consider the impacts (beneficial and detrimental) these behaviours have on maintaining and promoting a safe and supportive learning environment.

Table 3.1 Learner behaviour in class

Behaviour supporting learning	Potential impact	Behaviour disrupting learning	Potential impact

Comment

Experts tend to agree that disruptive behaviour has many negative impacts in terms of teacher and learner motivation, learners' social development, engagement and achievement (Massey, 2013).

Overall, promoting appropriate behaviour and respect for others relates to the following principles:

1. Teachers model appropriate, professional behaviour.

2. Learners are aware of appropriate/inappropriate behaviour and corresponding rewards/sanctions.

3. Behaviour policy is understood and administered fairly and consistently throughout the organisation.

Principle 1: teachers model appropriate, professional behaviour

Modelling professional behaviour to learners is something you should always do. This is in your control, so is the starting point of all your approaches to managing learners' behaviour. A positive appearance is vital, even when this does not match your inner feelings. Being prepared and arriving in good time to suitably arrange the learning environment is also crucial. A positive, enthusiastic and professional attitude supported by thorough preparation, varied resources and activities may take time to succeed in changing persistent disruptive behaviour – but the opposite will certainly fail.

Principle 2: learners are aware of appropriate/inappropriate behaviour and corresponding rewards/sanctions

It is easy to focus on challenging or disruptive behaviour, however, remember that developing behaviour which supports learning is also about promoting responsibility, independence, creativity and social skills such as the ability to work as a group.

Nevertheless, behaviours hindering learning need to be swiftly and consistently addressed before they undermine the learning environment. ATL (2013) categorises inappropriate behaviour as where learners are withdrawn, disaffected or aggressive. While teachers are often quick to take action with disaffected or aggressive learners, withdrawn learners can be forgotten as they are not actively disrupting the lesson. However, this represents an equally important behaviour issue, as there could be serious issues preventing learner contributions and it also makes non-participation acceptable for other learners, therefore limiting class development. Aggressive learners require swift disciplinary measures including possible exclusion, especially where learners or staff are endangered, such as in a workshop. When we consider that a key purpose of education is to develop the social skills necessary for employment, it is clear such behaviours need to be addressed before our learners can be considered *work-ready* regardless of their subject expertise.

Critical task

Copy and try to complete the following table which lists problematic behaviours. You should focus on those most relevant to your practice.

Behaviour	Strategies to tackle this behaviour	Reflections on the effectiveness of strategies
Poor punctuality		
Poor attendance		
Chatting		
Not paying attention		
Reluctant/no class contributions		
Inappropriate/offensive comments		
Not submitting/late submission of work		
Bullying		
Not respecting turn-taking rights in discussions		
Not complying with reasonable instructions		
Other		

Comment

Consider engaging with informal and constructive peer observations to learn how other teachers manage some of these behaviours.

Classroom contracts are a means of raising awareness of appropriate behaviour in the learning environment (UCU, 2013), so creating these may form part of learner induction to be regularly reviewed throughout the course. These can be a useful means of engaging learners in a behaviour improvement process though organisational policy compliance is still required as well as specific information such as health and safety guidance. While it's easy to consider disruptive behaviour as a personal challenge to your role and authority as a teacher, Higgins and Byrne (2008) found that learners expect discipline and order in the classroom, even when their own behaviours are disruptive. Coffield (2008) concurs, noting learners' frustration when they feel a teacher is not in control:

> students know what behaviour is expected of them, and they have specific and reasonable expectations of their tutors, whom they want to be strict as well as kind. They want to participate far more than at present, they want to be more active and involved in lessons, which they don't want to be disrupted.
>
> Coffield (2008, p 40)

Clearly displayed rules or principles highlight when behaviour is falling short of your (and their) expectations (DfE, 2014). As with all communication with learners, try to phrase these in a constructive manner, since it is positive behaviour you are trying to promote (ATL, 2013).

Safeguarding learners

Reece and Walker (2007) cite Maslow (1962), suggesting that to provide the best learning environment it is important that learners feel emotionally safe and secure. It is also a legal duty to ensure learners are free from discrimination, harassment or victimisation (Equality Act 2010, cited in EHRC, 2014), with Ofsted inspectors evaluating how well 'Teaching, learning and assessment promote equality, support diversity and tackle discrimination, victimisation, harassment, stereotyping or bullying' (Ofsted, 2014, p 51). According to the DfE (2010), bullying is a direct or indirect, but deliberate and repeated intention to harm, leading to physical or emotional hurt in the victim. It tends to involve abuse of power relating to differences in age, physical strength or psychological resilience. Bullying causes emotional distress and has also been linked to academic underachievement (DfE, 2010). SEN learners are often targeted, a problem compounded if they do not understand what is happening or are unable to articulate concerns (ATL, 2013). DfE (2011) recommend that learners should have clear and repeated opportunities to raise issues, as early intervention could prevent distress to the victim and enable the perpetrator to reform at an early stage.

With the growth of interactive online technology and associated social media, cyber bullying has become an issue, potentially occurring at any time or location. DfE (2011) recommends that action should be taken for reported incidents even if they occur outside the organisation. Byron (2010) advocates ensuring up-to-date policies regarding technology as well as a proactive stance, for example by not revealing personal data, blocking inappropriate communication and immediately informing a teacher about any inappropriacy. Given the speed of technological developments, organisational policy and training must be regularly updated.

It is your legal responsibility to safeguard your learners and ensure that they are able to work in a safe and secure environment free from bullying. DfE (2011) states that successful organisations *'have clear policies in place to deal with bullying and poor behaviour which are clear to parents, pupils and staff so that, when incidents do occur, they are dealt with quickly'* (DfE, 2011, p 3). Policy can be categorised as being preventative or responsive (ATL, 2013). To prevent the development of a culture of bullying, learners need to understand that difference is celebrated, bullying is not tolerated and that the consequences of any such action are clear for the perpetrator. ATL recommends awareness raising with posters and Taylor (2011) insists that all punishments for misbehaviour are clear and consistently enforced. Should any incidents occur, then the response must be swift, proportionate and consistently follow the clear behaviour policy which the learners have understood (Massey, 2013). Failure to act is not an option.

ATL (2013) advises that it is important for the teacher to try and understand any reasons which might be causing inappropriate behaviour. Tutorial time could give the learner the appropriate space to explain issues such as anxiety or stress which have been contributing to emotional and behavioural difficulties. When discussing behaviour issues, focus on the behaviour rather than personal admonishments, encouraging reflections on the impact their actions have on their own and others' learning (ATL, 2013). In such situations, a brief statement of facts followed by tutor silence may encourage learner reflection – even if not verbally articulated. *Telling off* the learner may be ineffectual – especially if this is something they are used to – as it enables them to escape responsibility for thinking about the impact of their actions. As a tutor you can offer a way out for learners, by directing them to appropriate support such as a learning mentor as well as setting achievable yet sufficiently challenging tasks to begin a cycle of positive experiences in education – something they might not have experienced previously. ATL (2013) recommends that behaviour targets are focused, concentrating on one issue at a time, giving learners achievable developmental goals, though this runs the danger of inconsistent application undermining organisational policy (Taylor, 2011).

Critical questions

Consider whether your learners have a clear understanding of:

o   what constitutes appropriate and inappropriate learning behaviour;

o   the processes of how inappropriate behaviour will be dealt with;

o   the sanctions for inappropriate behaviour.

Do any of your guidelines need to be clarified and how might you do this?

Principle 3: behaviour policy is understood, administered fairly and consistently throughout the organisation

Never believe that a learner is *not motivated*. All learners have interests and are motivated by something – so it's your task to try and direct this enthusiasm towards your subject. However, changes to the FE population, being no longer 'post-compulsory', require updated policies and practices to support the move away from its traditional base of self-motivated adult learners in employment to a more diverse population including younger learners:

> *Policies which enable colleges to build a positive, consistent and safe learning environment in which behaviour is well-managed and in which individual needs are identified and addressed, will promote a more satisfying education experience for all students, including those for whom college may be a last chance at success in education.*
>
> (Taubman and Parry, 2013, p 6)

Goodman's (2010) research for the Joseph Rowntree Foundation (JRF) found that the behaviour, attitudes and aspirations of parents are strongly linked to achievement of their children. Therefore, when working with younger learners (14–19), Massey (2013) strongly advocates involving parents/carers in terms of raising awareness of disciplinary issues and organisational procedures. As for mature learners studying HE in FE organisations, King and Widdowson (2012) found that they are more likely to have barriers to achievement in terms of personal and work commitments, so are more likely than full-time university students to withdraw or underperform.

A practical, coherent and consistently applied organisational behaviour policy is essential for creating an environment where poor behaviour and a lack of respect for diversity are not tolerated (Taylor, 2011; Massey, 2013; and Parry and Taubman, 2013). Inconsistent application of sanctions for bad behaviour undermines teachers' credibility, meaning learners are less likely to change behaviour if they feel unfairly treated. Similarly, teachers should also recognise and reward learners' positive contributions. Massey (2013) therefore recommends clear leadership and support for teachers and regular training for all levels of staff to develop consistent application of the organisation's policy and practice. Higgins and Byrne (2008) concur, stressing the importance of actively planning whole-organisation approaches to improving behaviour rather than reactively tackling disruption as it occurs. In a positive environment, inappropriate behaviour is less likely when the learner sees that they risk stepping outside of the social norms within the organisation. Conversely, tolerance of poor behaviour coupled with an ineffectual and inconsistently applied behaviour policy quickly creates a spiral of decline (Higgins and Byrne, 2008).

Case study

After being given a final warning a learner repeats the behaviour. According to the organisation's policy, the learner should be removed from the course. However, mindful of this affecting retention and achievement statistics negatively, the manager gives the learner another final warning and they stay on the course.

Critical question

What could be the impact of such actions?

Comment

The learner now has no reason to avoid repeating the behaviour – giving a final warning and then not following it up is worse than doing nothing. Enforcing policy could have been developmental for the learner as they would have had to face the consequences of their own actions – a key social and employment skill. Failure to implement policy also negatively impacts on other learners; unchecked disruptive behaviour tends to worsen and spread (Higgins and Byrne, 2008), sending a clear sign to others that there is no extrinsic motivation to behave appropriately. Furthermore, the rest of the staff now feel powerless as the organisation's behaviour policy appears to be toothless. Finally, this approach avoids organisational learning (Argyris, cited in Smith, 2013); whether such behaviour is a common institutional problem, how provision could be improved and what staff could do to engage learners more. Sanctions should always be proportional to the behaviour and in accordance with the organisation's policies and procedures, but must be consistently enforced.

Reflections: equality and diversity organisational analysis

Critical task

Use the following chart (see overleaf) to analyse your organisation's ability to promote inclusive and safe learning, referring to information such as its most recent Ofsted report about equality, inclusion and behaviour management. How is the organisation responding to any issues?

How effective is my organisation at:	Judgement (Outstanding, Good, Requires improvement, Inadequate)	Justify your decision
ensuring a safe and supportive learning environment?		
tackling discrimination, victimisation, bullying and harassment?		
managing equality and diversity in the workplace for staff and learners?		
analysing and acting on equality and diversity data?		
embedding equality and diversity in the curriculum?		
making reasonable adjustments to accommodate disability in the classroom?		
managing challenging behaviour consistently?		
challenging assumptions that learners and others have around equality and diversity?		

SUMMARY

Creativity expert Ken Robinson (2010) strongly criticises using age as a basis for school organisation. Conversely, FE colleges can provide education tailored to the individual learner if course selection is informed by an IA process focusing on individual needs, aspirations, ability and potential. Ideally, IA occurs well before a learner starts their studies, enabling teachers to check that learners are correctly enrolled, have appropriate support in place and make necessary teaching adjustments. Efficiently organised IA creates a good first impression for learners, whereas incompetence, disorganisation, long queues, disinterested staff and lack of feedback or action from the results will take a long time to dispel – if the learner actually returns. Effective IA therefore makes financial good sense, so consistent professional practice must be a key management duty; therefore Green (2003) argues that learner feedback on the IA process is important to inform continual quality improvement. Learners should always have opportunities to develop their skills and be given appropriate guidance to reach achievable goals – academic and behavioural. This is what makes support powerful – not doing work for a learner or pandering to their every whim, but promoting responsibility for their choices, actions and achievements. Researching different literature on behaviour management provides strategies to inform your everyday practice, though these only have a limited impact if disruptive behaviour is organisationally tolerated. Without a clear, consistent and effectively enforced policy, classroom management is much more difficult, so consider how you can contribute to overall strategy development. Finally, wherever learners have an opportunity to give feedback, also ask for reflections on what they can do to improve their contribution to the class.

 Check your understanding

You will find suggested answers to some of these questions at the back of this book.

Question 1: What problems are associated with IA and how may these be overcome?

Question 2: What activities do you use to develop ILPs?

Question 3: What do your learners think about your IA process?

Question 4: Compare your organisation's behaviour-related policy/policies with another organisation. What similarities and differences are there?

Question 5: Review your workshop, classroom and office – make sure you are aware of the relevant HSE guidance and organisational emergency procedures. What equipment do you use? Are there any potential health and safety issues?

End-of-chapter reflections

o Value initial assessment – when effectively implemented, it ensures learners are on the right courses and helps you to plan efficiently.

o Gain feedback from learners to continually improve your institution's recruitment and initial assessment processes.

o Behaviour improvement is everyone's responsibility. Ensure you and your learners are fully aware of your institution's policy.

o Consider how you can contribute towards fair and consistent application of your institution's behaviour policy.

TAKING IT FURTHER

In addition to the literature already commented upon in this chapter, you may find the following of interest:

British Dyslexia Association. [Online]. Available at: www.bdadyslexia.org.uk/ (accessed April 2014).

Coffield, F (2007) *Just Suppose Teaching and Learning Became the First Priority.* London: LSN.

Coffield, F, Moseley, D, Hall, E and Ecclestone, K (2004) *Should We Be Using Learning Styles? What Research Has to Say about Practice.* Trowbridge: Cromwell Press.

Cowley, S (2004) *Getting the Buggers to Behave (2).* London: Continuum International.

DfE (2014) *Behaviour and Attendance.* London: DfE. [Online]. Available at: www.gov. uk/schools-colleges/behaviour-attendance (accessed April 2014).

Dix, P (2010) *The Essential Guide to Taking Care of Behaviour.* 2nd edn. Gosport: Longman.

NIACE (2012) *Managing Challenging Behaviour within Skills Provision for Unemployed Adults.* London: BIS, http://shop.niace.org.uk/media/catalog/ product/m/a/managing-challenging-behaviour_web_final.pdf (accessed April 2014).

Royal National Institute for the Blind (RNIB). [Online]. Available at: www.rnib.org.uk/ (accessed May 2014).

Tuckman, B (1965) Developmental sequence in small groups. *Psychological Bulletin*, 63: 384–99. The article was reprinted in *Group Facilitation: A Research and Applications Journal*, 3, Spring 2001, http://dennislearningcenter.osu.edu/ references/GROUP%20DEV%20ARTICLE.doc (accessed May 2014).

UK Council for Child Internet Safety (UKCCIS). [Online]. Available at: www.gov.uk/ government/groups/uk-council-for-child-internet-safety-ukccis (accessed April 2014).

Vizard, D (2012) *How to Manage Behaviour in Further Education.* 2nd edn. London: Sage.

Wallace, S (2007) *Managing Behaviour in the Lifelong Learning Sector.* Exeter: Learning Matters.

REFERENCES

ATL (2013): *Achievement for All: Working with Children with Special Education Needs in Mainstream Schools and Colleges.* London: ATL, www.atl.org.uk/publications-and-resources/classroom-practice-publications/special-education-needs.asp (accessed April 2014).

Barnard, H and Turner, C (2011) *Poverty and Ethnicity: A Review of Evidence.* York: JRF, www.jrf.org.uk/sites/files/jrf/poverty-ethnicity-evidence-summary.pdf (accessed May 2014).

Byron, T (2010) *Do We Have Safer Children in a Digital World?* London: DfE, http://webarchive.nationalarchives.gov.uk/20100407120701/dcsf.gov.uk/byronreview/ (accessed April 2014).

Coffield, F (2008) *All You Wanted to Know about Teaching and Learning but Were Too Cool to Ask.* London: LSN.

DfE (2010) *Reducing Bullying amongst the Worst Effected.* London: DfE, www.webarchive.nationalarchives.gov.uk/20130401151715/https://www.education.gov.uk/publications/eOrderingDownload/Reducing%20Bullying%20Amongst%20the%20Worst%20Affected.pdf (accessed June 2014).

DfE (2011) *Preventing and Tackling Bullying.* London: DfE, www.gov.uk/government/publications/preventing-and-tackling-bullying (accessed April 2014).

DfE (2013) *Special Education Needs Code of Practice and Regulations (Consultation).* [Online]. Available at: www.gov.uk/government/consultations/special-educational-needs-sen-code-of-practice-and-regulations (accessed April 2014).

DfE (2014) *Behaviour and Discipline in Schools.* London: DfE, www.gov.uk/government/publications/behaviour-and-discipline-in-schools (accessed April 2014).

DfES (2006) *Improving Initial Assessment: Guide to Good Practice.* Bristol: Portishead Press.

EHRC (2014) *Specific Guidance for Further Education Providers.* [Online]. Available at: www.equalityhumanrights.com/advice-and-guidance/further-and-higher-education-providers-guidance/ (accessed April 2014).

ETF (2014) *Professional Standards for Teachers and Trainers in Education and Training: England.* London: Education and Training Foundation, www.et-foundation.co.uk/our-priorities/professional-standards-2014/ (accessed 30 July 2014).

Goodman, A (2010) *The Importance of Attitudes and Behaviour for Poorer Children's Educational Attainment.* York: JRF, www.jrf.org.uk/sites/files/jrf/poorer-children-education-summary.pdf (accessed April 2014).

Green, M (2003) *Improving initial assessment in work-based learning.* London: LSDA.

Higgins, J and Byrne, M (2008) *Behaviour Management: A Whole Organisation Approach.* Belfast: LSDA NI.

HSE (2014) *About HSE.* [Online]. Available at: HSE (2009) Health and Safety at Work Act 1974 (Summary), www.hse.gov.uk/pubns/law.pdf (accessed May 2014).

ICO (2014) *Guide to Data Protection.* [Online]. Available at: http://ico.org.uk/for_organisations/data_protection/the_guide (accessed April 2014).

Jones, C (2006) *Assessment for Learning.* London: LSN.

King, M and Widdowson, J (2012) *Inspiring Individuals: Teaching Higher Education in a Further Education College.* [Online]. Available at: www.heacademy.ac.uk/assets/documents/heinfe/Inspiring_Individuals_HE_in_FE_MEG3.pdf (accessed April 2014).

Knasel, E, Meed, J, Rossetti, A and Read, H (2006) *Improving Initial Assessment: Guide to Good Practice.* Portishead Press: Bristol.

LSIS (2013) *Qualification Guidance for the Level 5 Diploma in Education and Training.* Coventry: LSIS.

Martinez, P (2001) *Great Expectations: Setting Targets for Students.* London: LSDA.

Massey, A (2013) *Best Behaviour: School Discipline, Intervention and Exclusion.* London: Policy Exchange. Available at: www.policyexchange.org.uk/publications/category/item/best-behaviour-school-discipline-intervention-and-exclusion (accessed May 2014).

Ofsted (2014) *Handbook for the Inspection of Further Education and Skills.* (Revised 25 April 2014). Manchester: Ofsted, www.ofsted.gov.uk/resources/handbook-for-inspection-of-further-education-and-skills-september-2012 (accessed April 2014).

Parry, D and Taubman, D (2013) *Behaviour Management: Final Report.* Birmingham: UCU, http://cpd.web.ucu.org.uk/files/2013/11/UCU-Whole-College-Behaviour-Policy-Project-Final-Report.pdf (accessed April 2014).

QIA (2008) *Skills for Life Improvement Programme: 5 Initial Assessment.* Reading: CfBT.

Reece, I and Walker, S (2007) *Teaching, Training and Learning: A Practical Guide.* 6th edn. Sunderland: Business Education Publishers.

Robinson, K (2010) *Changing Education Paradigms.* TED talks/RSA Animate. [Online]. Available at: www.ted.com/talks/ken_robinson_changing_education_paradigms (accessed April 2014).

Smith, M (2013) *Chris Argyris: Theories of Action, Double-loop Learning and Organizational Learning: The Encyclopaedia of Informal Education.* [Online]. Available at: http://infed.org/mobi/chris-argyris-theories-of-action-double-loop-learning-and-organizational-learning/ (accessed May 2014).

Taylor, C (2011) *Behaviour Checklists.* London: DfE, www.gov.uk/government/publications/good-behaviour-in-schools-checklist-for-teachers (accessed April 2014).

UCU (2013) *Classroom Management.* Birmingham: UCU, http://cpd.web.ucu.org.uk/files/2013/07/CPD-factsheet-6.pdf (accessed April 2014).

4 Assessment principles, practices and processes

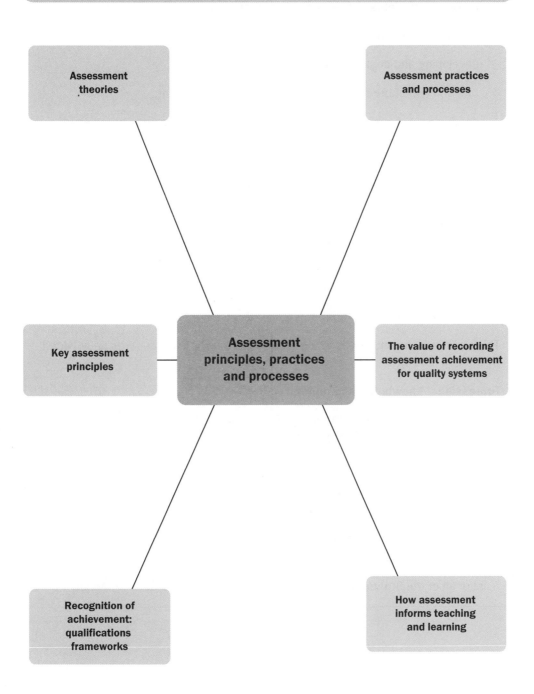

- Assessment theories
- Assessment practices and processes
- Key assessment principles
- **Assessment principles, practices and processes**
- The value of recording assessment achievement for quality systems
- Recognition of achievement: qualifications frameworks
- How assessment informs teaching and learning

PROFESSIONAL LINKS

This chapter assists understanding of the following LSIS (2013, p 28) mandatory content:

o   theories, principles and models of assessment;

o   types and methods of assessment;

o   developing and designing assessments;

o   role and use of questioning and feedback in assessment;

o   conducting assessments using assessment approaches and strategies to meet individual learning needs;

o   demonstrating flexibility and adaptability in using assessment approaches and strategies in response to individual learning needs;

o   achievement, attainment and progress;

o   using assessment data in monitoring of progress, setting targets and planning subsequent lessons;

o   recording and reporting on assessments;

o   awarding organisation requirements for assessments.

This chapter also contributes to the following Professional Standards as provided by the ETF (2014).

Professional knowledge and understanding

9   *apply theoretical understanding of effective practice in teaching, learning and assessment, drawing on research and other evidence*

Professional skills

17   *enable learners to share responsibility for their own learning and assessment, setting goals that stretch and challenge*

18   *apply appropriate and fair methods of assessment and provide constructive and timely feedback to support progression and achievement*

A list of all of the Standards can be found at the back of this book (Appendix 7).

KEY DEFINITIONS

Assessment of learning	Measuring learning to inform learner and teacher of current ability, often for a qualification.
Assessment for learning	Measuring learning to inform learner and teacher of future development needs.
Assessment-led learning	An approach to education which values the result of the assessment over the process of learning.
Assessment methods	Different approaches to assessing learning such as examination, practical work-based tasks and assignments.
Feedback (to learners)	Informing learners of progress and future development needs.
Formal assessment	Assessment with clear procedures, structure and outcomes.
Formative assessment	Assessment approach focusing on learner development.
Individual goals	Specific steps towards achieving long-term aspirations.
Informal assessment	Checking learning, usually as a part of everyday teaching practice.
Objectivity	Evidence-based judgement without prejudice.
Reliability	The consistency of an assessment process.
Subjectivity	Judgement based on opinion and not supported by clear evidence.
Sufficiency	The breadth of assessment coverage in relation to the overall subject syllabus.
Summative assessment	Final assessment, usually at the end of a course, to evidence learner achievement.

→

Transparency	The extent to which the assessment process is clear and understood by all involved.
Validity	The extent an assessment tests the required skills.

INTRODUCTION

This chapter introduces key theories and principles underpinning assessment, how it measures learning, informs development, teacher planning and quality systems. It illustrates some of the many different assessment tools to facilitate your evaluation of their appropriacy for promoting inclusive learning. It therefore aims to support you in:

○ investigating theories, models and principles of assessment;

○ reflecting on the impact of different types and methods of assessment that promote inclusive learning;

○ identifying elements of good practice in developing and designing assessments;

○ evaluating assessment approaches/strategies/methods/techniques to meet individual learning needs;

○ developing understanding of the role of accurately recording and reporting assessment;

○ monitoring progress, setting targets and planning subsequent lessons;

○ recording and reporting on assessments to meet institutional quality requirements;

○ meeting awarding organisation (AO) requirements for assessments.

STARTING POINT

What do you already know about reflecting and evaluating your own practice?

○ What assessment methods do you have experience of as a learner?

○ What assessment methods do you have experience of as a teacher?

○ What other assessment methods are you aware of?

○ Why do we assess learning?

THEORIES, PRINCIPLES AND MODELS OF ASSESSMENT

Even if you are not involved in formal assessment processes you will, as a teacher, constantly be assessing your learners and as Broadfoot et al. (2002) note:

> *Assessment is one of the most powerful educational tools for promoting effective learning. But it must be used in the right way. There is no evidence that increasing the amount of testing will enhance learning. Instead the focus needs to be on helping teachers use assessment, as part of teaching and learning, in ways that will raise pupils' achievement.*
>
> (Broadfoot et al., 2002, p 12)

Race (2001) identifies several positive and negative feelings that learners may undergo during various assessment processes. Negative feelings include fear, vulnerability, inadequacy and frustration, whilst positive feelings include adrenaline, comradeship and expectancy of successful results opening further employment or learning opportunities. Teachers can influence learners' feelings regarding assessment by ensuring that learners are motivated and are given support and effective assessment practice before any final assessment process takes place. This way learners approach assessment with more expectation than fear.

Critical questions

What emotional factors contributed to your success/failure in an assessment?

What impact did these experiences have on your self-esteem?

ASSESSMENT THEORIES

Rust (2002) argues that assessment is not just about grading, but also about identifying strengths and weaknesses. As general concepts, assessment can be considered in terms of assessment of learning, assessment-led learning and assessment for learning.

Assessment of learning

Assessment of learning measures learners' ability in a chosen area of knowledge or skill to provide a clear decision about whether they have met the required criteria. Often formal, using assessment tools such as examination or work-based observation of practice, such assessments may also be summative, meaning that they pass final judgement on achievement at the end of a learning process. A benefit of such a measurement is that it leads to recognised qualifications or professional competencies which can enhance learners' employment opportunities or academic progression (Black et al., 2003). Assessment of learning can therefore motivate learners who value the resulting qualification as well as raising their self-esteem:

This sense of achievement often derives from the 'second chance' element of post-compulsory education, but seems to be articulated in 'affective' terms, relating to an overall sense of achievement, identity change and social progress rather than directly related to acquisition of skills or competences.

(Torrance et al., 2005, p 35)

Making assessment of learning judgements: criterion, competency and norm-referencing

Torrance et al. (2005) identify key approaches to making assessment judgements as criterion, competency-based and norm-referenced. The criterion-based approach judges success or failure on the individual's ability to evidence achievement of clear abilities, skills or behaviours. The achievement of any cohort therefore depends solely on their ability to reach these criteria, rather than on how well they perform in relation to others. Rather than using assessment to divide learners into achievers and failures, potentially all learners succeed as criteria provide learners with a transparent basis for success (Rust, 2002). Similarly, competency-based approaches are often used for evidencing practical skills in work-based learning. Learners may have to pass every criterion to demonstrate the competence and achievement of professional skills required for accreditation and qualification.

However, criterion and competence-based assessments face criticism of being too easy. Improved results are commonly interpreted in the media as evidencing simplification rather than better quality teaching, as opposed to traditional perceptions of education's role being to divide achievers and non-achievers (Torrance et al., 2005). Indeed, while finding that coaching learners raises achievement, learning can become so assessment led that learners may develop little more than the ability to pass tests. This emphasis on achievement, often supported by multiple opportunities to reassess until a competency has been achieved, adds sustenance to such viewpoints (Wolf, 2011). Unless assessed competencies build on previous achievements, there is a danger that knowledge and skills are lost after the assessment.

Government policy appears to be moving towards more traditional approaches to assessment such as single, summative assessments (DfE, 2013). While these also have criteria to reach, examinations such as GCSEs also have an element of norm referencing included to set boundaries between grades. A norm-referenced approach is therefore used to divide groups in terms of their achievement by making judgements based on how well learners perform in relation to each other: *'The practice derives both from a belief in there being a fixed "pool" of ability, or capacity to achieve, and from which therefore the most talented individuals should be identified ... so that selection was the main purpose of assessment'* (Torrance et al., 2005, p 20). Criticisms of norm referencing are therefore roughly the opposite of criteria-based assessments. It assumes that each cohort's ability is static and therefore results cannot be compared with previous years to ascertain the relative quality of national provision. Furthermore, shifting pass rates lack transparency and potentially demotivate the majority who fail to achieve the highest grades (Broadfoot et al., 2002; Torrance et al., 2005); although Ofqual (2013) proposes that such percentile scores should be introduced for learners. With successful Ofsted inspections reliant on high achievement rates compared with national benchmarks, the renewed emphasis on norm-referenced assessment may lead to a static portion of institutions may be judged as inadequate (Stewart, 2013).

Critical questions

Which of these approaches do you use and why?

To what extent is assessment used to divide learners in terms of ability or evidence competence?

Assessment-led learning

The ability to engage with and perform well in a variety of approaches to assessment is clearly a useful skill for a learner to develop to maximise their ability to achieve. However, beyond the development of assessment technique, assessments should be sufficiently engaging to be seen as a regular part rather than a distraction from the learning process. Flórez and Sammons (2013) warn against assessment-led learning, linking this to theories of learning which implicitly view knowledge and understanding as being clearly quantifiable, measurable and permanently retained (see Chapter 6). Though learners should practise using techniques required in the final assessment, excessive preparation is counter-productive, detracting from broader personal, social and employability development purposes of learning. Faced with pressures to demonstrate achievement, focusing on the summative assessment rather than instilling learner enthusiasm for the subject itself might be appropriate for motivated and experienced learners needing a quick update to pass a qualification, but should not be used in longer courses or where your learners' initial motivation to achieve is in doubt. Such an approach leads to uninspiring teacher-led repetition of key facts and examination practice which fail to raise achievement anyway (Petty, 2009). Assessment practice should therefore clearly be seen as part of a learner's overall development.

Assessment for learning

Assessment for learning (AfL) takes place throughout the learner journey (QIA, 2008b), with the Assessment Reform Group (ARG, 2002, p 2) summarising it as '*the process of seeking and interpreting evidence for use by learners and their teachers to decide where the learners are in their learning, where they need to go and how best to get there*'. Flórez and Sammons (2013) view AfL as a constructivist approach to learning, with its emphasis on developing personal understanding rather than rote memorisation of facts (see Chapter 6). Such assessment is formative, providing information to both learner and teacher of achievement and future development needs: '*Teachers who assess in this way are concerned not just to confirm and verify what their learners have learnt, but also to help their learners and themselves understand what the next steps in learning should be and how they might be attempted*' (Flórez and Sammons, 2013, p 2). Flórez and Sammons' (2013) review of AfL found that it could have numerous benefits for learners and teachers; for example, improving results and developing learners' self-concept and confidence to engage more in classroom activities as a whole. Rather than viewing assessment as a competition of winners and losers, focusing on achievement helps to build more positive self-esteem, developing personal responsibility for learning. Teachers may also benefit in terms of moving away from the limitations of an overly behaviourist approach (see Chapter 6):

Teachers, like learners, change their role in classroom interaction when AfL is introduced. Their participation is said to shift from the prime concern to be a content deliverer who largely controls the classroom dynamics, to a moderator and facilitator of learning who collaborates with learners during the class, supporting and monitoring their progress.

(Flórez and Sammons, 2013, p 18)

However, unless AfL becomes an institution-wide policy, its impact can be limited, with some professionals resisting giving learners more responsibility for fear of losing control (Flórez and Sammons, 2013). Flórez and Sammons highlight the work of Dunn and Mulvenon (2009), whose review of American AfL research concluded that it tended to be small scale, and therefore potentially unreliable, and was weakened by a lack of agreed terminology and concepts. Furthermore, where AfL failed, they found researchers tended to blame other factors rather than question the validity of the concept itself, with a lack of detailed research into which techniques work best. Figure 4.1, developed from QIA (2008a), demonstrates how AfL aims to enhance learner achievement and experiences.

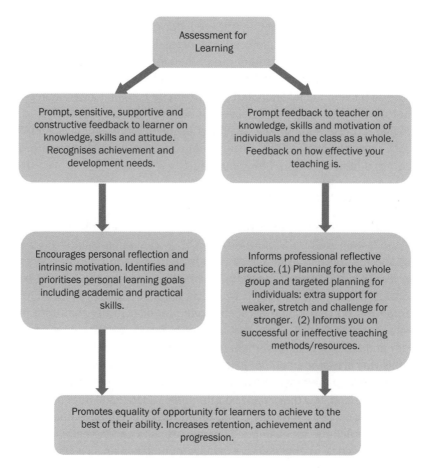

Figure 4.1 AFL: enhancement of learner experiences and achievement

Critical question

'Right you all did badly on this subject in the test, so let's go through the PowerPoint again.'

What is wrong with this approach?

Comment

Formative assessment findings inform you of the content which needs to be covered and also the effectiveness of teaching and learning methods. As the technique was ineffective the first time, repetition is unlikely to work, especially as learner boredom might cause behavioural issues to further compound a lack of engagement. Therefore, it can be useful to discuss the following:

o successes and challenges with your learners after assessments to develop understanding of what helped or hindered their achievement;

o how you can support them, and more crucially, what can they change to help themselves.

Critical questions

Which assessments have you had that you thought fairly judged your abilities? Which ones did not? Explain your answers.

Once you have read the text on pages 78–81, evaluate your responses to these questions in relation to the key assessment principles.

Figure 4.2 Promoting equality of opportunity to succeed

KEY ASSESSMENT PRINCIPLES

Figure 4.2 illustrates how certain key principles contribute to the overall purpose of assessment, which is to provide equality of opportunity for your learners to achieve to the best of their ability.

Validity

Assessment validity relates to the extent that the means of testing are appropriate to evaluate the required knowledge, skills and abilities.

 Case study

Teacher: '*So when they've completed the level 3 qualification they have full professional accreditation.*'

Observer: '*So you'd employ any successful student on your building site then?*'

Teacher: '*What – this lot? You must be joking.*'

> ## *Critical questions*
>
> To what extent do the qualifications you offer meet their stated professional com-
> petencies? How do you know this?
>
> To what extent do employers value the qualifications you teach?
>
> To what extent do employers consider successful learners to be work-ready?

Reliability

Rust (2000, p 2) defines assessment reliability in terms of our approach to forming judgement: '*If a particular assessment were totally reliable, assessors acting independently using the same criteria and mark scheme would come to exactly the same judgement about a given piece of work.*' Race (2001, p 12) concurs, arguing that reliability is synonymous with consistency, fairness and (as far as can be achieved) lack of subjectivity. Reliability can therefore be considered in terms of the extent to which:

o markers assess work using standard criteria, interpreting these as objectively as possible;

o different assessments for the same level and qualification are equitable;

o assessment conditions are similar at each assessment site through rigid adherence to AO guidelines.

This means that all learners should undergo assessment in as similar conditions as possible or appropriate. AOs therefore advise on:

o assessment location and environment (this includes room layout to prevent copying);

o when an assessment is set (national examinations often have specific dates and durations so that on completion learners cannot communicate content to others);

o course-specific instructions (this must be followed so that the assessment is fair for all learners; for example permitted equipment guidance is typically found in mathematics examinations).

Each AO has specific provision for learners with SEN. Typical examinations of reasonable adjustments which an AO may recommend could include:

o allowing a reader;

o extra time allowances;

o specially recorded listening examination for language skills assessments;

o assessment papers with large print.

Critical question

According to your AO, what provision is available for your learners with SEN?

Comment

Contact the AO and make any necessary adjustments well in advance of the assessment, including raising awareness of these to learners with SEN.

Transparency

Transparency relates to the clarity of assessment processes, for learners, teachers and external organisations such as Ofsted. It is not sufficient for a learner to be given a mark or grade without understanding the grading process. Race (2001, p 12) states that transparency is '*about the goalposts being clearly defined, so that learners are well aware of the standards expected of them to gain particular awards, and the nature of the evidence that they will need to furnish to demonstrate their achievement of the published intended learning outcomes*.' Teachers must therefore understand and carefully adhere to the marking criteria (Rust, 2002). This is especially important where there is no clear *right* or *wrong* answer; academic writing or professional competency judgements may be interpreted differently, and so require prior agreement through standardisation. This should be undertaken before commencing assessment, for example by marking sample scripts or performing a joint observation of practice.

Learners should be made aware of the criteria throughout the learning process so that they understand how their work is assessed. When criteria use language that is above the level of learners' understanding it should, if possible, be simplified and supported by sample work demonstrating different levels of achievement. You need to be able to defend your judgement clearly to AOs, your learners and, as appropriate, other stakeholders. A poor result may be disappointing for a learner, especially if the course cost them a good deal of money or hinders their career aspirations, but this must not have any bearing on your judgement which must be based on the criteria alone. You therefore need to be able to explicitly refer to the agreed criteria in your feedback so that it is clear why the mark has been awarded.

Critical question

How do you justify grades to your learners and how do you ensure assessment transparency?

Sufficiency

Assessments rarely cover everything taught as they would become too long and impractical. Sufficiency therefore relates to the scope of the assessment in terms of the extent to which its content is a reasonable reflection of the overall course syllabus content and required skills.

Practicality

There will never be a perfect assessment in relation to the above principles. Generally speaking, the more reliable, valid and sufficient we attempt to make our assessment, the less practical and therefore more costly it will become. Assessment is always a balancing act between what is practical – and affordable – and giving learners the best learning and assessment environment in order to succeed.

Authenticity

Assessment authenticity refers to ensuring that work submitted is the learner's own so AOs require learners to bring some form of personal identification. Any assessment which takes place outside of such controlled conditions runs the risk of not being the learner's own work; this could be plagiarised – taken from an unacknowledged source – or completed by a friend or relative. Qualifications therefore often involve a variety of assessments to validate authenticity – such as supplementing coursework with an examination.

Critical questions

How do you ensure the authenticity of assessed work?

What guidance does your AO give on ensuring authenticity?

What processes do you follow if you suspect work is not authentic?

Currency

Currency relates to the value of the qualification in relation to other qualifications and with employers or professional bodies. The Wolf Review (DfE, 2011) strongly criticised many vocational qualifications as lacking rigour or value for employers, resulting in the DfE reducing the number of funded qualifications.

Critical questions

What do employers think about the qualification/s that you teach?

→

Are the qualifications relating to the course/s that you teach and your AO well recognised nationally and even internationally?

Are your assessments compliant with the latest laws, policies and codes of practice as stipulated by relevant professional bodies and government agencies?

HOW ASSESSMENT INFORMS TEACHING AND LEARNING

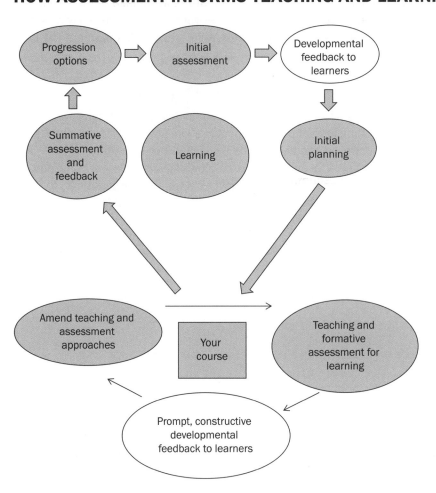

Figure 4.3 Approach to diagnostic assessment

Initial assessment, feedback and planning

Diagnostic assessments inform both teacher and learner of current abilities and specific future needs (see Figure 4.3). Essentially, initial assessment (IA) is diagnostic, but specifically refers to the first assessment, ideally taken before courses begin (see Chapter 2).

Further diagnostic assessments may be taken at any point during the course to identify changing learner needs.

Self- and peer assessment

Self- and peer assessment engage learners in assessment and develop key transferable employment skills of responsibility, autonomy, analysis, evaluation and reflection (Race, 2001). Self-assessment encourages learner reflection on their progress and understanding of assessment processes, thereby informing development priorities. When used in conjunction with your assessment judgement, it can inform the learner of how accurately they perceive their own abilities. Peer assessment refers to learners judging each other's work. As with self-assessment, this encourages learners to actively take responsibility for their progress by developing an understanding of the assessment criteria. Peer assessment may increase the reliability of assessments as it ensures that judgement has been made by more than one assessor (Race, 2001). Table 4.1 illustrates some of the possible approaches to self- and peer assessment.

Table 4.1 Approaches to self- and peer assessment

Assessment tool	Description	Reflections on my practice
Colour code criteria according to confidence in achieving goal	Self-assessment to focus learners on the criteria	
Self-marking	Learners mark their own work, using the criteria to justify their judgement	
Comment only marking	Peer assessment to focus on aspects of the work rather than grading. Can be tailored to be constructive comments only	
Medals and mission	Peer assessment which highlights achievement and sets key future goal	
Paired marking	In pairs, learners mark each other's work, justifying the feedback based on the criteria	
Question setting	Learners set questions for each other based on the topic. Can be turned into a team-based quiz	

Source: Adapted from Flórez and Sammons (2013) and QIA (2008)

Critical question

Teacher: *'Peer assessment sounds great but we can't do any of that on our courses. We have so much content to cover that we have to stick to teacher-led delivery.'*

What advice could you give to this teacher?

Comment

You could advise the teacher to:

o focus on active learning of the key points in the syllabus for your teaching, signposting learners to self-study less important areas (Petty, 2009);

o consider alternative forms of delivery, for example could any of the content be delivered through a virtual learning environment?

Challenges of self- and peer assessment

Nevertheless, self- and peer assessment can present problems as learners may under- or over-assess their ability (DfES, 2006) so it is not recommended for summative assessment purposes (Knasel et al., 2006). AOs often use complicated language to aid precise judgements which learners may not understand (Flórez and Sammons, 2013), so consider what they are capable of assessing and retain more complex criteria for your expertise. To familiarise your learners with assessment rubrics (the language of assessments), you must carefully explain key terms first. For example, tasks including define, outline, illustrate, compare, analyse and evaluate require increasing levels of learner cognition (Bloom, 1956, cited in Petty, 2009). Learners need to develop skills to sensitively and constructively deliver and receive feedback, using evidence-based judgements rather than opinion. You can avoid potential disputes by initially asking learners to mark previous groups' anonymous work (Rust, 2002). Flórez and Sammons (2013) contend that learners may consider peers' feedback more credible and are therefore more likely to take action.

However, Knasel et al. (2006) warn that poorly articulated feedback could be upsetting as learners might lack the subtlety of language which teachers use to accurately, yet sensitively, outline weaknesses. Jones (2006) concurs, warning that the potential for peers to publicly rank each other's ability can be highly demotivating for less able learners and conversely, more able learners may not be stretched when reviewing an activity which they completed successfully. Furthermore, your class may be reluctant to accurately highlight legitimate criticisms of each other's work. Flórez and Sammons (2013), focusing on school education, and Race (2001), on higher education, therefore concur that developing effective self- and peer learning takes time and careful planning.

Individual and group assessment

Summative assessments in FE are usually individually based for ease of accreditation and accountability. Alternatively, group assessments develop interpersonal communication skills through leading or contributing to a team and so are clearly useful for developing employability (Race, 2001). Therefore, group assessments are useful for IA processes and team building (Jones, 2006). However, Rust (2002) warns of difficulties of fairly allocating marks – a key argument against its use in summative assessment. Marks could be given to the group overall, emphasising the value of teamwork, but could lead to complaints over the fairness of the group's organisation due to differing initial levels of each group's ability. Individually based marking is also problematic because of difficulties quantifying the extent and quality of individual contributions (Race, 2001).

Summative assessment, feedback and progression

Summative assessment and subsequent feedback informs learners of their overall achievement. As well as an overall grade, learners need opportunities to explore progression options – whether they have passed or failed. What are their interests, career options or aspirations? (See Chapter 9 for more discussion about learners' progression.)

Table 4.2 Skills assessment

Assessed skill	Required on my course?	How is this currently assessed?	What alternatives are there?
Accessing information/ researching topic			
Demonstrating subject knowledge			
Demonstrating planning skills			
Designing/creativity			
Communication			
Problem solving			
Practical tasks/ performing work-based procedures			
Making judgements			
Personal and professional development (reflective skills)			

Source: Adapted from Dunn (2002)

Critical task

Think about your practice in terms of the key assessment principles. How are the skills outlined in Table 4.2 evidenced in your assessment practices?

THE VALUE OF RECORDING ASSESSMENT ACHIEVEMENT FOR QUALITY SYSTEMS

According to Perry et al. (2010) Callaghan's *Great Debate* speech (1976) paved the way for the principle of financial accountability justifying political control of education. Standardised national testing provides measured outcomes so is integral to organisational quality assurance systems. Learner achievement provides accountability data on teachers', departments' and education organisations' performance and informs international comparisons. In return for public funding, teachers are expected to develop well-qualified and employable learners, defined by qualification achievements. The Programme for International Student Assessment evaluates education systems worldwide every three years by assessing 15 year-olds' competencies in three subjects (reading, mathematics and science), and is used for international comparisons of education system success.

The UK's mediocre PISA standing, in spite of steadily improving national achievement rates, has been used to justify reforms to education initiated in the White Paper, the Importance of Teaching (DfE, 2010), subsequent reforms emanating from the Education Act 2011 and the response to the Wolf Report (DfE, 2011), which argued that such performance measurement had led institutions to direct learners away from the skills they needed towards qualifications which were easier to attain to boost their achievement results. Nevertheless, this accountability focus of assessment remains and has met varied criticisms. Professors Frank Coffield and Bill Williamson (2011) highlight the potentially negative emotional impacts of constant testing and targets on learners and their teachers. Robinson (2010) contends that the education system is outdated, being over-reliant on testing a narrow range of abilities at the expense of creative thinking. In addition to these concerns, over 100 academics protested that PISA led to short-term quick-fix policies focused on improving the international ranking rather than developing a broad and engaging education system (Andrews et al., 2014).

RECOGNITION OF ACHIEVEMENT: QUALIFICATION FRAMEWORKS

Assessment is an important part of promoting employment opportunities through recognition of achievement for all learners. Nationally recognised qualifications are regulated by the Office of Qualifications and Examinations Regulation (Ofqual). These qualifications will be part of the Qualifications and Credit Framework (QCF) or the National Qualifications Framework (NQF) (Ofqual, 2013). More information about the QCF can be found in the Introduction at the beginning of this book.

The Qualifications and Credit Framework

Qualifications that use the QCF rules are made up of units which provide flexible ways to get a qualification. Each unit has a credit value and units build up to make qualifications. The three different types of qualification in the QCF are the Award, Certificate and Diploma. Units and qualifications are each given a level according to their difficulty, from entry level to level 8.

The National Qualifications Framework

Qualifications that do not meet the rules of the QCF have been developed to fit the NQF, which provides an indication of the relative demand of different qualifications. Here again qualifications are given a level from entry level to level 8 based on the standards of knowledge, skill and competence needed.

Each qualification is assessed at a certain level, allowing for qualifications in different subjects to be recognised as having the same academic value as can be seen in Figure 4.4. If you are unsure about the levels of the qualifications you teach, go to the Ofqual register of regulated qualifications or your AO.

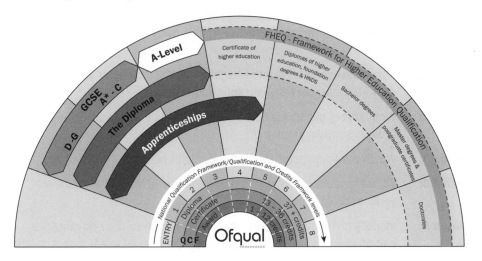

Figure 4.4 Guide to qualification levels

The European Qualifications Framework

UK qualification levels are comparable with European levels using the EQF (European Commission 2013). Learners from outside the European Union can find out the value of their qualifications in relation to the English system through the National Recognition Information Centre (NARIC) (Ectis, 2014).

Other schemes

Not all subjects are linked to a qualification, though there may be opportunities for formal recognition of achievement in your courses. For example the National Institute of

Adult Continuing Education (NIACE) has the Recognising and Recording Progress and Achievement (RARPA) scheme. This is '*a framework for ensuring that progress and achievement could be evidenced for learners and teachers in learning where there is no formal accreditation*' (NIACE, 2013).

SUMMARY

Whether assessment is formal or informal it is potentially a powerful motivator for learners' future development. For example, the attainment of formal qualifications opens up career opportunities, such as enabling learners to gain promotion or to practise a trade. Often learners' progression is only considered at the end of a course but, to motivate and raise their aspirations further, learning opportunities should be discussed and promoted throughout the course (see Chapter 9).

 # Check your understanding

You will find suggested answers to some of these questions at the back of this book.

Question 1:   What assessment strategies are most successful at actively engaging learners? Explain your answer.

Question 2:   What sort of questions could promote self- and peer assessment? Provide some examples.

Question 3:   Which qualifications have had the most impact on your life? Why?

Question 4:   What are your organisation's requirements for internal and external verification of assessments?

Question 5:   Identify different assessment tools and analyse their advantages and challenges in relation to the key principles of assessment.

End-of-chapter reflections

o   Remember: all forms of assessment have differing advantages and challenges; reflect on how your practice can improve in relation to the key principles of assessment.

o   Assessment takes place throughout the learner's journey, informing your planning as well as your learners' achievements and future development focus.

o Summative assessment preparation is useful for learners, but should not become the only focus of your teaching.

o Contact your AO for guidance on adjustments for Special Educational Needs well in advance of assessments. Ensure your learners are fully aware of any support opportunities.

o Assessment informs quality assurance and improvement processes, so accurate recording and reporting is an essential part of your professional practice.

 TAKING IT FURTHER

In addition to the literature already commented upon in this chapter you may find the following of interest.

BBC (2012) Do Schools Make a Difference? *BBC Radio 4 Podcast.* [Online]. Available at: www.bbc.co.uk/programmes/b01b9hjs (accessed May 2014).

Gravells, A (2011) *Principles and Practice of Assessment in the Lifelong Learning Sector.* 2nd edn. Exeter: Learning Matters.

Green, M (2002) *Initial Assessment: A Learner-centred Process.* London: LSDA.

Moorse, R and Clough, L (2002) *Recognition and Reward: Using Feedback for Learner Success.* London: LSDA.

OECD. *Programme for International Student Attainment (PISA).* [Online]. Available at: www.oecd.org/pisa/aboutpisa/ (accessed May 2014).

REFERENCES

Andrews et al. (over 100 academics) (2014) *OECD and Pisa Tests Are Damaging Education Worldwide.* [Online]. Available at: www.theguardian.com/education/2014/may/06/oecd-pisa-tests-damaging-education-academics (accessed May 2014).

ARG (2002) *Assessment for Learning: 10 Principles.* London: Nuffield Foundation, www.aaia.org.uk/content/uploads/2010/06/Assessment-for-Learning-10-principles.pdf (accessed May 2014).

Black, P, Harrison, C, Lee, C, Marshall, B and Wiliam, D (2003) *Assessment for Learning: Putting It into Practice.* Maidenhead: OUP.

Broadfoot, P, Daugherty, R, Gardner, J, Harlen, W, James, M and Stobart, G (2002) *Beyond the Black Box.* London: Assessment Reform Group/Nuffield Foundation.

Coffield, F and Williamson, B (2011) *From Examination Factories to Communities of Discovery.* London: Institute of Education.

DfE (2010) *Reducing Bullying amongst the Worst Effected*. London: DfE, www.webarchive. nationalarchives.gov.uk/20130401151715/https://www.education.gov.uk/publications/ eOrderingDownload/Reducing%20Bullying%20Amongst%20the%20Worst%20Affected. pdf (accessed June 2014).

DfE (2011) *Wolf Review of Vocational Education: Government Response*. London: DfE, www. gov.uk/government/uploads/system/uploads/attachment_data/file/180868/Wolf- Review-Response.pdf (accessed April 2014).

DfE (2013) *Wolf Recommendations Progress Report*. London: DfE, www.gov.uk/government/ publications/wolf-recommendations-progress-report (accessed April 2014).

DfES (2006) *Improving Initial Assessment: Guide to Good Practice*. Bristol: Portishead Press.

Dunn, L (2002) *Selecting Methods of Assessment*. Oxford: Oxford Brookes.

Dunn, K and Mulvenon, S (2009) A critical review of research on formative assessment: the limited scientific evidence of the impact of formative assessment in education practical assessment. *Research and Evaluation*, 14(7): 1–11.

Ectis (2014) *UK NARIC: What We Do*. [Online]. Available at: www.ecctis.co.uk/naric/ What%20we%20do.aspx (accessed May 2014).

ETF (2014) *Professional Standards for Teachers and Trainers in Education and Training: England*. London: Education and Training Foundation, www.et-foundation. co.uk/our-priorities/professional-standards-2014/ (accessed 20 July 2014).

European Commission (2013) *The European Qualifications Framework*. [Online]. Available at: http://ec.europa.eu/eqf/home_en.htm (accessed May 2014).

Flórez, M and Sammons, P (2013) *Assessment for Learning*. Reading: CfBT, www.cfbt.com/ en-GB/Research/Research-library/2013/r-assessment-for-learning-2013 (accessed May 2014).

Jones, C (2006) *Assessment for Learning*. London: LSN.

Knasel, E, Meed, J, Rossetti, A, Read, H and Record, D (2006) *Improving Initial Assessment: Guide to Good Practice*. Bristol: Portishead Press.

LSIS (2013) *Qualification Guidance for the Level 5 Diploma in Education and Training*. Coventry: LSIS.

NIACE (2013) *Recognising and Recording Progress and Achievement*. [Online]. Available at: www.niace.org.uk/current-work/rarpa (accessed May 2014).

Ofqual (2013) *Comparing Qualifications Levels*. [Online]. Available at: www.ofqual.gov.uk/ help-and-advice/comparing-qualifications/ (accessed May 2014).

Perry, A, Amadeo, C, Fletcher, M and Walker, E (2010) *Instinct of Reason: How Education Policy Is Made and How We Might Make It Better*. Reading: CfBT, www.cfbt.com/en-GB/ Research/Research-library/2010/r-instinct-or-reason-2010 (accessed 19 October 2013).

Petty, G (2009) *Evidence Based Teaching*. 2nd edn. Cheltenham: Nelson Thornes.

QIA (2008a) *Quick Start Guide: Assessment for Learning*. [Online]. Available at: http://tlp. excellencegateway.org.uk/tlp/pedagogy/assets/documents/qs_assessment_learning. pdf (accessed June 2014).

QIA (2008b) *Skills for Life Improvement Programme: 5 Initial Assessment*. Reading: CfBT.

Race, P (2001) *A Briefing on Self, Peer and Group Assessment.* York: LTSN.

Robinson, K (2010) *Changing Education Paradigms.* TED talks/RSA Animate, www.ted.com/talks/ken_robinson_changing_education_paradigms (accessed April 2014).

Rust, C (2000) *Principles of Assessment.* York: HEA, www.medev.heacademy.ac.uk/assets/documents/resources/database/id436_basic_assessment_issues.pdf (accessed June 2014).

Rust, C (2002) *Purposes and Principles of Assessment.* Oxford: Oxford Brookes University.

Stewart, W (2013) Is there no way up for results? *Times Educational Supplement*, 24 April, www.tes.co.uk/article.aspx?storycode=6329987 (accessed April 2014).

Torrance, H, Colley, H, Garret, D, Jarvis, J, Piper, H, Ecclestone, C and James, D (2005) *The Impact of Different Modes of Assessment on Achievement and Progress in the Lifelong Learning Sector.* London: LSRC.

Wolf, A (2011) *Review of Vocational Education: The Wolf Report.* London: DfE, www.gov.uk/government/publications/review-of-vocational-education-the-wolf-report (accessed May 2014).

5 Communication

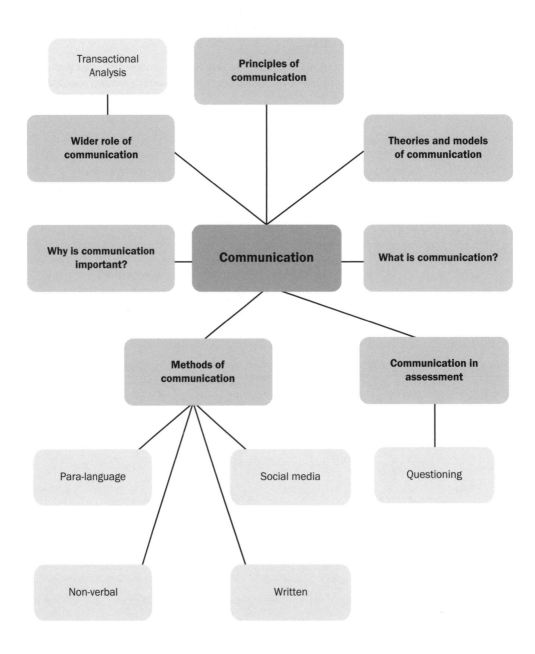

PROFESSIONAL LINKS

This chapter assists with your understanding of the following LSIS (2013, p 28) mandatory content:

○   theories and models of communication;

○   principles of communication;

○   methods of communication;

○   communicating with learners, other learning professionals and other relevant parties;

○   the role and use of questioning and feedback in assessment.

It also contributes to the following Professional Standards as provided by the ETF (2014).

Professional values and attributes

Develop your own judgement of what works and does not work in your teaching and training.

6   *Build positive and collaborative relationships with colleagues and learners*

Professional knowledge and understanding

Develop deep and critically informed knowledge and understanding in theory and practice.

9   *Apply theoretical understanding of effective practice in teaching, learning and assessment drawing on research and other evidence*

Professional skills

Develop your expertise and skills to ensure the best outcomes for learners.

15   *Promote the benefits of technology and support learners in its use*

18   *Apply appropriate and fair methods of assessment and provide constructive and timely feedback to support progression and achievement*

A list of all of the Standards can be found at the back of this book (Appendix 7).

KEY DEFINITIONS

Kinesics	The study of body movements and gestures.
Medal and mission	An approach to providing feedback.
Non-verbal communication	Communication via a means other than speech.
Para-language	Analysis of tone, pitch or speed in verbal communication.
Transactional analysis	Theory based on the ego states adopted by people when communicating.

INTRODUCTION

Communication is at the heart of everything that you do as a teacher, whether with learners, colleagues or other professionals and is a skill that will continue to be developed throughout your career. This chapter, through its alignment to literature, asking questions and providing activities, is designed to support you in your understanding of how to apply theories, principles and models of effective communication to develop your practice. It therefore aims to support you in:

○   identifying and exploring principles of communication;

○   identifying, exploring and critiquing some of the key theories and models of communication;

○   considering and developing your approaches to communication in assessment;

○   considering and developing the wider role of communication in relation to your practice.

STARTING POINT

What do you already know about communication?

○   What methods of communication are you already aware of?

○   What do you understand by principles of communication?

○   What models and theories of communication are you already aware of?

○   How can you ensure effective communication within
assessment?

○   What do you understand about the wider role of
communication?

WHY IS COMMUNICATION IMPORTANT?

As a teacher in FE you will require excellent communication skills in a variety of situations, with a range of people and at differing levels. As you start your DET qualification
you will already have some strengths in this area; however, there are likely to be some
that you need to develop more fully so that you can swiftly remove any barriers to effective communication between you and your learners and also, as necessary, with other
stakeholders (eg parents, other teachers). Your understanding and skills in all of these
areas can be developed by engaging critically with key principles and relevant communication theory.

WHAT IS COMMUNICATION?

Communication relates to the giving, receiving and imparting information, thoughts,
ideas, feelings and values. Communication takes place between two or more people.
However, Hargie puts forward a wide range of factors, including '*perceptual, cognitive,
affective and performative factors*', that can all influence communication (Hargie, 2004,
p 11).

PRINCIPLES OF COMMUNICATION

A number of basic principles underlie any discussion of interpersonal communication
and contributions are many and varied. However, you may find the following particularly
relevant in your teaching role:

○   *interpersonal communication is unavoidable;*

○   *interpersonal communication is irreversible;*

○   *interpersonal communication is rule governed.*

(West, 2006, pp 26–7)

You cannot avoid communicating. For example, even if you are in a room with a group
of learners and do not say anything your body language will convey a message, whether
intentionally or otherwise. The irreversibility element of communication means that
whether you like it or not, once something has been said it cannot be unsaid and this
emphasises the need to think carefully before you speak. Even the act of not speaking will itself convey a message to learners. Knowledge of the often unwritten *rules*
and *social knowledge* required in effective communication is essential. Hartley (1999,
p 89) acknowledges that these can vary for reasons including cultural background and
gender. This is something to consider as you communicate with your learners and, for

example, your managers and colleagues, as how you communicate to different groups of people will differ and require the application of different rules of discourse.

 Case study

Pat is a new member of a teaching team and is usually a confident communicator. She has been asked by her manager to deliver a new course but has been given very little information about the proposed course structure and content and is concerned about having to deliver it. She is nervous about raising her concerns about this and doesn't know what to say or how to say it.

Critical question

How might consideration of the rules of communication apply to any discussion that Pat plans to have with her line manager?

Comment

The rules of communication here are related to the relationship between manager and staff member. Pat should remain calm and polite and enquire if there is any further information that will help her deliver the course or to ask if someone else can help her locate the information.

THEORIES AND MODELS OF COMMUNICATION

A basic model of communication is that proposed by Shannon and Weaver (1949) in which they recognise the two participants in a communication scenario and refer to these as '*source*' and '*receiver*' (Hill et al., 2007, p 8). A conversation between yourself and a learner would position one of you as the source (the sender) and the other as the receiver. A shortcoming of this model lies with its origins as a model of technical communication. Shannon and Weaver's (1949) model also includes the notion of '*interference*' or '*noise*' (Hill et al., 2007, p 8), which relates to the distortion of the original message. Noise can take a wide range of forms including visual or auditory distractions, disabilities or learning difficulties and languages or jargon. When considering your communication you should therefore carefully consider the environment, the learners and your own communication skills.

With recognition of the technical origins of Shannon and Weaver's model, Berlo (1960) included wider elements within his model of communication. He suggests that a range of further factors could influence the effectiveness of interpersonal communication. These factors include the '*communication skills, attitudes, knowledge, social system and cultural factors*' of the participants and are a core influence on the effectiveness of communication (Hill et al., 2007, p 12).

COMMUNICATION IN ASSESSMENT

Effective communication is imperative at every stage of teaching, learning and assessment. Skills in assessment can range from those required in giving feedback to those necessary when questioning your learners.

Formative assessment can serve a dual purpose in terms of checking whether learning has taken place and supporting learners to improve their skills and knowledge. The key factor in achieving this is the use of effective feedback. Shute (2008, p 153) supports this and considers formative feedback in terms of '*information communicated to the learner that is intended to modify his or her thinking or behaviour to improve learning*'.

This use of formative feedback is a significant move away from more traditional methods of assessment that only considered a grade important. The way that formative feedback is provided to learners may be verbal or it may be written. Some recent innovators have even trialled the use of audio or video feedback to learners. This relevance of variety is noted by Race (2005) who suggests that as teachers you should not limit yourself to one particular way of providing feedback to learners. Rather he suggests that a wider variety of approaches can help to meet learners' own preferences or individual needs. For example, when using the *praise sandwich* approach the teacher starts dialogue or written feedback with a positive, then notes the development area and concludes with a final positive. The aim of this is to sandwich the development point to ensure that the feedback does not demotivate the learner. However, there is a danger that the learner will only focus on the first or last comment made by the tutor and fail to recognise the development area.

The importance of feedback is further noted by Petty (2009, pp 66–7) who suggests three key aspects to effective feedback which he refers to as '*goals, medals and missions*':

Goals: *Feedback needs to be explicit in what the learner is looking to achieve overall, so for example, if they are working towards an assignment, the goal will be specified by the learning outcomes or assignment criteria.*

Medals: *Medals are similar to the positives suggested by the praise sandwich approach. They should note what the learner did well.*

Missions: *Missions are clear targets in how to move from the current situation to achieve the specified goals.*

(Petty, 2009, p 66–7)

Case study

Sue teaches study skills and academic writing to a group of 18 year-olds on an art foundation degree course. Many of the learners are very competent, however, she is aware that one learner (Paula), despite reading widely to support her writing, is struggling with the structure of her written work and her sentences are too long and confusing. On her last feedback sheet and in discussions Sue advised Paula that she needs to work on the structure of her written work, but the re-submission received shows no improvement.

Critical question

How can Sue provide Paula with more effective feedback?

Comment

Sue could use the medal and mission approach. The goal here would be to create a piece of clearly written academic work, therefore the medal and mission should reflect this, for example:

○ medal – you have drawn on a wide range of literature to support what you say;

○ mission – you should examine your longer sentences and split them in order to improve the flow of your argument.

Questioning skills

Questioning skills are essential for all teachers, however they are often skills that can take some time to develop. With a little guidance you can develop your skills in questioning in order to both engage learners and to ensure that learning has taken place. A common mistake made by teachers is to leave insufficient thinking time for the learners before providing them with hints or often answering the questions themselves. The gap between asking a question and receiving an answer can seem like an awfully long time if you are a new teacher, but you should avoid any desire to fill the gap until you are certain that you have given the learners adequate time to consider their response. Patience, therefore, is one of the key skills to effective questioning and forms part of the *pose, pause, pounce* approach:

Pose: put a question to the class.

Pause: allow the learners thinking time depending on the nature of the question.

Pounce: nominate a learner to answer.

When questioning you should also be aware of the nature of the questions that you ask and whether you seek a brief answer or a deeper insight into the area that you are examining. Closed questioning involves a learner being asked a question that will expect short answers, whereas with open questioning the learner is encouraged to provide a more in-depth answer.

 Case study

Bob is on his first teaching placement and is teaching history in a sixth form college. His mentor has suggested that he use questioning whilst delivering the short lecture elements of the course. Bob has tried this a few times with the group and is struggling to get detailed answers from any of the learners. One of the questions that he asked is: *Do you think that the Treaty of Versailles was a good thing?*

Critical question

What is the problem with this question?

Comment

Bob is asking a closed question which encourages a *yes* or *no* answer from the learners. Closed questions can, however, form the basis of further questioning. So he could start with *Do you think that the Treaty of Versailles was a good thing?* And depending on whether Bob received a *yes* or *no* response, he could probe deeper with Socratic questioning and ask '*why*' or '*why not*'?

THE WIDER ROLE OF COMMUNICATION

As a teacher you will be required to use your communication skills in team discussions, meetings with managers and other stakeholders (including parents and guardians if you teach 16–18 year-old learners). You will take different approaches, depending on who you communicate with, therefore the analysis of this, in relation to theory, can aid the development of your skills.

Transactional analysis

Whoever you converse with, it is important that you convey the best possible image on behalf of your organisation. Berne's (1964) theory of transactional analysis may help you to do this and is relevant to your interactions with learners and with colleagues in a range of settings, for example office discussions and within meetings (Huddleston and Unwin, 2013). The theory of transactional analysis (TA) considers the way in which you interact with others. Berne (1964) suggests that you can adopt one of three ego states at different times.

Berne's ego states

Parent (P) In a Parent ego state you take on the role of a parent. This can be either as a controlling or nurturing parent.

Adult (A) In an Adult ego state you take on the role of an adult. The adult ego state is responsible, rational and logical.

Child (C) In a Child ego state you take on the role of a child. This can be either as a free or adapted child (a free child responds without any concern for others, whereas an adapted child will comply with adult expectations).

(Berne, 1964)

Berne's theory suggests that for effective communication to take place complementary transactions should be used. For example, if two adults are engaging in logical, rational and responsible communication this means that both of the adults are in an adult to adult state, talking and responding as an adult.

To effectively analyse communication using transactional analysis, you need to consider how the person you are communicating with is responding to you, ie what ego state they are in. For example, if a learner asks you for a pen because they have forgotten theirs, they are using a child to parent transaction. If you respond as a parent and reply in a nurturing manner, providing a pen for them to use, you are responding as parent to child. This is a complementary transaction because you are responding in the state to which you were addressed.

TA relies on concepts of complementary transactions and also crossed transactions. The effective communication that can result from complementary transactions is contrasted by crossed transactions which can lead to communication breakdown. Whereas complementary transactions occur when the other party replies in the same ego state in which they were addressed, in crossed transactions the other party replies in a different ego state to that in which they were addressed. Interestingly though, crossed transactions can, occasionally, be beneficial, especially when adult to adult transactions are introduced. If, for example, a learner says that they don't want to do a classroom activity (child ego state) and you respond in an adult to adult ego state you can prevent the situation from escalating.

METHODS OF COMMUNICATION

You will communicate verbally, non-verbally and also in writing as part of your teaching and wider role. In recognition of the evolving nature of communication you may also utilise social media in order to engage learners.

Non-verbal communication

Non-verbal communication (NVC) explores the aspects of communication that are conveyed by means other than the words used. NVC was explored by Albert Mehrabian (1981) who recognised that communication also included vocal aspects such as volume, tone and facial expressions (McKay et al., 2009). Hargie (2004, p 69) also notes the importance of proxemics which he considers in terms of '*how we perceive and make use of personal space*'. Within this he notes aspects of '*territoriality, interpersonal distance and personal space*'.

Further evidence of the complexity of communication can be seen by the importance of kinesics. Kinesics refers to the study of body movements and gestures, including eye contact, expressions and even hand gestures. Facial expressions are further considered by Hargie (2004, p 66), who notes '*six basic emotions that are consistently decodable*' stating that these are '*sadness, anger, disgust, fear, surprise and happiness*'. However, Rayudu (2010) cautions that non-verbal gestures do not have universal meaning. Given the diverse cultures around the world, an innocent gesture in one culture may be offensive to another. Equally, whilst you should be informed and guided by learners' non-verbal communication, you should be careful not to make incorrect assumptions. If your learners are sitting with their arms crossed, they may be cold, rather than defensive.

Para-language

Verbal communication is complex and can be analysed in terms of tone, pitch or speed, as noted by Mehrabian (1981) in his consideration of NVC (McKay et al., 2009). This aspect of communication is referred to as para-language and '*gives communication the distinctive characteristics that make it unique*' (Hasson, 2012, p 8). Hasson further notes that para-language in particular conveys emotions and attitudes. For example, you may be aware that when you are angry your voice can become louder or when you are sad your voice becomes softer, but your voice can also convey other emotions without you realising it. You may be abrupt to others when you are feeling defensive, your speech may slow down if you are unhappy or if you are excited or nervous your speech may speed up (Hasson, 2012).

Written communication

You should also consider the approach that you take in your written communication to ensure that it suits the needs and expectations of the recipient. For example, you may use email to converse with friends but the structure and style would be very different than when you send an email to a potential student or a colleague.

Critical question

How does your email communication to your friends and learners differ?

Comment

The key distinction here is between informal and formal communication. In an email with friends you might start with '*Hi Louise*', whereas in a more formal email to a learner you should instead start with '*Dear Louise*' *or* '*Hello Louise*'. When you conclude the email to your friends you might be very informal with '*Bye*' or '*See you later*', however with a learner you should use '*Regards*' or '*Best wishes*'. The structure of formal emails should be in complete sentences and should avoid '*idioms, clichés and colloquialisms*' (Machin, 2009, p 68).

Social media

The changing nature of communication is particularly relevant given the rise of social media over the past decade. Social media may include blogs and social networking sites allowing the sharing of images, text, audio and video. You may find that whereas learners rarely check their student email they engage with social media on numerous occasions throughout the day. Therefore, the use of a microblogging application like Twitter could be an excellent way of providing learners with reminders and important announcements. You might even use this approach to issue prompts to engage with homework or specific course elements. Online social networking sites also provide opportunities for learners to develop their skills in collaborative learning and can be used to encourage engagement and interaction with peers outside of the traditional classroom environment.

A word of caution must be noted in relation to the use of social media for learning. You should be careful not to assume that all learners have access to technology and ensure that any choices you make will include all of the learners. You should be particularly aware of the blurring of boundaries and the potential pitfalls that can occur with social media. If used appropriately such technology can be an excellent way of engaging and motivating learners, however, it is important to maintain the professional nature of your interaction.

SUMMARY

The role and effectiveness of any teacher in FE is dependent on successful communication, not only with learners but with a wide range of professionals and other stakeholders. By drawing on relevant theories and principles of communication and carefully analysing your own practice and approaches to communication you will further enhance your knowledge and, consequently, develop both your teaching and professional skills.

Check your understanding

You will find suggested answers to some of these questions at the back of this book.

Question 1: In one or two sentences provide a definition of communication.

Question 2: What are the implications of rules of communication and why are they important?

Question 3: What are the components of Shannon and Weaver's (1949) model of communication?

Question 4: What are the similarities and differences between Berlo's (1960) model of communication and that proposed by Shannon and Weaver?

Question 5: Consider some feedback that you have given to a learner. Does this feedback fit with the *praise sandwich* or *medal and mission* approach? If neither of these, consider how you might adapt the feedback to fit with these models.

Question 6: What is an advantage and what is a disadvantage of providing feedback using a range of methods?

Question 7: What is the difference between kinesics and para-language?

End-of-chapter reflections

○ Exploring and applying communication theory to your practice will help you to develop your communication skills.

○ Communication is inevitable and involves a range of both verbal and non-verbal communication.

○ Feedback should be used to guide the learner to improve.

○ As a teacher you will communicate with a range of professionals and interested parties via a variety of media.

○ How do you think you will be able to use your learning from this chapter to develop your practice?

TAKING IT FURTHER

In addition to the literature already commented upon in this chapter you may find the following of interest.

Appleyard, N and Appleyard, K (2010) *Communicating with Learners in the Lifelong Learning Sector (Achieving QTLS Series).* Exeter: Learning Matters.

Mehrabian, A (2007) *Nonverbal communication.* Piscataway, NJ: Aldine Transaction.

Thompson, N (2011) *Effective Communication: A Guide for the People Professions.* Basingstoke: Palgrave Macmillan.

REFERENCES

Berne, E (1964) *Games People Play: The Psychology of Human Relationships.* London: Penguin Books.

ETF (2014) *Professional Standards for Teachers and Trainers in Education and Training: England.* London: Education and Training Foundation, www.et-foundation.co.uk/our-priorities/professional-standards-2014/ (accessed 30 July 2014).

Hargie, O (2004) *Skilled Interpersonal Communication: Research, Theory and Practice.* Hove: Routledge.

Hartley, P (1999) *Interpersonal Communication.* 2nd edn. London: Routledge.

Hasson, G (2012) *Brilliant Communication Skills: What the Best Communicators Know, Do and Say.* Harlow: Pearson Education.

Hill, A, Watson, J, Rivers, D and Joyce, M D (2007) *Key Themes in Interpersonal Communication.* Maidenhead: McGraw Hill Education.

Huddleston, P and Unwin, L (2013) *Teaching and Learning in Further Education: Diversity and Change.* 4th edn. Abingdon: Routledge.

LSIS (2013) *Qualification Guidance for the Level 5 Diploma in Education and Training.* Coventry: LSIS.

Machin, L (2009) *The Minimum Core for Literacy and Language: Audit and Test.* Exeter: Learning Matters.

Mckay, M, Davis, M and Fanning, M (2009) *Messages: The Communication Skills Book.* Oakland, CA: New Harbinger Publications.

Petty, G (2009) *Teaching Today.* Cheltenham: Nelson Thornes.

Race, P (2005) *Making Learning Happen: A Guide for Post Compulsory Education.* London: Sage.

Rayudu, C (2010) *Communication.* Mumbai: Himalaya Publishing.

Shute, V J (2008) Focus on formative feedback. *Review of Educational Research*, 78(1): 153–89.

West, R (2006) *Understanding Interpersonal Communication: Making Choices in Changing Times.* Boston, MA: Wadsworth, Cengage Learning.

6 Inclusive learning and managing behaviour in the classroom

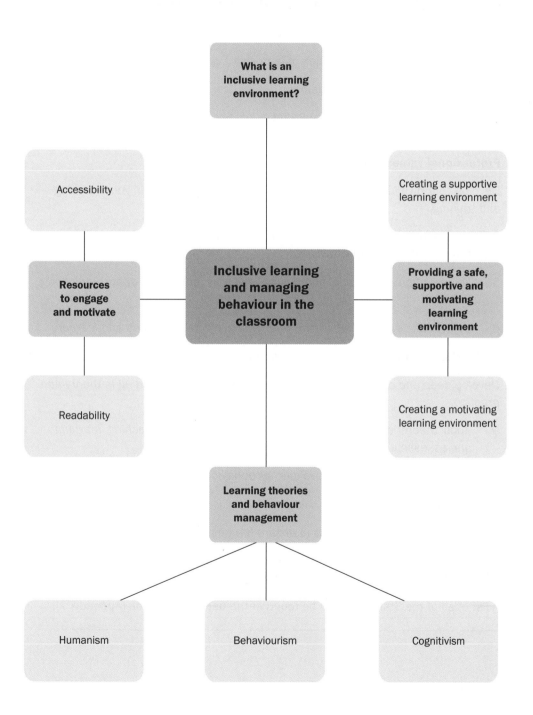

What is an inclusive learning environment?

Accessibility

Creating a supportive learning environment

Resources to engage and motivate

Inclusive learning and managing behaviour in the classroom

Providing a safe, supportive and motivating learning environment

Readability

Creating a motivating learning environment

Learning theories and behaviour management

Humanism

Behaviourism

Cognitivism

PROFESSIONAL LINKS

This chapter assists with your understanding of the following LSIS (2013, p 28) mandatory content:

○ providing a safe, supportive and motivating learning environment;

○ creating and maintaining an inclusive learning environment;

○ theories, models and principles of learning;

○ theories of behaviour management.

It also contributes to the following Professional Standards as provided by the ETF (2014).

Professional values and attributes

Develop your own judgement of what works and does not work in your teaching and training.

3 *Inspire, motivate and raise aspirations of learners through your enthusiasm and knowledge*

5 *Value and promote social and cultural diversity, equality of opportunity and inclusion*

6 *Build positive and collaborative relationships with colleagues and learners*

Professional knowledge and understanding

Develop deep and critically informed knowledge and understanding in theory and practice.

9 *Apply theoretical understanding of effective practice in teaching, learning and assessment drawing on research and other evidence*

11 *Manage and promote positive learner behaviour*

Professional skills

Develop your expertise and skills to ensure the best outcomes for learners.

14 *Plan and deliver effective learning programmes for diverse groups or individuals in a safe and inclusive environment*

A list of all of the Standards can be found at the back of this book (Appendix 7).

KEY DEFINITIONS

Behavioural approaches	Psychological approaches that suggest behaviours could be shaped or modelled by use of positive reinforcement, negative reinforcement and punishment.
Cognitive approaches	Psychological approaches that recognise the role of thinking and cognitive processes in shaping behaviour.
Extrinsic motivation	Desire to achieve that is provided by external rewards.
Fog index	A measure of the readability of text.
Inclusivity	Using approaches that will involve all learners however diverse they may be.
Intrinsic motivation	Desire to achieve that comes from within.

INTRODUCTION

As a teacher it is your responsibility to provide an environment that meets the needs of all learners. This not only involves you making sure that all learners are actively engaged in learning, but also addresses essential and integral issues of managing behaviour in the classroom so that an optimal learning environment is sustained and maintained. In this way this chapter aims to meet the following objectives:

○ identifying and exploring ways of providing a safe, supportive and motivating learning environment;

○ identifying and exploring ways of creating and maintaining an inclusive learning environment;

○ identifying, exploring and critiquing some of the key learning theories and theories of behaviour management;

○ identifying and evaluating resources including learning technologies.

STARTING POINT

What do you already know about inclusive learning and managing behaviour in the classroom?

○   What do you currently understand by the term *inclusive learning environment*?

○   In relation to your role as a teacher, what issues of managing classroom behaviour concern you?

○   What approaches do you use to evaluate resources?

○   What learning theories and theories of managing behaviour are you already aware of?

WHAT IS AN INCLUSIVE LEARNING ENVIRONMENT?

Step into any classroom and you should see learners engaged in activities, either individually, in pairs, small groups, large groups or as a whole class. The learners are likely to have different backgrounds, experiences and learning needs. Your responsibility to these learners is to create an environment that will actively include them all in each and every lesson. When you meet the needs of your learners in this way you are creating an inclusive learning environment (Huddleston and Unwin, 2013).

The rise of inclusivity and inclusive practice can be traced to the Tomlinson Report (FEFC, 1996), more formally referred to as the 1996 Report of the Committee on Students with Learning Difficulties and/or Disabilities. The outcomes of the report emphasised the needs for FE organisations to ensure that they met the needs of learners with learning difficulties or disabilities. However, the report moved beyond this by advising that inclusivity should be extended to meeting the diverse needs of all learners. The expectation developed that organisations should adapt to learners rather than learners having to adapt to the needs of the organisation.

Critical questions

Identify at least three ways in which your learners can differ.

How can your teaching practice accommodate these learner differences?

> **Comment**
>
> You may have thought about differences in terms of age, gender, culture, ethnicity, socio-economic background or learning experiences. You can accommodate all learners through, for example, your communication with them (see Chapter 5), by drawing on their experiences as part of your teaching and learning activities (ice-breaker activities, peer learning, shared activities) and by your use of learning resources.

PROVIDING A SAFE, SUPPORTIVE AND MOTIVATING LEARNING ENVIRONMENT

Chapter 3 considered essential elements and legislation with regard to the safety of learners and maintaining a safe learning environment, drawing on key issues of bullying and types of disruptive behaviours. A supportive learning environment is also essential and has implications on how the learners view your course, your teaching and your attitude towards them.

Creating a supportive learning environment

Analysis of a supportive learning environment requires you to reflect on your approach to developing a safe and supportive teaching and learning environment. Kyle and Rogien (2004, p 116) suggest that this can be considered in terms of the VIABLE acronym:

Valued, **I**ncluded, **A**ccepted, **B**elonging, **L**istened to, **E**ncouraged

These VIABLE concepts are essential in creating an inclusive and supportive environment and can be incorporated in a number of ways. One of the easiest ways is by listening to your learners and understanding their needs (Huddleston and Unwin, 2013). Learners will know better than anyone what they need and by demonstrating active listening skills you are conveying your willingness to engage with them. To be an active listener you need to make a concerted effort to relate to your learners and pay attention to their verbal and non-verbal communication, making encouraging comments and nodding or smiling to encourage them to continue (see Chapter 5). Creating a learning contract can be useful whereby you, as the teacher, and the learners, agree to behave in a particular way. You could also take on board some of the suggestions by Kyle and Rogien (2004, p 116) and allocate roles to the learners, perhaps as *'peer tutors, homework buddies or to assign classroom responsibilities'*. Hootstein (1994, p 216) makes similar recommendations, suggesting that teachers should *'provide opportunities that allow students to perceive a sense of control in their learning activities'*.

Research carried out by Stipek (2006) identified that adolescents worked harder for teachers who treated them as individuals and expressed interest in their personal lives. Taking an interest should always remain within the professional boundaries of your role as a teacher (you should see Chapter 2 for further discussion in relation to professional boundaries).

Critical question

Can you see any problems that could occur when teachers follow Stipek's suggestion?

Comment

It is crucial that you maintain the professional boundaries relating to you as a teacher. It is completely acceptable for a teacher to enquire how a learner got on in a football match, enjoyed a book that they have read or had a good holiday. However, you should be careful not to become overfamiliar and to maintain an appropriate level of detachment.

Creating a motivating learning environment

Meeting the needs of learners requires an understanding of what drives or motivates them and, as noted by Armitage et al. (2003), learner motivations for attending courses are many and varied. Following the Education and Skills Act 2008 learners need to remain in education or training until they reach the age of 18. This, along with the necessity for some learners to attend functional skills or GCSE English and mathematics classes will mean that the motivation and reasons for learners being in your classes will continue to change.

Motivation can be considered in terms of intrinsic and extrinsic motivation. Intrinsic motivation is drawn from within the learner themselves. When they choose to attend a course for the sense of satisfaction it gives them they are intrinsically motivated. When they are driven by external factors or rewards, perhaps a pay rise, a qualification or recognition by their peers, they are extrinsically motivated.

As with many education concepts and ideas, motivation is supported by relevant theory and the most widely known of these is that provided by Maslow (1954). In his theory, Maslow noted the needs that drive human beings and documented these in a hierarchy, recognising that lower needs needed to be met before people can progress to having their higher needs satisfied. This hierarchy is frequently represented by a pyramid and is reproduced in Figure 6.1:

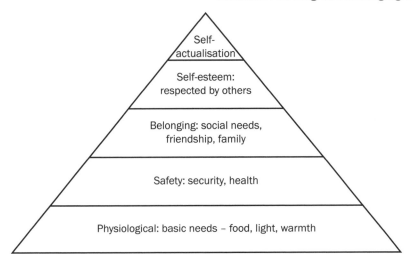

Figure 6.1 Maslow's (1954) hierarchy of needs

The application of Maslow's hierarchy to your own teaching practice can be considered in terms of examining the learners' current position. Achieving their potential as human beings requires that they progress through the levels, however if learners are cold or hungry in your lessons it is unlikely that they will be motivated to learn – they will not be able to move beyond the low level physiological needs of the hierarchy.

Critical question

Consider each of the stages in Maslow's Hierarchy. How might your classroom environment take into consideration each stage?

Comment

Your answer might have included some of the following:

physiological: ensuring that the classroom is neither too hot nor too cold, that the lighting in the classroom is adequate;

safety: ensuring that all health and safety legislation is adhered to and that any machinery is safe and guarded if necessary. You might also consider ensuring that learners feel safe psychologically and are not bullied or pressured;

belonging: do learners have friends within the class? Are you aware of any family issues that might impact on learning? Do they contribute to whole class and group discussions?;

self-esteem: do you provide all learners with an opportunity to develop their self-esteem? Do you praise appropriately and challenge any comments that may negatively impact on learners' self-esteem?;

self-actualisation: do your learners have attainment goals? Are they on target for meeting the requirements of any assessments? Do they have a vision and long-term goals about what they want to be or achieve in the future?

LEARNING THEORIES AND BEHAVIOUR MANAGEMENT

The origins of learning theories lie with behavioural psychology and date back to the early twentieth century. These early theories suggested that behaviour could be shaped or modelled by drawing on the outcomes of experiments with animals (Thorndike, 1898; Skinner, 1938). In particular it focused on observed behaviours and did not consider the cognitive processes that may lie behind such behaviours and ignored the complexity of the learning process (Gould, 2009). A cognitive approach focuses on cognitive processes and '*emphasises the importance of explaining behaviour in terms of internal events, the meaning of concepts, and processes, beliefs, attitudes and intentions*' (Buckler and Castle, 2014, pp 18–19).

In addition to the behavioural and cognitive approaches, a humanistic approach is often considered and emerged as a '*deliberate reaction against behaviourism*' (Curzon and Tummons, 2013, p 85). The humanistic approach recognises the teacher, not as a classroom manager or a director of learning but rather as a facilitator and supporter of learners in guiding their journey and '*encouraging the broader growth of the whole person*' (Curzon and Tummons, 2013, p 95). The implications of this to teaching practice are important as there is a seemingly ever increasing move towards a teacher as a facilitator of practice in discussions and group work. Building positive relationships with learners will therefore play a key part in supporting this facilitator role.

Behavioural approaches

Despite the previously noted shortcomings of behavioural theories in terms of their lack of consideration of cognitive processes, behaviourist theories are still highly relevant. They can be used to effectively inform your approach to behaviour management and you may find that three strategies prove particularly useful:

○ *Positive reinforcement*

○ *Punishment*

○ *Negative reinforcement.*

(Buckler and Castle, 2014, p 14)

Positive reinforcement

Positive reinforcements are positive actions following a specific behaviour. In behavioural research the initial reinforcement may have been a reward of food for a cat who escaped from a box (Thorndike, 1898) or a rat who pressed a lever (Skinner, 1938). This can be applied to your own practice in the classroom, for example if you praise a learner who does well in an assignment you are applying positive reinforcement. Praise is an excellent tool to ensure learner engagement and its use is well documented, however, Kohn (1993) maintains it is not without its shortcomings and suggests that the overuse of reward systems and praise can reduce learner autonomy and motivation.

Critical question

Why do you think that the overuse of reward systems and praise can reduce learner autonomy and motivation?

Comment

If overused, the learners can become accustomed to praise and reward systems and they can lose their value. For example, a learner who gets a reward on a daily basis will not feel the need to put in additional effort, whereas the learner who is praised less frequently may make additional effort and strive for praise or reward. (See Chapter 5 for further consideration of effective use of praise.)

Punishment

Punishments are implemented following an undesired action – perhaps a learner refuses to do work in class and is given a verbal warning. The aim of a punishment is to reduce the likelihood of a recurrence of the behaviour. In order for the behaviour to be discouraged, it is particularly important that any classroom rules and consequences are applied consistently (Gould, 2009).

Negative reinforcement

Negative reinforcements are often confused with punishments, however, there is a clear distinction that should be noted. Whereas punishments are actions designed to prevent a repeat of an undesirable behaviour, negative reinforcements are actions taken to avoid a negative consequence. In terms of your own practice consider the learner who pays attention in class to prevent them being moved to another seat or a learner who hands in their homework early to avoid a sanction.

Cognitive approaches

The behaviourist approach fails to recognise that learners need to understand the reason behind rules and consider what drives learners' thinking. For example, when applying rules in terms of health and safety, you do of course want learners to apply them, however, some learners may not do this automatically. By engaging learners in an understanding of the rules cognitively, you are helping them to develop their wider application in the workplace or outside of your organisation. The active role of learners and the suggestion that they be involved in the formulation of rules is suggested by Fontana (1994), who suggests that learners will also become responsible for upholding them.

Gould (2009, p 73) also suggests that the cognitive approach builds on the holistic approach to learners and recognises that their behaviour should be *'viewed as merely one part of a more complex picture'*. Recognition of individuality and the holistic approach to learners when considering behaviours builds on learners' prior experiences, which can influence their thinking, and suggests that there are usually reasons behind learners' reluctance to engage in the classroom (Gould, 2009). Supporting learners to develop skills of reflection and to challenge their assumptions (see Chapter 1) can help them to develop new thinking skills and therefore new behaviours.

The cognitive approach forms a key element of the proactive approach to behaviour management as advocated within the Elton Report (1989) and recognised by Ellis and Tod (2012). The proactive approach considers actions that a teacher makes to encourage desired behaviours from learners, rather than relying on the need for reprimands and sanction to programme behaviours. This may involve allowing learners regular breaks, planning a variety of activities within a lesson or, as noted by Hootstein (1994), providing learners with opportunities to take control of their learning.

 Case study

Tom is halfway through his DET qualification. He has been receiving positive feedback from his mentor and course tutor in relation to his teaching practice and has not experienced any problems in terms of behaviour management. He has now been given a new class to teach and his colleagues have warned him that the group are difficult to manage. He has done some investigation into previous approaches to classroom management and considers that his colleagues have previously concentrated perhaps too much on a sanctions and punishment approach.

Critical question

What suggestions do you have that might help Tom move away from the sanctions- and punishment-based approach?

Comment

You might have suggested the introduction of a reward system, perhaps awarding learners points or golden tickets when they do something well, arrive early or display positive behaviours. Perhaps you also considered trying to identify the learners who displayed the most disruptive behaviours and giving them a role of responsibility in the class where they can gain positive, rather than negative, attention.

RESOURCES TO ENGAGE AND MOTIVATE

The use of a variety of resources will play a key part in motivating learners and as a teacher you should be aware of the implications in relation to inclusivity. The importance of appropriate resource selection is noted by Armitage et al. (2003), who suggest that they should be used purposefully to engage learners and develop their learning. If you provide your learners with too many handouts and resources, it is quite possible that the essential messages you are trying to convey will be missed amongst the quantity that you have provided.

Identifying and evaluating resources

Whatever resources you use, you need to evaluate them to ensure that they meet the needs of your intended audience. This will involve considering images and phrases used to ensure that they demonstrate diversity. You might consider whether you tend to use male or female images in your resources or whether different cultures and ethnicities are represented.

Accessibility

Presentation software is a popular way to engage and motivate learners and enhance communication. However, new teachers often make the mistake of creating presentations to share with their learners that contain large paragraphs of text that are illegible from the back of the classroom. You should always check that the font size used can be read by all of your learners. You might also include images to further aid communication visually and maintain the learners' attention. Be careful not to go overboard though. There is nothing more annoying than a multitude of images on every slide.

Critical task

Review any of your own presentation slides. Have you overloaded the slide with text or is it accessible to learners? Do your slides represent different cultures, ages and genders? Are they interesting?

Readability

You should also consider the readability of the resources that you use. They may be books, articles or online resources but it is particularly important that the text is suitable for its intended audience; this can be considered in terms of the Fog index as proposed by Gunning (1952). The index comprises a calculation that provides a numerical value equivalent to the number of years of education a person would require in order to be able to understand the text.

Calculation for the Fog index

1. From your chosen text, select a paragraph of around 100 words.

2. Divide the number of words in the chosen text by the number of sentences – this will give the average sentence length.

3. Count the numbers of words that have three or more syllables in your chosen 100 words.

4. Add the results from points 2 and 3 together and multiply the total by 0.4.

Gunning (1952)

SUMMARY

Providing an inclusive learning environment for all of your learners will inform a wide range of aspects in relation to your teaching practice, including the resources that you use. By considering your approaches to behaviour management and inclusive practice and drawing on relevant theory you can provide an environment where all learners feel safe and supported and where all learners are engaged in the learning process. In doing this you will become a more inclusive practitioner and continue to develop the essential professional relationships necessary as a teacher in FE.

 Check your understanding

You will find suggested answers to some of these questions at the back of this book.

Question 1:   What is an inclusive learning environment?

Question 2:   Why is it important to create a motivating learning environment?

Question 3:   What is the difference between intrinsic and extrinsic motivation?

Question 4:   Write down at least three examples of extrinsic motivators.

Question 5:   Why is it important to satisfy the lower stages of Maslow's hierarchy of needs?

Question 6:   Find out what motivates a group of your learners attending a course that you teach. What implications does this knowledge have for your teaching practice?

Question 7:   Why is it important to evaluate your resources?

End-of-chapter reflections

o   A key teacher responsibility is creating and maintaining an inclusive learning environment.

o   A supportive and motivating learning environment will engage learners and encourage positive behaviours.

o   Will you adopt a behavioural, cognitive or combined approach to behaviour management?

o   How do you think you will be able to use your learning from this chapter to develop your practice?

 TAKING IT FURTHER

In addition to the literature already commented upon in this chapter you may find the following of interest.

Race, P (2005) *Making Learning Happen: A Guide for Post Compulsory Education.* London: Sage.

Scruton, J and Ferguson, B (2014) *Teaching and Supporting Adult Learners.* Northwich: Critical Publishing.

Tummons, J and Powell, S (2011) *Inclusive Practice in the Lifelong Learning Sector (Achieving QTLS Series).* Exeter: Learning Matters.

Wallace, S (2007) *Managing Behaviour in the Lifelong Learning Sector (Achieving QTLS Series).* Exeter: Learning Matters.

REFERENCES

Armitage, A, Bryant, R, Dunnill, R, Renwick, M, Hayes, D, Hudson, A and Lawes, S (2003) *Teaching and Training in Post Compulsory Education.* 2nd edn. Maidenhead: Open University Press.

Buckler, S and Castle, P (2014) *Psychology for Teachers.* London: Sage.

Curzon, L B and Tummons, J (2013) *Teaching in Further Education: An Outline of Principles and Practice.* London: Bloomsbury.

Ellis, S and Tod, J (2012) Motivation and Behaviour. In J Arthur and A Peterson (eds), *The Routledge Companion to Eduation.* Abingdon: Routledge.

Elton, R (1989) *Enquiry into Discipline in Schools.* London: HMSO.

ETF (2014) *Professional Standards for Teachers and Trainers in Education and Training: England.* London: Education and Training Foundation, www.et-foundation.co.uk/ our-priorities/professional-standards-2014/ (accessed 30 July 2014).

FEFC (1996) *Inclusive Learning: Report of the Learning Difficulties and/or Disabilities Committee.* London: HMSO.

Fontana, D (1994) *Managing Classroom Behaviour.* Leicester: BPS Books.

Gould, J (2009) *Learning Theory and Classroom Practice.* Exeter: Learning Matters.

Gunning, R (1952) *The Technique of Clear Writing.* New York: McGraw Hill Education.

Hootstein, E W (1994) Motivating Students to Learn. *Clearing House*, 67(4): 213–16.

Huddleston, P and Unwin, L (2013) *Teaching and Learning in Further Education: Diversity and Change.* 4th edn. Abingdon: Routledge.

Kohn, A (1993) *Punished by Rewards: The Trouble with Gold Stars, Incentive Plans, A's, Praise and Other Bribes.* New York: Houghton Mifflin.

Kyle, P and Rogien, L (2004) *Classroom Management: Supportive Strategies.* Bethesda: National Association of School Psychologists.

LSIS (2013) *Teaching and Training Qualifications for the Further Education and Skills Sector in England: Guidance for Higher Education Institutions.* Coventry: Learning Skills Improvement Services.

Maslow, A H (1954) *Motivation and Personality.* New York: Harper and Row.

Skinner, B F (1938) *The Behavior of Organisms: An Experimental Analysis.* New York: Appleton-Century.

Stipek, D (2006) Relationships Matter. *Educational Leadership*, 64(1): 46–9.

Thorndike, E L (1898) *Animal Intelligence: An Experimental Study of the Associative Processes in Animals.* New York: Columbia University.

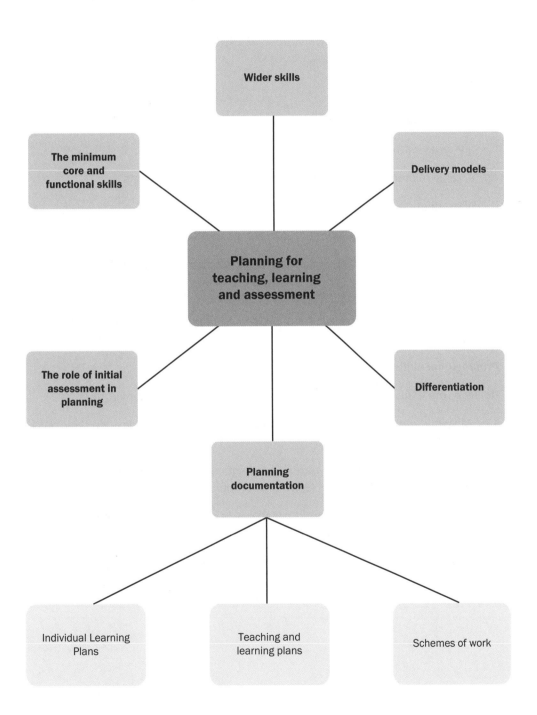

PROFESSIONAL LINKS

This chapter assists with your understanding of the following LSIS (2013, p 27) mandatory content:

- delivery models;

- role and use of initial and diagnostic assessment;

- programmes/sessions/lessons;

- schemes of work;

- teaching and learning plans;

- individual learning plans;

- learning related to learning outcomes/curriculum requirements;

- differentiation;

- integrating English, mathematics, ICT and wider skills;

- knowledge understanding of literacy, language, numeracy and ICT;

- own personal skills in literacy, language, numeracy and ICT.

It also contributes to the following Professional Standards as provided by the ETF (2014).

Professional skills

Develop your expertise and skills to ensure the best outcomes for learners.

13   *Motivate and inspire learners to promote achievement and develop their skills to enable progression*

14   *Plan and deliver effective learning programmes for diverse groups or individuals in a safe and inclusive environment*

16   *Address the mathematics and English needs of learners and work creatively to overcome individual barriers to learning*

A list of all of the Standards can be found at the back of this book (Appendix 7).

KEY DEFINITIONS

Affective domain	Relates to attitudes, values and beliefs gained by learners.
Cognitive domain	Relates to knowledge and understanding gained by learners.
Differentiation	Teaching to meet the varying needs of all learners at all levels within the teaching environment.
Individual learning plan	Learner-centred document that records the learner journey, targets and progress.
Minimum core	The minimum skills and knowledge in literacy and language, numeracy and ICT required by teachers in FE.
Psychomotor domain	Relates to physical or practical skills gained by learners.
Scheme of work	Long-term planning document.
Teaching and learning plan	Short-term planning document.

INTRODUCTION

Before you enter a classroom to deliver your first lesson, there will be a range of planning processes that will need careful consideration. You will need to plan and prepare an array of organisational documents; for example schemes of work, teaching and learning plans and individual learning plans. This chapter, through its alignment to literature, asking questions and providing activities, is designed to support you in your understanding of how to develop your skills and knowledge of planning your delivery to meet the needs of learners in FE. It therefore aims to support you in:

○ identifying and exploring the range of planning documents used to inform your own teaching practice;

○ identifying and exploring the role of initial assessment in your planning;

○ considering the application of differentiation within your planning;

○ evaluating your own personal skills in literacy, language, numeracy and ICT;

○ identifying and exploring ways to integrate English, mathematics, ICT and wider skills.

DELIVERY MODELS

Before you start your planning you will need to consider which delivery model/s you intend to use. You may consider using a traditional classroom model with a teacher at the front of the class or you may plan for a more learner-engaged model where you act as a facilitator of learning in a workshop session. Other approaches that you might also consider include blended and distance learning models.

Within an individual lesson you may alternate between different teaching and learning models, with you taking different roles varying between facilitator and lecturer. When you create your planning documents, you should consider the model being used and ensure that your documentation is appropriate to that model. A scheme of work for a college-based course may have specific delivery dates whereas a flexible or distance learning approach may have broader module delivery and learner engagement dates. However, both would have specific assignment deadlines that you would expect learners to meet.

PLANNING DOCUMENTATION

Schemes of work

> *A scheme of work is a forward plan of the topics and skills to be covered in different sessions over the period of a learning programme/course.*
>
> (LSIS, 2013)

Schemes of work provide an overview of the course being delivered and are usually maintained by the teacher, though some organisations do assign this responsibility to more experienced staff and have the expectation that all staff use the structure to inform their delivery. You may find that this is the case in your organisation or placement, but it would be good practice (and a requirement of the DET qualification) that you take the time to devise your own scheme of work and consider the learning objectives or outcomes, your teaching methods, assessment methods (initial, formative and summative) and resources.

Most organisations have their own organisational template for schemes of work. If your organisation does not have a preferred template, you may find the template provided in Appendix 5 useful as it contains the required sections of a scheme of work, eg timing (in terms of course, module and lesson length), content, methods, resources and assessment. A scheme of work need not be a rigid document so don't be afraid to stray from it temporarily if the needs of the learners require it during your course. Being able to do this and evidencing flexibility is an excellent skill in terms of Schön's (2002) reflection in action (see Chapter 1).

Teaching and learning plans

Creation of a comprehensive scheme of work will not only ensure that your course has clear structure, it will aid you in your individual lesson planning. You should use the scheme of work for each lesson as the basis for developing your teaching and learning plan. Your planning will draw on the relevant theories of curriculum, noting both the process and the product of learning which are discussed in Chapter 9.

> *Lesson planning should commence with a consideration of the ends and means; the topic of the lesson will define the ends; the activities necessary to accompany the ends will suggest the instructional means.*

> (Curzon and Tummons, 2013, p 293)

Your teaching and learning plan will usually build around expected learner outcomes as required by your organisation and awarding body in order to meet curriculum requirements. In order to ensure this you are required to use clear aims and objectives, evidencing these in your planning and sharing with learners at the start of every lesson.

You will commence your planning with a general statement of what you want to achieve in a lesson and then break this down further to create your objectives. Your objectives should be a clear distance apart from the generalist nature of your aims. They should be specific statements that will include a verb to specify what learners are expected to do at the end of the lesson that they couldn't at the beginning. Consider the example below:

○　List at least three activities that will engage children in an early years environment

The objective noted above considers learners' knowledge and draws on the cognitive domain as proposed by Benjamin Bloom et al. (1956). Any objectives that draw on the thinking skills or knowledge (for example with verbs including *list*, *state*, *explain* or *analyse*) will be linked to the cognitive domain. The cognitive domain has levels of increasing complexity, ranging from the basic recall of facts at the lowest level to evaluation at the highest.

You might be developing your learners' practical or physical skills in addition to their knowledge and thinking skills. This is where you should draw on objectives related to the psychomotor domain as attributed to Simpson (1966) or Dave (1970). Verbs used in writing psychomotor objectives will include *build*, *draw* and *create*. The psychomotor domain has similar levels of complexity to the cognitive domain, ranging from imitation at the lowest level (copying the movements of someone else) to naturalisation at the highest.

The teaching of attitudes, values and beliefs can similarly be evidenced within teaching and learning plans and relate to the affective domain (Krathwohl, Bloom and Masia, 1956). Verbs used in writing affective objectives will include *accept*, *comply* or *argue* and the levels in the affective domain range from *receive* (be willing to accept the beliefs and values stated) to *internalise* (acting in accordance with those values).

Critical question

Consider the objectives below and in each case identify the relevant domain being considered:

o   evaluate a written assignment;

o   create a small clay sculpture;

o   comply with organisational health and safety rules.

Comment

You should have noted the following.

o   Evaluate a written assignment – cognitive domain.

o   Create a small clay sculpture – psychomotor domain.

o   Comply with organisational health and safety rules – affective domain.

Individual Learning Plans

Individual Learning Plans (ILPs) are an excellent way of documenting learners' journeys whilst supporting them in a range of FE environments. In particular, they are a key document in encouraging learners to take *more responsibility for their personal, employability and vocational skill development* (Ofsted, 2012a, p 1).

Your organisation will normally provide you with an ILP template to use with your learners. However, if these are not used in your organisation consider using the template in Appendix 4. By using the ILP as a *'dynamic working document'* (QIA, 2013, p 2) and recording not only background information about learners but also targets, achievements and learner self-assessment, you will continue to engage the learner and enhance motivation.

THE ROLE OF INITIAL ASSESSMENT IN PLANNING

You will have encountered key issues in relation to initial assessment in Chapter 3 and explored its necessity in allowing you to identify individual learner needs. The best time for initial assessment to occur is prior to the start of a course on a one-to-one or perhaps a small-group basis. By doing this you are providing yourself with a wealth of evidence about your learners that will be essential in informing your planning regarding their learning requirements. Additionally, recognition and consideration of these needs will further aid you in removing possible barriers to learning (Francis and Gould, 2009).

Initial assessment can be informed by a range of elements including classroom activities, application forms and documents (see Table 7.1).

Table 7.1 Initial assessment in practice

Element	Example
Documents	Application forms, certificates, letters of reference, school reports
Self assessment	Learner evaluation of their own skills, abilities and motivations for completing the course
Discussions	Formal – interview style or informal semi-structured chat
Work-based observation	Observing the learner in practice
Structured activities	Group/team activity
Tests	Generic English and mathematics tests as well as subject understanding tests. Assessing English and mathematics skills in the context of the subject may also be beneficial.

Adapted from DfES (2006, p 8)

Critical question

Consider your own current or future teaching practice. How will each of the methods of initial assessment in Table 7.1 influence your knowledge of learners to aid your planning?

Comment

You might have considered some of the following.

o   Documents – Application forms and other documentation about the learner will give information about qualifications and prior experience and help you to target your delivery and materials at the correct level.

o   Self-assessment – This would give you an insight into learner knowledge, skills and confidence, with some learners having more confidence in their ability than others.

o   Discussions – You will gain an understanding about your learners' knowledge, levels of confidence and communication skills.

o   Work-based observation – This will give you the opportunity to see your learners in a natural environment and to identify their practical skills.

o   Structured activities – These are less daunting than tests and give you an insight into learners' wider skills and communication depending on your subject area. You could then plan your delivery to develop these wider skills.

o   Tests – These can provide information rapidly to feed into your planning in relation to learner knowledge and application, however, some learners may struggle with tests so you should take this into account when reviewing test results.

DIFFERENTIATION

Application of the cognitive, psychomotor and affective domains can assist you in evidencing differentiation in your planning. Differentiation is considered in detail in Chapter 8 and particularly the notion of differentiation by outcome. This recognises that for any given task or activity you may have varying expectations of learners based on their prior knowledge, skills and ability. By recognising the different levels in each of the domains, you can use verbs which relate to increasing levels of complexity to evidence these varying expectations (Bouchard, 2011).

On your teaching and learning plan you will probably be asked to write objectives using the following headings and this is where you can evidence how you differentiate by outcome.

o   *All learners must …* (this is what you expect everyone to achieve but should provide stretch and challenge).

o   *Some learners will …* (the objectives under this heading will start to stretch the learners further).

o   *A few learners may …* (the objectives under these headings will provide the greatest stretch and challenge).

Consider the example provided earlier in this chapter (List at least three activities that will engage children in an early years environment). This is a low level objective in the cognitive domain (because of the use of *list*) and can be differentiated by exploring higher level verbs to specify expectations, for example:

○ ***all learners must*** list at least three activities that will engage children in an early years environment;

○ ***some learners will*** explain how at least three activities will engage children in an early years environment;

○ ***a few learners may*** evaluate at least three activities and how they may engage children in an early years environment.

As with schemes of work, the organisation where you work or your ITE provider will usually have their own template for schemes of work. However, you may find the template provided in Appendix 5 at the back of this book useful.

 Case study

Helen is a former school cook who has decided to move into teaching. One of her friends, who has some experience in teaching, has given her a teaching and learning plan as a guide to a lesson she will shortly be required to teach. The plan does not have differentiated objectives.

Critical question

Differentiate the following objectives to evidence how Helen can stretch and challenge all learners.

1. List five ways in which food can be spoiled.
2. List three ways in which food can be contaminated.

Comment

Your answer may vary from the examples below, however you should have noted the increase in expectations of the learner as the objective is differentiated.

1. Explain five ways in which food can be spoiled.

   Analyse five ways in which food can be spoiled and suggest ways that this can be avoided.

→

> **2.** Describe three ways in which food can be contaminated.
>
> Analyse three ways in which food can be contaminated and explain the strategies that should be implemented to avoid this occurring.

THE MINIMUM CORE AND FUNCTIONAL SKILLS

As a teacher you will have an active part in developing your learners' skills in literacy, language, mathematics and ICT (functional skills). You might incorporate written work or reading tasks to develop learners' literacy and language, ask learners to perform calculations to develop their numeracy skills or require them to use word processors and presentation software to develop their ICT skills. You will also need to continue to develop your minimum core – the minimum skills and knowledge in literacy and language, numeracy and ICT that are expected of you as a teacher. In developing your minimum core you will become proficient in supporting learners whose *'levels of literacy, language, numeracy and ICT skills would otherwise undermine their chance of success'* (LLUK, 2007, p 2).

Within each of the minimum core areas you will need to develop two elements, represented by Part A and Part B:

○ *Part A – knowledge and understanding*

○ *Part B – personal skills.*

(LLUK, 2007)

Your knowledge and understanding of each of the minimum core areas is represented by Part A. Amongst other factors it considers how numeracy, literacy and language or ICT skills vary with age and the influence of gender, cultural and socio-economic factors on your learners' development in these areas. Part B relates to the practical application of your skills in each of the minimum core areas (see Chapter 12 for further discussion in relation to the minimum core).

At the start of your DET qualification you may be asked to complete an audit or self-assessment of your knowledge and skills in each of the minimum core areas and this should then be used as the basis of an action plan of how you will develop in each of the areas as your teaching practice progresses.

> *Critical question*
>
> Consider your own strengths and development areas in literacy and language, numeracy and ICT. What areas do you need to develop? What evidence have you on which to base your decision?

Comment

You will probably have identified that you have both strengths and areas for development in the minimum core areas. The next step is to start to consider how you will ensure that you develop in order to meet the requirements by the end of the DET qualification. Try not to develop all areas at the same time, instead decide where your priorities lie and focus on developing those skills and knowledge before moving on to the next. You might want to explore these further or speak to your DET tutor and use this as the basis of one of your own personal targets.

Wider skills

As a teacher in FE you are in a key position to develop learners' wider skills. With youth unemployment standing at 881,000 in February 2014 (Mirza-Davies, 2014) employability needs to have a key focus in any learning environment in order to provide young (and those not so young) people with the best possible chance of securing employment. This is further noted by Ofsted who stress the importance of wider skills: '*Helping people to improve their chances of finding work, especially those who have few or no qualifications or specialist vocational skills is a vital task for those in the FE and skills sector and one which presents considerable challenges*' (Ofsted, 2012b, p 4). As Ofsted recognises, it is increasingly important for learners to be equipped with the skills necessary for them to be able to work in a global society. Therefore, when you plan your lesson you should also consider what strategies you can use in order to develop learners' employability skills. This is relatively straightforward to do, with many skills required in the workplace being readily applied to those you will expect of your own learners in the classroom. For example:

○ communication (verbal and non-verbal – see Chapter 5);

○ time management (being on time for class, handing in work on time);

○ problem solving (research activities, working with others in the class, teamwork);

○ organisational skills (being prepared for lessons);

○ motivation (engaging in class activities and discussions, supporting others).

Critical question

What further examples, other than those provided above, can you give regarding the development of employability skills in the classroom?

Comment

You might have considered some of the following:

- ○ teamwork (engaging learners in activities including group and pair work);

- ○ leadership skills (alternating the role of leader in group work);

- ○ independent working (allowing learners the choice and interpretation of a project).

SUMMARY

Planning and preparing documentation contributes to the effective delivery of learning and further builds on your ability to meet learners' individual needs. This will be enhanced by the use of differentiation, individualised targets and engagement with individual learning plans. By reviewing and evaluating your practice in planning you will continue to develop as an effective teacher in FE.

 Check your understanding

You will find suggested answers to some of these questions at the back of this book.

Question 1:   An institution conducts initial assessment centrally for efficiency. The results are sent to the manager and are stored ready for auditing or inspection visits but not given to the learners' teacher. The learners never see the findings of this assessment. What are the implications on learning and teaching of this practice?

Question 2:   Why do you need to consider the cognitive, psychomotor and affective domains as part of your planning?

Question 3:   Why are you required to evidence clear aims and objectives in your planning?

Question 4:   What is the difference between a scheme of work and a teaching and learning plan?

Question 5:   What purpose does an ILP serve?

Question 6:   Why do you need to embed employability skills within your teaching?

Question 7:   Why is it important as a teacher in FE that you develop your skills in each of the minimum core areas?

End-of-chapter reflections

○ Engaging learners in maintaining and reviewing their own ILP will encourage them to take ownership of their own learning.

○ Planning to incorporate elements of the cognitive, psychomotor and affective domains will ensure that you fully consider the different aspects of the courses that you teach.

○ Differentiation should always be evidenced at the planning stage in order to ensure that the needs of learners of all abilities, knowledge and experience are met.

○ Your planning needs to encompass more than delivery of course subject matter and also consider skills required in future courses and employment.

○ How do you think you will be able to use your learning from this chapter to develop your practice?

 TAKING IT FURTHER

In addition to the literature already commented upon in this chapter you may find the following of interest.

Forsyth, I, Jolliffe, A and Stevens, D (1999) *Planning a Course (Complete Guide to Teaching a Course)*. Oxon: Routledge.

Gronlund, N E and Brookhart, S M (2009) *Gronlund's Writing Instructional Objectives*. 8th edn. Upper Saddle River, NJ: Pearson Education.

The following books are particularly useful if you plan to undertake an audit of your skills and knowledge in each of the minimum core areas:

Machin, L (2009) *The Minimum Core for Language and Literacy, Audit and Test*. Exeter: Learning Matters.

Murray, S (2009) *The Minimum Core for ICT, Audit and Test*. Exeter: Learning Matters.

Patmore, M and Woodhouse, S (2009) *The Minimum Core for Numeracy, Audit and Test*. Exeter: Learning Matters.

REFERENCES

Bloom, B S, Englehar, M D, Furst, E J, Hill, W H and Krathwohl, D R (1956) *Taxonomy of Educational Objectives: The Classification of Educational Goals. Handbook I: Cognitive Domain*. New York: David McKay.

Bouchard, G J (2011) In full bloom: helping students grow using the taxonomy of educational objectives. *Journal of Physician Education*, 22(4): 44–6.

Curzon, L B and Tummons, J (2013) *Teaching in Further Education: An Outline of Principles and Practice.* London: Bloomsbury.

Dave, R H (1970) Psychomotor levels. In R J Armstrong, *Developing and Writing Educational Objectives*. Tucson, AZ: Educational Innovators Press.

DfES (2006) *Improving Initial Assessment: Guide to Good Practice.* Bristol: Portishead Press.

ETF (2014) *Professional Standards for Teachers and Trainers in Education and Training: England.* London: Education and Training Foundation, www.et-foundation.co.uk/our-priorities/professional-standards-2014/ (accessed 30 July 2014).

Francis, M and Gould, J (2009) *Achieving Your PTLLS Award.* London: Sage.

Krathwohl, D R, Bloom, B and Masia, B (1956) *Taxonomy of Educational Objectives, the Classification of Educational Goals – Handbook II: Affective Domain.* New York: Mckay.

LLUK (2007) *New Overarching Professional Standards for Teachers, Tutors and Trainers in the Lifelong Learning Sector.* London: LLUK.

LSIS (2013) *Schemes of Work*. Retrieved from Excellence Gateway. [Online]. Available at: www.excellencegateway.org.uk/node/2753 (accessed 29 May 2014).

Mirza-Davies, J (2014) *Youth Unemployment Statistics.* London: HMSO, www.parliament.uk/business/publications/research/briefing-papers/SN05871/youth-unemployment-statistics (accessed 29 May 2014).

Ofsted (2012a) *Good Practice Resource: Using Individual Learning Plans to Improve Personal and Vocational Skill Development: HMP and YOI Low Newton.* Manchester: Ofsted.

Ofsted (2012b) *Skills for Employment.* Manchester: Ofsted.

QIA (2013) *Guidance for Assessment and Learning.* Reading: QIA.

Schön, D (2002) *The Reflective Practitioner*. Aldershot: Ashgate Publishing.

Simpson, E J (1966) The classification of educational objectives: psychomotor domain. *Illinois Journal of Home Economics*, 10(4): 110–44.

8 The practice of teaching

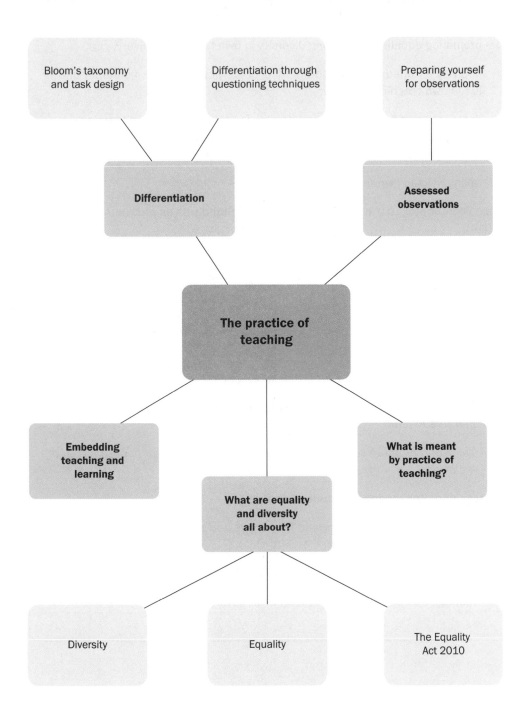

PROFESSIONAL LINKS

This chapter assists with your understanding of the following LSIS (2013, p 28) mandatory content:

○   using teaching and learning approaches/strategies/methods/techniques and resources, including learning technologies to meet individual learning needs;

○   promoting equality and valuing diversity in own teaching/delivery;

○   applying knowledge and understanding of literacy, language, numeracy and ICT in own teaching/delivery;

○   demonstrating flexibility and adaptability in using teaching and learning approaches/strategies/methods/techniques in response to individual learning needs;

○   taking risks in own teaching/delivery.

It also contributes to the following Professional Standards as provided by the ETF (2014).

Professional values and attributes

Develop your own judgement of what works and does not work in your teaching and training.

1   *Reflect on what works best in your teaching and learning to meet the diverse needs of learners*

2   *Evaluate and challenge your practice, values and beliefs*

4   *Be creative and innovative in selecting and adapting strategies to help learners to learn*

5   *Value and promote social and cultural diversity, equality of opportunity and inclusion*

Professional knowledge and understanding

Develop deep and critically informed knowledge and understanding in theory and practice.

10   *Evaluate your practice with others and assess its impact on learning*

11   *Manage and promote positive learner behaviour*

Professional skills

Develop your expertise and skills to ensure the best outcomes for learners.

14 *Plan and deliver effective learning programmes for diverse groups or individuals in a safe and inclusive environment*

15 *Promote the benefits of technology and support learners in its use*

16 *Address the mathematics and English needs of learners and work creatively to overcome individual barriers to learning*

17 *Enable learners to share responsibility for their own learning and assessment, setting goals that stretch and challenge*

A list of all of the Standards can be found at the back of this book (Appendix 7).

KEY DEFINITIONS

Differentiation	Teaching to meet the varying needs of all learners at all levels within the teaching environment.
Diversity	Promoting progress and achievement in learners of all backgrounds, heritages and abilities.
Equality	Ensuring all learners have been given a fair chance to succeed.
Protected characteristics	Groups who are protected under the Equality Act 2010.

INTRODUCTION

Whether you are a new or experienced teacher this chapter is designed to support you in the professional practice of your teaching and help you make the most of your observations by ensuring you are prepared and able to show your teaching and learning at its most effective. It therefore aims to support you in:

○ identifying and exploring some of the key teaching and learning approaches and resources, including learning technologies to meet individual learning needs;

○ considering approaches to promoting equality and valuing diversity in own teaching/delivery;

○   developing your knowledge and understanding of embedding in own teaching/ delivery;

○   understanding and demonstrating flexibility and adaptability in response to individual learning needs;

○   exploring risk taking in own teaching and delivery.

STARTING POINT

What do you understand by practice of teaching?

○   What do you currently understand about embedding?

○   Are you aware of the different forms differentiation can take?

○   How do you ensure that equality and diversity are included in your lessons?

○   What do you think a safe and inclusive teaching environment is?

WHAT IS MEANT BY PRACTICE OF TEACHING?

To some extent the practice of teaching is governed by what is expected of you at a national and local level. For example, your practice of teaching is governed by Ofsted (2014) and the Professional Standards (ETF, 2014) as well as what is expected of you by your own educational establishment. Another dimension could be added to that: what you expect of yourself. All of this is wrapped up in a reflective cycle of continuous improvement. So, if you have been teaching for a while, some of the things regarding your practice that were expected of you five years ago will be different to what is expected of you today. Similarly, what is expected of you at the start of the DET qualification is not what is expected of you at the end of the DET qualification.

ASSESSED OBSERVATIONS

As part of your DET qualification you will need to undertake 100 hours of teaching in an appropriate educational setting and also be observed eight times. As discussed later in this chapter there is an expectation that, by the end of your training, you will have achieved at least a Grade 2 (according to Ofsted requirements) in your observed practice. It is also a good idea to take any opportunities offered to observe others' practice as this can give you a great insight into strategies, resources and planning by other teachers. Your mentor may well offer you the opportunity to observe them or if you have heard great things about another teacher, even in a completely different area, ask if you could observe them and then reflect and act on what you have observed (see Chapter 4 regarding assessment).

Following a review in 2012 (see the Introduction of this book) LSIS developed guidance for awarding organisations (AOs) and higher education institutions (HEIs) and it is this guidance that this section is based upon. The criteria listed below, distilled by LSIS (2013, p 16), is taken from Ofsted's (2014) handbook for the Inspection of Further Education and Skills:

○ *learners benefit from high expectations, engagement, care, support and motivation from staff;*

○ *staff use their skills and expertise to plan and deliver teaching, learning and support to meet each learner's needs;*

○ *staff initially assess learners' starting points and monitor their progress, set challenging tasks, and build on and extend learning for all learners;*

○ *learners understand how to improve as a result of frequent, detailed and accurate feedback from staff following assessment of their learning;*

○ *teaching and learning to develop English, mathematics and functional skills, and support the achievement of learning goals and career aims;*

○ *appropriate and timely information, advice and guidance support in learning effectively;*

○ *equality and diversity are promoted through teaching and learning.*

(LSIS, 2013, table 1)

Critical task

Look at the criteria listed above and consider which areas of teaching and learning you would focus on in order to improve your practice. Put together a plan of action on how to focus on the areas identified.

Comment

Reflecting on your practice is a significant part of your continuing development as a teacher. The information in Chapter 1 can support you in doing this.

The observations that you have for your DET may be graded. Outlined overleaf are the Ofsted criteria for an outstanding and a good lesson. What you are aiming for, by the end of your DET, is a good lesson with some examples of outstanding teaching. However, what you are probably hoping for is an outstanding lesson. Remember that even with an outstanding lesson there is always room for improvement and development, both in the short and longer term.

Outstanding (Grade 1)

o *Much teaching, learning and assessment for all age groups and learning programmes is outstanding and rarely less than consistently good. As a result, the very large majority of learners consistently make very good and sustained progress in learning sessions that may take place in a variety of locations, such as the classroom, workplace or wider community;*

o *all staff are highly adept at working with and developing skills and knowledge in learners from different backgrounds;*

o *staff have consistently high expectations of all learners and demonstrate this in a range of learning environments;*

o *drawing on excellent subject knowledge and/or industry experience, teachers, trainers, assessors and coaches plan astutely and set challenging tasks based on systematic, accurate assessment of learners' prior skills, knowledge and understanding. They use well-judged and often imaginative teaching strategies that, together with sharply focused and timely support and intervention, match individual needs accurately;*

o *consequently, the development of learners' skills and understanding is exceptional. Staff generate high levels of enthusiasm for participation in, and commitment to, learning;*

o *teaching and learning develop high levels of resilience, confidence and independence in learners when they tackle challenging activities;*

o *teachers, trainers, and assessors check learners' understanding effectively throughout learning sessions;*

o *time is used very well and every opportunity is taken to develop crucial skills successfully, including being able to use their literacy and numeracy skills on other courses and at work;*

o *appropriate and regular coursework contributes very well to learners' progress;*

o *high quality learning materials and resources including information and communication technology (ICT) are available and are used by staff and learners during and between learning and assessment sessions;*

o *marking and constructive feedback from staff are frequent and of a consistent quality, leading to high levels of engagement and interest;*

o *the teaching of English, mathematics and functional skills is consistently good with much outstanding;*

o *teachers and other staff enthuse and motivate most learners to participate in a wide range of learning activities;*

o *equality and diversity are integrated fully into the learning experience. Staff manage learners' behaviour skilfully; they show great awareness of equality and diversity in teaching sessions;*

○ advice, guidance and support motivate learners to secure the best possible opportunities for success in their learning and progression.

Good (Grade 2)

○ *Teaching, learning and assessment are predominantly good, with examples of outstanding teaching. All staff are able to develop learners' skills and knowledge regardless of their backgrounds. As a result, learners make good progress;*

○ *staff have high expectations of all learners. Staff in most curriculum and learning programme areas use their well-developed skills and expertise to assess learners' prior skills, knowledge and understanding accurately, to plan effectively and set challenging tasks. They use effective teaching, learning and assessment strategies that, together with appropriately targeted support and intervention, match most learners' individual needs effectively;*

○ *teaching generally develops learners' resilience, confidence and independence when tackling challenging activities. Staff listen perceptively to, carefully observe and skilfully question learners during learning sessions;*

○ *teaching deepens learners' knowledge and understanding consistently and promotes the development of independent learning skills;*

○ *good use of resources, including ICT, and regular coursework contribute well to learners' progress;*

○ *staff assess learners' progress regularly and accurately and discuss assessments with them so that learners know how well they have done and what they need to do to improve;*

○ *the teaching of English, mathematics and functional skills is generally good. Teachers and other staff enthuse and motivate most learners to participate in a wide range of learning activities;*

○ *equality and diversity are promoted and learners' behaviour is managed well, although some work is still needed to integrate aspects of equality and diversity into learning fully;*

○ *advice, guidance and support provide good opportunities for learners to be motivated and make the necessary connection between learning and successful progression.*

(Ofsted, 2014, pp 43–6)

Critical questions

Read through the Grade 1 and Grade 2 Ofsted requirements.

What makes a good lesson into an outstanding lesson?

→

What grade would you have given your last teaching lesson, and why?

What areas do you feel you need to improve?

When you have considered these points come up with a list to use against your next observed lesson.

Comment

It might help you if you share your list with your mentor and construct an action plan to develop the knowledge and skills that you consider will improve your practice.

As well as the requirements and standards set by Ofsted and LSIS there is also a set of Professional Standards from the Education and Training Foundation, which was set up in 2013. At the start of every chapter, you will notice the Professional Standards that are appropriate for that chapter. They are set out into three sections:

o   *Professional values and attributes*

o   *Professional knowledge and understanding*

o   *Professional skills*

(ETF, 2014)

Critical task

Visit the ETF (2014) website and read through the new Professional Standards. Do these align and support what is noted in the Ofsted framework and the LSIS requirements for ITE?

Preparing yourself for observations

Pre-observation checklist

Your tutor may provide you with a checklist to help you prepare for an observation. If not the following quick checklist could be used to help you prepare for an observation.

☐	If this is your first observation, do you feel that you understand the observation process? (If you do not, please talk to your observer or course tutor.)
☐	If this is not your first observation, do you have the feedback from your previous observation to reflect upon and use for your next observation?

☐	Do you have a spare copy of your paperwork and resources to give to your observer (such as lesson plan, scheme of work, sample ILPs and resources)?
☐	In your lesson planning have you thought out your strategy to assess learning (differentiated) so it is clear to the learners what they need to achieve and how?
☐	Are you showing excellent subject knowledge?
☐	Have you explicitly identified equality and diversity opportunities?
☐	Are you challenging all of your learners and building up their independence?
☐	Do your lesson plan and delivery show how you are developing LLN and ICT skills, embedding them within the lesson?
☐	Do you have extension exercises (or homework) prepared to suit the lesson?
☐	Do you have good quality, age-appropriate resources?
☐	Are you spacing your observations out over the duration of the Diploma?
☐	Are you using your reflective log to inform future teaching and learning?
☐	Do you have time and a quiet place to receive feedback on your observed lesson?
☐	Are you familiar with the Ofsted and Professional Standards for Teaching and Learning in the Lifelong Learning Sector, against which your observation may be assessed?

To ensure that you make the most of your observations, always be prepared for your lesson, reflect on the lesson at your earliest opportunity, preferably with your mentor, and record any action points for your next teaching lesson.

WHAT ARE EQUALITY AND DIVERSITY ALL ABOUT?

Equality

An essential part of teaching and learning is about equality. This is about treating your learners fairly and ensuring everyone is given a fair chance. This is not the same as everyone needing to be treated the same. Equality recognises the many different needs of people to be able to access the same opportunities.

Diversity

Diversity is a celebration of the fact that everyone is different.

> *It is about visible and non-visible differences. While equality is about treating everyone equally in terms of rights, status and opportunities, with an emphasis on eradicating discrimination, diversity is about making sure that everyone is valued and included.*

(Gravells and Simpson, 2009, p 30)

The Equality Act 2010 brought together *equality* and *diversity* and consolidated all of the existing acts regarding discrimination under the umbrella of one act. The Equality Act also makes it law that public bodies must encourage good relations and ensure everyone has equality of opportunity. This is known as Public Sector Equality Duties (PSED). This effectively means that public sector organisations, such as educational establishments, must not only uphold equality and diversity but also promote it.

Critical question

Reflect on your teaching and learning sessions and consider how you could promote equality and diversity in the classroom or in your organisation.

Comment

For some practical classroom ideas on this see Adult Education in Gloucestershire (2012). In addition, the Equality Act 2010 has produced a list of *protected characteristics*. These are groups of people or qualities that may be easily discriminated against, in one way or another, and therefore need protecting (see Chapters 2 and 3 for further information about this act). For more information about the protected characteristics and discrimination see Chapter 3.

You can see a more in-depth definition of the protected characteristics on the GOV.UK website.

The Equality Act 2010

The Equality Act 2010 also describes seven types of discrimination that can be legally protected against.

1. Direct discrimination – where someone is treated less favourably than another person because of a protected characteristic.

2. Associative discrimination – this is direct discrimination against someone because they are associated with another person who possesses a protected characteristic.

3. Discrimination by perception – this is direct discrimination against someone because others think that they possess a particular protected characteristic. They do not necessarily have to possess the characteristic, just be perceived to.

4. Indirect discrimination – this can occur when you have a rule or policy that applies to everyone but disadvantages a person with a particular protected characteristic.

5. Harassment by a third party – employers are potentially liable for the harassment of their staff or customers by people they don't themselves employ, ie a contractor.

6. Harassment – this is behaviour that is deemed offensive by the recipient. Employees can now complain of the behaviour they find offensive even if it is not directed at them.

7. Victimisation – this occurs when someone is treated badly because they have made or supported a complaint or grievance under this legislation.

Critical question

Are there any occasions within your teaching practice when it might be possible to inadvertently or indirectly discriminate against someone? Explain your answer.

Comment

Insufficient planning and consideration of resources could possibly result in indirect discrimination, as could an inability to challenge pre-held assumptions (see Chapter 1 for further information about challenging assumptions).

An excellent booklet on equality and diversity in the classroom is Adult Education in Gloucestershire (2012), with practical applications. Also, see Chapters 3 and 7 for ideas about planning and delivering for equality and diversity.

DIFFERENTIATION

Equality and diversity are very much a part of differentiation. Differentiation is making sure that the work given to learners is suitable for the individual or group of learners. Differentiation must be incorporated into lesson planning, teaching and learning. Another teacher when looking at your lesson plan must be able to clearly identify where you have built differentiation into the lesson. A part of differentiation is making sure that all learners are challenged. Make sure that all learners are able to access a lesson but also that all learners feel challenged by the learning (see Chapter 6). We differentiate for:

○   a whole group;

○   groups within the class;

○   individuals.

Bloom's taxonomy and task design

Research Bloom's taxonomy (Bloom et al., 1956) and evaluate its use to help to create differentiated and challenging tasks for learners. Look at Chapter 7 to see how Bloom's taxonomy fits into lesson planning at the activity and assessment levels.

Critical task

Look at the ideas for differentiation below and fill in the boxes with an appropriate teaching and learning activity that incorporates the idea. Think about how the differentiated tasks might be judged against Bloom's taxonomy. As some of the suggested answers may not be specific enough to your area of teaching, there are no suggested answers, however, for any that you find problematic, discuss them with your mentor or with a study buddy on your DET.

○ Differentiation by content: learners study different materials within the same topic area but do the same activities.

○ Differentiation by activities: learners study the same content but do different activities.

○ Differentiation by negotiation: learners study different materials within the same topic area and also do different activities. Teachers help learners to select appropriate materials.

○ Differentiation by support: learners study the same materials and do the same activities but receive different amounts of support from the teacher or from extra printed information.

○ Differentiation by extension: learners study the same materials and do the same activities. Extension work is given to the most able after they have finished the basic activities.

○ Differentiation by response: learners are set open-ended assignments that can be interpreted at different levels.

○ Differentiation by group work: learners work in mixed-ability groups. Learners help each other by working together and interpreting the tasks at different levels.

○ Differentiation by gradation: learners are given the same information and activities. The activities become progressively more difficult. The learners work through the activities at different rates and therefore only the more able do the more difficult tasks.

○ Differentiation by role: learners carry out different activities depending on the role they are playing in a simulation. The roles are matched to the abilities, aptitudes and needs of the pupil. The worksheets are differentiated by content, activities, extension, response, support, gradation, group work and role.

Differentiation through questioning techniques

A teacher who is a skilful questioner will be able to mix up question types and carefully direct them to learners in an appropriate manner. So, for some learners they will get a question that has a simple *yes* or *no* answer whereas others will be asked more complex questions. Or questions will be scaffolding, beginning with simple questions and gradually building to more complex ones that test learners' understanding. One thing to remember is that not all work needs to be differentiated.

EMBEDDING TEACHING AND LEARNING

Embedded teaching and learning combines the development of literacy, language (ESOL) or numeracy with vocational and other skills. The skills acquired provide learners with the confidence, competence and motivation necessary for them to succeed in qualifications, life and work.

(Excellence Gateway, 2014)

A really good paper to read is one entitled *You Wouldn't Expect a Maths Teacher to Teach Plumbing* (Casey et al., 2006). It explains why a teacher of any subject also needs to think about the literacy, language and numeracy levels and needs of the learners. This feeds into differentiation and, again, your lesson plan should clearly show where you have planned to support learners during the lesson (see Chapter 7 regarding planning of lessons).

A very simple illustration embedding literacy and language is during a practical hairdressing lesson on dyeing hair. As part of the lesson the teacher is explaining the mixing ratios of colour to developer or peroxide. If the learners do not understand ratios or how to work them out then the teacher needs to support them with this. The consequence for getting it wrong could be disastrous, for example a client's scalp could be burnt. So whilst a hairdressing teacher would say that they were not a maths teacher, they have a responsibility to ensure that the learners' mathematics skills are up to the level needed for the vocational application.

The notion of embedding literacy, language and numeracy translates beyond the classroom and into the learners' workplace. An employer wants to be confident that the new employee has the skills needed to carry out their job (see Chapter 7 regarding fitting employability skills into planning).

Critical task

Read the summaries of the Leitch (2006) and Wolf (2011) Reviews and reflect on what implications these have for you. Review your last lesson plan and (using the personal audit and lesson plan templates that can be located within the appendices at the end of this book if necessary) consider how, in your lessons, you could embed:

o literacy;

o language;

o numeracy;

o ICT;

o employability skills.

> ### Comment
>
> You may find that you have nothing explicitly embedded, so plan your next lesson with these areas at the forefront of your mind. If it is not in a lesson plan then it is hard to prove that you had planned for the embedding to take place.

SUMMARY

When you are observed you will know what the observer is looking for in terms of planning and delivery. It should not come as a surprise. With careful preparation, reflection and full use of your mentor, each observed lesson will build on your skills as a teacher. Welcome the opportunity to be observed rather than see it as a problem. Take on board any developmental points and be aware of the professional standards expected of you as a teacher.

 Check your understanding

You will find suggested answers to some of these questions at the back of this book.

Question 1:   Make notes about what you think you should be doing at the following points:

   ○   before the lesson;

   ○   at the beginning of the lesson;

   ○   in the lesson;

   ○   towards the end of the lesson;

   ○   at the end of the lesson.

Question 2:   Why do we differentiate and what are the benefits to the learner and to the teacher?

Question 3:   Read through the case studies on pages 147–8 and consider the questions that follow. The case studies have been taken from the excellent Equality and Human Rights Commission (EHRC, 2014) website.

Case study 1

I use a wheelchair to get around and I'm finding it very hard to get a place at my local college. I want to study science and the labs are on the first floor. The college hasn't got a lift and they say they can't afford to have one put in just for me so I must go somewhere else. Travelling any distance is really difficult and expensive so I don't want to go to another college.

○ What protected characteristic is potentially being discriminated against?

○ Could this be unlawful discrimination under the Equality Act 2010?

○ What action could the person take?

 Case study 2

I was refused an apprenticeship at a local hairdresser's because I wear the hijab and they say that all staff must wear their hair in trendy styles to impress the customers. I'm not prepared to do this as it is against my beliefs.

○ What protected characteristic is potentially being discriminated against?

○ Could this be unlawful discrimination under the Equality Act 2010?

○ What action could the person take?

 Case study 3

I am an Irish Traveller. We live on a permanent site now and so we don't move around anymore, which is great because I get to stay at the same school. But the other day I was in school and I heard a teacher making horrible comments about gypsies and travellers. They were saying our site should be shut down and we are all trouble.

→

○ What protected characteristic is potentially being discriminated against?

○ Could this be unlawful discrimination under the Equality Act 2010?

○ What action could the person take?

 Case study 4

I am at college and I'm pregnant. I am required to attend parenting class at the same time as my science GCSE class. Both classes are really important and it seems unfair that I can't attend them both.

○ What protected characteristic is potentially being discriminated against?

○ Could this be unlawful discrimination under the Equality Act 2010?

○ What action could the person take?

End-of-chapter reflections

○ Always reflect on each episode of teaching.

○ Make sure you are aware of what criteria your observer is using to observe you against.

○ Use your mentor.

○ Take any opportunities to observe teaching and learning.

○ Make sure your lesson plan and teaching and learning explicitly demonstrate how you are embedding equality and diversity, LLN, ICT and employability skills.

○ During a lesson, make sure you can say that you have done your best to make sure everyone is included in the lesson and able to achieve at an appropriate level.

○ How do you think you will be able to use your learning from this chapter to develop your practice?

TAKING IT FURTHER

In addition to the literature already commented upon in this chapter you may find the following of interest.

Excellence Gateway (2013) *Equality and Diversity*. [Online]. Available at: http://www.excellencegateway.org.uk/edresource (accessed 5 August 2014).

REFERENCES

Adult Education in Gloucestershire (2012) *Equality and Diversity in the Classroom*. [Online]. Available at: http://adulteducation.gloucestershire.gov.uk/pluginfile.php/4438/mod_resource/content/1/2.3%20ED%20in%20the%20classroom.pdf (accessed 26 May 2014).

Bloom, B S, Englehar, M D, Furst, E J, Hill, W H and Krathwohl, D R (1956) *Taxonomy of Educational Objectives: The Classification of Educational Goals. Handbook I: Cognitive Domain*. New York: David McKay.

Casey, H, Cara, O, Eldred, J, Grief, S, Hodge, R, Ivanič, R, Jupp, T, Lopez, D and McNeil, B (2006) *You Wouldn't Expect a Maths Teacher to Teach Plastering*. London: NRDC.

EHRC (2014) *Creating a Fairer Britain*. [Online]. Available at: www.equalityhumanrights.com/ (accessed 26 May 2014).

ETF (2014) *Professional Standards for Teachers and Trainers in Education and Training*. [Online]. Available at: www.et-foundation.co.uk (accessed 26 May 2014).

Excellence Gateway (2014) *Embedding*. [Online]. Available at: http://rwp.excellencegateway.org.uk/Embedded%20Learning/ (accessed 26 May 2014).

GOV.UK (2010) *Equality Act 2010*. London: HMSO.

Gravells, A and Simpson, S (2009) *Equality and Diversity in the Lifelong Learning Sector (Further Education and Skills)*. Exeter: Learning Matters.

Leitch, S (2006) *Prosperity for All in the Global Economy*. [Online]. Available at: http://dera.ioe.ac.uk/6322/1/leitch_finalreport051206.pdf (accessed 26 May 2014).

LSIS (2013) *Qualification Guidance for Awarding Organisations: Assessed Observations of Practice within the Education and Training Suite of Qualifications*. Coventry: LSIS.

Ofsted (2014) *Handbook for the Inspection of Further Education and Skills*. Manchester: Ofsted.

Wolf, A (2011) *Review of Vocational Education*. [Online]. Available at: http://dera.ioe.ac.uk/11621/1/DFE-00031-2011.pdf (accessed 26 May 2014).

9 Curriculum development and evaluation

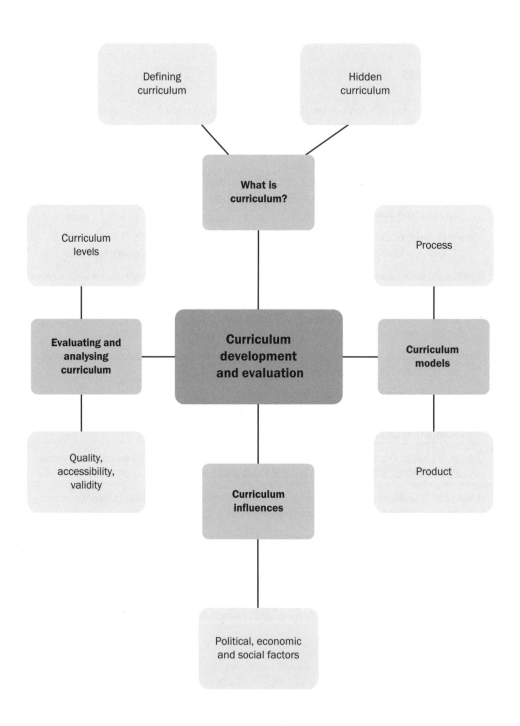

PROFESSIONAL LINKS

This chapter assists with your understanding of the following LSIS (2013, p 28) mandatory content:

o theories and models of curriculum development;

o impact of social/political/economic context on curriculum development;

o evaluating curriculum.

It also contributes to the following Professional Standards as provided by the ETF (2014):

Professional knowledge and understanding

Develop deep and critically informed knowledge and understanding in theory and practice.

9 *Apply theoretical understanding of effective practice in teaching, learning and assessment drawing on research and other evidence*

10 *Evaluate your practice with others and assess its impact on learning*

Professional skills

Develop your expertise and skills to ensure the best outcomes for learners.

14 *Plan and deliver effective learning programmes for diverse groups or individuals in a safe and inclusive environment*

A list of all of the Standards can be found at the back of this book (Appendix 7).

KEY DEFINITIONS

Hidden curriculum	Elements of course content delivered unintentionally.
Process model	A model of curriculum design that focuses on the learning experiences.
Product model	A model of curriculum design that focuses on the outcomes of learning.

INTRODUCTION

At the heart of FE lies the notion of curriculum, informing every element of a teacher's practice, from planning through to teaching and finally to evaluation. This chapter therefore aims to guide you to explore this further, through examination and critical analysis of a range of aspects, influences and models of curriculum and to draw on these to support you in:

○   defining curriculum;

○   identifying, exploring and critiquing key theories and models of curriculum;

○   recognising and analysing influences on your curriculum;

○   evaluating the effectiveness of your own curriculum.

STARTING POINT

What do you already know about curriculum?

○   What do you currently understand by the term *curriculum*?

○   What influences on curriculum design are you already aware of?

○   What theories and models of curriculum design are you already aware of?

WHAT IS MEANT BY THE TERM *CURRICULUM*?

Critical question

What do you understand by the term *curriculum*?

Comment

In your answer you may have suggested curriculum being a course of study, as an overarching term for the courses in an organisation or perhaps as the content that you teach.

Your answer to the above Critical question may have identified uncertainty in relation to a unique definition of curriculum. This lack of decisiveness is often evidenced in any examination of literature, with an array of possible definitions, varying in scope, structure and breadth. Gray, Griffin and Nasta (2000, p 71) note that at its narrowest curriculum can be considered as a '*body of knowledge or skills*', whereas, Armitage et al. (2003, p 194) note an array of definitions including those which consider the curriculum as '*a teacher's intentional plan or formal timetabled lessons*'.

Whilst it may be tempting to accept simple definitions, as teachers it is essential that you look to analyse and evaluate every element of your curriculum and this requires consideration of the broader view. Gray, Griffin and Nasta (2000, p 71) note that '*in the broadest sense, the curriculum stands for just about everything that happened in the educational setting*'. They further suggest that this broader view should encompass any of the numerous factors that influence the learning process, including consideration of issues of staffing, buildings and policies. Print (1993, p 9) concurs in this view of a broad curriculum and suggests that '*curriculum is defined as all the planned learning opportunities offered to the learners by the educational institution and the experiences learners encountered when the curriculum is implemented*'.

Hidden curriculum

Not all curriculum is specifically taught. The notion of a hidden curriculum explores the idea that some learning can be unintentional. Kelly (2011) suggests that a hidden curriculum may include the transmission of values or attitudes. Such values may be those of your own punctuality, commitment, motivation and professionalism. If you repeatedly turn up late to a class, you are conveying the message that arriving late is acceptable, however, if you are always on time or early, you are conveying the message that punctuality is important.

Critical question

Consider your own qualities in terms of commitment, motivation and professionalism. How might these influence what learners unintentionally learn from you?

Comment

You might have considered how you demonstrate enthusiasm for the varying components of your subject, perhaps by how you communicate with your learners, by drawing on notions of transactional analysis (see Chapter 5). Your learners are likely to model and learn from your behaviour, therefore when you reflect on your own practice, you should also consider the unintended consequences of your own actions.

CURRICULUM MODELS

The examination of curriculum, as with all areas of education, is supported by a range of relevant models and theories. Gray et al. (2000) suggest that these models are useful in helping us to organise our thinking about our practice. Various models consider curriculum as a process, a product or even as a body of knowledge to be transmitted from teacher to learners. Given the diverse contexts within which you may teach, some have more relevance than others.

The product or objectives model

One of the most commonly known and used curriculum models is Tyler's (1949) objectives model. In his model he considers curriculum planning as originating from the answers to four questions:

1. *What educational purposes should the [organisation] seek to attain?*

2. *What educational experiences can be provided that are likely to attain these purposes?*

3. *How can these educational experiences be effectively organised?*

4. *How can we determine whether these purposes are being attained?*

(Tyler, 1949, p 1)

This model, based on behavioural approaches, has essential links to questions about aims and objectives which can usually be found embedded within organisational documentation, including schemes of work and teaching and learning plans.

Critical task

Explore the documentation within your own organisation or that provided by your training organisation. To what extent are aims and objectives included?

Comment

Your answer may differ according to your organisation, however, you may have found some of the following:

o   lesson aims noted on teaching and learning plans and schemes of work;

o   differentiated objectives required on teaching and learning plans;

o   aims and objectives evidenced in documentation provided by awarding bodies.

As objectives are usually integral to teaching and learning plans, adopting an objectives model enables closer attention to be paid regarding whether the objectives have been met. This is supported by Wilson (2009) who notes that the advantage of an objectives model is the way in which evidence of learning can be standardised, although she adds a note of caution that this approach may have a tendency to provide shallow learning over a range of topics.

The process model

A process model, as proposed by Stenhouse (1975), focuses predominantly on activities that enable learners to develop their cognitive skills without allowing the objectives to dominate. Stenhouse produced his model in response to Tyler's model, which he felt was more relevant to the learning of skills rather than a deeper understanding of the topic. The process model, rather than focusing on outcomes, focuses on the journey taken.

The process model sees the teacher in a different role than that suggested by the product model. Rather than taking the traditional teacher role, the teacher becomes a fellow learner with a senior role (Gould, 2009). This model therefore takes a humanistic approach and places the learners at the centre of learning, with teachers supporting, rather than directly teaching their learners. Whilst the learner-centred positioning of the process model appears attractive in engaging learners, Stenhouse (1975) notes a clear limitation in relation to the assessment of learners' work and suggests that it should not form the basis of an examination-driven course.

Critical question

Consider your own curriculum and the approach that you take to curriculum planning. Do you take a product or a process approach? Can you explain the reasons for your approach?

Comment

In your answer to this reflective task you may have found elements of both models. Perhaps you need learners to complete an examination at the end of the course but you have also tried to engage their deeper learning skills by your choice of activity and your role in the classroom.

CURRICULUM INFLUENCES

Education does not exist in a vacuum and it is important to consider your own delivery, approaches and outcomes. However, as teachers it is equally important that you consider the range of influences which are often out of your control. The courses that you teach will be affected by a range of political, economic and social issues. Changing government policies and priorities may influence the type of courses offered and the number of places available. Economic issues may influence the availability of course funding and the ability of learners to pay for courses. Social factors including the culture, experience, attitudes and background of learners may influence the teaching and learning approaches that you need to take.

Case study

James has a background in business and has completed a placement for his DET qualification at a local sixth form college teaching on a business studies course. The sixth form college serves an affluent local area and learners were mainly aged 16–18 years old. For the next part of his course, he will be teaching at another college. This college is situated in an area of high unemployment and learners range from 16 years old to retired people taking recreational courses.

Critical question

If James were to analyse the curriculum in his second placement, what political, economic and social factors might he consider?

Comment

You might have suggested some of the following.

Political: perhaps employability is a key focus for the government. It may be that some learners have been advised that they must attend James' course and are therefore not as motivated as those who have signed up for the course willingly.

Economic: if the local population is unemployed James might find that no charge is made for the course. This could make the course attractive to learners who have previously been deterred by high course costs.

Social: James would need to think about the age and culture of the learners and he would need to focus on this to ensure his curriculum was inclusive. He might also note his lack of experience of teaching mixed-ability groups.

EVALUATING AND ANALYSING CURRICULUM

There are a range of factors that can influence your own curriculum and as your own teaching role develops, so do your responsibilities. You may find that you start to move from developing the curriculum provided by others to adapting and developing your own.

Curriculum levels

As a teacher and as part of your DET qualification, you will usually be asked to examine your own curriculum in detail and this can be aided by considering curriculum levels as suggested by Porter (2006). Porter suggests that curriculum may be analysed at one of four levels, those of intended, enacted, assessed and learned.

> *Intended: analyse the content of the curriculum.*
>
> *Enacted: analyse how the content is delivered to the learner.*
>
> *Assessed: analyse the assessment materials and expectations.*
>
> *Learned: analyse what the learners take away with them in terms of knowledge and skills.*
>
> (Porter, 2006, p 141)

Analysing the curriculum that you deliver may seem a daunting task, however, by considering your analysis in relation to these levels, you should find that you are able to examine in greater depth your own and organisational practice. This analysis will guide you in identifying your strengths and areas for development, to evaluate the courses that you teach and also to evaluate your curriculum in relation to the bigger picture – the wider curriculum of your department, faculty or organisation.

Quality, accessibility and validity

When you are tasked with evaluating your curriculum, you should move beyond evaluation of the day-to-day delivery of your lessons and teaching practice. One way that you can do this is to consider it in terms of the dimensions suggested by Nasta (1994, p 133), who refers to a report by County of Avon (1989) and suggests that course evaluation should focus on '*Quality, Accessibility and Validity*'.

> *Quality How effective is the course?*
>
> *Accessibility How accessible is the course to all of the proposed client group?*
>
> *Validity How relevant is the course? Does it meet the needs of employers? Does it meet the needs of learners?*
>
> (Nasta, 1994, p 133)

In an increasingly market-driven teaching and learning environment, consideration of these three dimensions is essential. Within FE, reliance on external funding and from learners themselves means that you will continually be called upon to justify the need for your course.

Case study

John is a French teacher. He has been graded as Outstanding in recent observations. The course he teaches is a GCSE course and takes place in the evening. A large proportion of his learners have joined his class following the closure of their conversational French class. Whilst they enjoy the class, they have already expressed their lack of interest in the examination.

Critical question

Can you foresee any long-term problems that John may have in terms of the quality of his course?

Comment

The important thing to note here is that the quality of the course need not necessarily be about John's teaching. He may be an outstanding teacher, however, the quality of his course may not be equally outstanding. Of concern here would be results and this is often how courses are judged. If a large proportion of his learners are not interested in the examination, this could influence their achievement. For example, they might decide not to take the examination or to take it in order to please John, and not be concerned whether they pass.

SUMMARY

In order for you to analyse, evaluate and develop your own practice, a key understanding and application of curriculum models, theories and influences is required. The application of each of these concepts will aid you in developing your own curriculum. It will also enable you to critically analyse the effectiveness of your own curriculum design and delivery and to contribute to discussions in relation to wider issues of curriculum.

Check your understanding

You will find suggested answers to some of these questions at the back of this book.

Question 1: Write down two different definitions of curriculum.

Question 2: What approaches can you use to analyse and evaluate your own curriculum?

Question 3: Consider the impact of current political, economic and social influences for your own practice. If you are an in-service lecturer, consider your place of work. Alternatively, if you are on a pre-service route, consider one of the placements that you have completed.

Question 4: Write down three reasons why it is important to analyse and evaluate your own curriculum.

Question 5: Nasta (1994) noted that the quality of a course was an important dimension of curriculum analysis. Why do you think that this is the case?

Question 6: This chapter has asked you to both analyse and evaluate your own curriculum. What is the difference between these two concepts?

End-of-chapter reflections

○ A range of political, economic and social factors will influence your curriculum.

○ Analysis and evaluation of your curriculum is an essential part of your teaching role.

○ How do you think you will be able to use your learning from this chapter to assist you in analysing and evaluating your curriculum?

 TAKING IT FURTHER

In addition to the literature already commented upon in this chapter you may find the following of interest.

Avis, J, Fisher, R and Thompson, R (2010) *Teaching in Lifelong Learning: A Guide to Theory and Practice.* Berkshire: Open University Press.

Tummons, J (2012) *Curriculum Studies in the Lifelong Learning Sector (Achieving QTLS Series).* London: Learning Matters.

REFERENCES

Armitage, A, Bryant, R, Dunnill, R, Renwick, M, Hayes, D, Hudson, A and Lawes, S (2003) *Teaching and Training in Post Compulsory Education*. 2nd edn. Maidenhead: Open University Press.

ETF (2014) *Professional Standards for Teachers and Trainers in Education and Training*. [Online]. Available at: www.et-foundation.co.uk (accessed 26 May 2014).

Gould, J (2009) *Learning Theory and Classroom Practice in the Lifelong Learning Sector*. Exeter: Learning Matters.

Gray, D, Griffin, C and Nasta, T (2000) *Training to Teach in Further and Adult Education*. Cheltenham: Stanley Thornes.

Kelly, A V (2011) *The Curriculum: Theory and Practice*. 6th edn. London: Sage Publications.

LSIS (2013) *Teaching and Training Qualifications for the Further Education and Skills Sector in England, Guidance for Higher Education Institutions*. Learning Skills Improvement Services: Coventry.

Nasta, T (1994) *How to Design a Vocational Curriculum: A Practical Guide for Schools and Colleges*. London: Kogan Page.

Porter, A (2006) Curriculum Assessment. In J L Green, G Camilli and P B Elmore (eds) *Complementary Methods for Research in Education*. Washington, DC: American Educational Research Association.

Print, M (1993) *Curriculum Development and Design*. 2nd edn. St Leonards: Allen and Unwin.

Stenhouse, L (1975) *An Introduction to Curriculum Research and Development*. London: Heinemann.

Tyler, R W (1949) *Basic Principles of Curriculum and Instruction*. Chicago: University of Chicago Press.

Wilson, L (2009) *Practical Teaching: A Guide to PTLLS and DTLLS*. Andover: Cengage Learning EMEA.

10 Wider professional practice

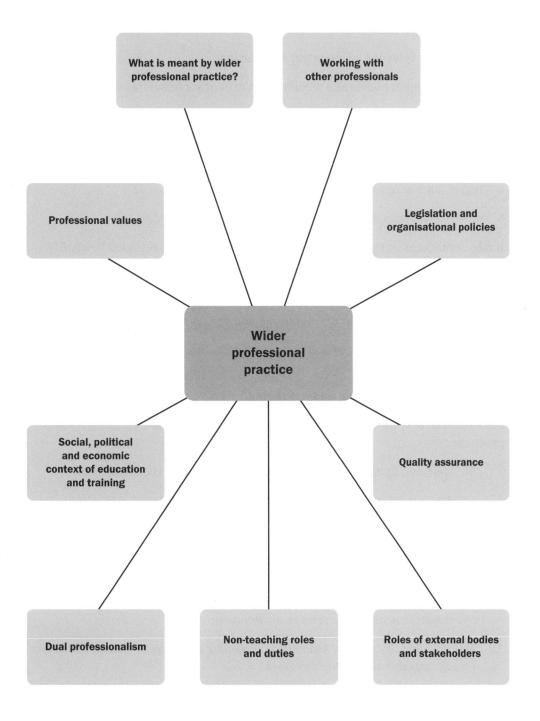

PROFESSIONAL LINKS

This chapter assists with your understanding of the following LSIS (2013, p 28) mandatory content:

- professionalism and professional values;

- dual professionalism;

- contemporary issues in education and training;

- roles of external bodies and stakeholders in education and training;

- social/political/economic context of education and training;

- accountability of education and training organisations to external bodies and stakeholders;

- organisational policies, codes of practice and guidelines;

- quality assurance and quality improvement arrangements.

It also contributes to the following Professional Standards as provided by the ETF (2014):

Professional values and attributes

Develop your own judgement of what works and does not work in your teaching.

5   *Value and promote social and cultural diversity, equality of opportunity and inclusion*

Professional knowledge and understanding

Develop deep and critically informed knowledge and understanding in theory and practice.

7   *Maintain and update knowledge of your subject and/or vocational area*

12   *Understand the teaching and professional role and your responsibilities*

Professional skills

Maintain and develop expertise and skills to ensure the best outcomes for learners.

14   *Plan and deliver effective learning programmes for diverse groups or individuals in a safe and inclusive environment*

19   *Maintain and update your teaching and training expertise and vocational skills through collaboration with employers*

20   *Contribute to organisational development and quality improvement through collaboration with others*

A list of all of the Standards can be found at the back of this book (Appendix 7).

KEY DEFINITIONS

Economic context of education   Change in education driven by economics.

Political context of education   Change in education driven by politics.

Social context of education   Social conditions that can change the way we learn.

Stakeholder   Anyone or any organisation invested in the success of an organisation.

INTRODUCTION

Wider professional practice, whilst vital to excellence in teaching and learning, is often something overlooked by teachers and observers. This chapter seeks to raise the importance of issues inside and outside of classroom practice. It therefore aims to support you in:

○   developing professionalism and professional values;

○   identifying and developing dual professionalism;

○   considering contemporary issues in education and training;

○   exploring the roles of external bodies and stakeholders in education and training;

○   considering social/political/economic context of education and training;

○   reflecting on the accountability of education and training organisations to external bodies and stakeholders;

○   identifying and applying organisational policies, codes of practice and guidelines;

○   identifying quality assurance and quality improvement arrangements.

STARTING POINT

What do you already know about wider professional practice?

○   What do you currently understand by wider professional practice?

○   In relation to you as a teacher, how do you feel concepts of wider professional practice impact on your teaching and learning?

WHAT IS MEANT BY WIDER PROFESSIONAL PRACTICE?

Wider professional practice involves you knowing about and engaging with internal and external requirements and practices that apply to you as a teacher. These may relate to assessment, quality assurance, government policy, quality improvement and your subject knowledge; all of which will be discussed and encountered as part of your DET qualification and in your workplace.

> ### Critical task
>
> Carry out some research to see what else is included in the term *wider professional practice*. How does the term relate to your teaching and learning?

PROFESSIONAL VALUES

The new Standards (ETF, 2014) that have been introduced by the ETF are listed below (Appendix 7 also outlines how they link to the chapters in this book). These Standards list the responsibilities that you have, as a teacher, to your learners, your educational organisation, stakeholders and the wider community.

> ### Critical task
>
> Read through the points below and highlight any areas that you had not previously considered as within your remit as a teacher. Then reflect on how they could be incorporated into your wider teaching and learning and how that will impact on your teaching and learning.

Professional values and attributes

Develop your own judgement of what works and does not work in your teaching.

1   *Reflect on what works best in your teaching and learning to meet the diverse needs of learners.*

2 *Evaluate and challenge your practice, values and beliefs.*

3 *Inspire, motivate and raise the expectations of learners with your own enthusiasm and knowledge.*

4 *Foster creativity and innovation in selecting and adapting strategies to help learners to learn.*

5 *Value and promote social and cultural diversity, equality of opportunity and inclusion.*

6 *Build positive and collaborative relationships with colleagues and learners.*

Professional knowledge and understanding

Develop deep and critically informed knowledge and understanding in theory and practice.

7 *Maintain and update knowledge of your subject and/or vocational area.*

8 *Maintain and update your knowledge of educational research to develop evidence-based practice.*

9 *Apply theoretical understanding of effective practice in teaching, learning and assessment drawing on research and other evidence.*

10 *Evaluate your practice with others and assess its impact on learning.*

11 *Manage and promote positive learner behaviour.*

12 *Understand the teaching and professional role and your responsibilities.*

Professional skills

Maintain and develop expertise and skills to ensure the best outcomes for learners.

13 *Motivate and inspire learners to promote achievement and develop their skills to enable progression to learning.*

14 *Plan and deliver effective learning programmes for diverse groups or individuals in a safe and inclusive environment.*

15 *Promote the benefits of technology and support learners in its use.*

16 *Address the needs of learners in English and mathematics and work creatively to overcome individual barriers to learning.*

17 *Enable learners to share responsibility for their own learning and assessment, setting goals that stretch and challenge.*

18 *Apply appropriate and fair methods of assessment and provide constructive and timely feedback to support progression and achievement.*

19 *Update your expertise and vocational skills through collaboration with the wider community and other agencies.*

20 *Contribute to organisational development and quality improvement through collaboration with others.*

(ETF, 2014)

You should also refer to Chapter 8 for information about LSIS and Ofsted requirements.

NON-TEACHING ROLES AND DUTIES

To identify what roles and duties you will carry out that are not directly related to your teaching, it is worth looking again at the ETF's (2014) Professional Standards to extract those areas that are not necessarily applicable to your practice in the classroom. Although this will not cover all of your roles and responsibilities relating to wider professional practice it will provide you with some insight about your role outside of the classroom:

Evaluate your practice with others and assess its impact on learning

Work with colleagues, peer observe and share good practice to improve teaching and learning. Some teachers have an attitude that if they have spent time creating resources, they should not have to share them. This is very short-sighted and sharing strategies and resources can be very rewarding. You could encourage this practice with your peers on your DET course.

Understand the teaching and professional role and your responsibilities

As a teacher it can sometimes be difficult to know where your role and responsibilities stop (see section on page 167 on *Working with other professionals*). It is imperative that you know what responsibilities you have outside of the classroom, for example, the completion of paperwork. That might be something as obvious as filling in ILPs to completing paperwork for external examinations. It is equally important to keep accurate records to contribute to your organisation's quality improvement strategy: recruitment, retention, achievement and progression.

Build positive and collaborative relationships with colleagues and learners

As a mentor and role model for learners your attitude to colleagues is vitally important. If you teach the same learners as another teacher it is important to communicate with them to make sure that any important information about the learners is known. Teaching can be a stressful occupation and you need the support of colleagues and, similarly, they will need your support.

Update your expertise and vocational skills through collaboration with the wider community and other agencies

You should ensure that you update your industrial skills as necessary and, where possible, keep good relations with local and national businesses to ensure that the information you are passing on to your learners is still vocationally relevant. Friendly links can also lead to visits to workplaces and visits to the classroom by specialists. There may well be employment leads that are open to your learners if a company knows that your learners are ready for the workplace.

Contribute to organisational development and quality improvement through collaboration with others

In a busy educational establishment work can sometimes be all engrossing and you feel you never have time to lift your head up and find out what else is happening in your field of teaching and learning. If you have the opportunity to take on an external role, such as a moderator or marker for an awarding organisation, it can be very beneficial. Remember when accepting a role you must let your place of work know.

Working with other professionals

Part of your professionalism as a teacher means providing learners with appropriate points of referral (internally and externally) as required. In terms of this, during the course, your primary aim is to enable each learner to achieve to the best of their ability through working in a safe and supportive environment. It is therefore your responsibility to know who your learners should contact if they need any additional support or specialist information, such as:

○   finance;

○   health;

○   study skills;

○   counselling.

Critical question

Study the list above. If any of your learners came to you with issues relating to any of these areas would you know where to send them, who to refer them to or what any referral process involved? If not, you need to carry out some research in order to find out so that you are able to give your learners speedy and reliable advice.

Comment

It is not your responsibility to try to solve all of your learners' problems. In fact, as a responsible teacher, you must be able to understand when to take action and signpost or refer learners to another (internal or external) agency. This is part of understanding your boundaries as a teacher.

DUAL PROFESSIONALISM

Dual professionalism is rooted in the understanding that a teacher in FE needs to have excellent, up-to-date subject specialist knowledge as well as excellent, up-to-date skills in teaching and learning. This could be demonstrated in a vocational tutor who teaches plumbing. The teacher would need to keep up to date with plumbing as well as with how to teach plumbing.

The Commission on Adult Vocational Teaching and Learning (CAVTL) explored the idea of excellent teaching and learning, allied with current subject knowledge: *'dual professional teachers and trainers … combine occupational and pedagogical expertise, and are trusted and given the time to develop partnerships and curricula with employers'* (CAVTL, 2013, p 13).

Case studies

Ofsted (2014) and the ETF (2014) have produced some very good quality case studies that highlight excellence in vocational teaching and learning in a variety of situations. Whether you see yourself as a vocational teacher or not, the case studies in the link below are worth reading and reflecting upon. They illustrate the need for professionalism and dual professionalism and the lessons learned from these could apply to any area of teaching.

Critical task

Read at least two of the case studies that can be found using the link below and reflect on how you can use the lessons learned in your own teaching and learning.

www.ofsted.gov.uk/resources/education-and-training-foundation-good-practice-case-studies-for-vocational-education-and-training

ROLES OF EXTERNAL BODIES AND STAKEHOLDERS IN EDUCATION AND TRAINING

As noted in Chapter 2 there are many external bodies and stakeholders that take an interest in, quality assure and have various levels of influence on teaching and learning within FE. Below are just some of these (see Chapter 2 for more information about legislation and statutory bodies).

The Department for Business Innovation and Skills (BIS) – the ministry responsible for further education and skills – provides finance for education. This is to promote trade, increase innovation and grow small businesses. BIS wants to ensure FE provides the skilled workforce which employers need in their workplaces.

The Office for Teaching Standards in Education (Ofsted), the Equality and Human Rights Commission (EHRC) and the Health and Safety Executive (HSE) are statutory bodies established by the government to uphold legislation. So, for instance, Ofsted was set up to enforce standards in education, EHRC to ensure all people are treated fairly and HSE to ensure that the health and safety of the workforce is maintained.

Teachers' unions such as the University and College Union (UCU) or the Association of Teachers and Lecturers (ATL) seek to protect the working rights of its members. Members usually pay to be part of a union.

Professional bodies such as the Education and Training Foundation (ETF) and any organisations related to your subject are usually non-profit organisations that endeavour to protect the professionals within that body whilst monitoring standards within their profession.

Many professions have their own professional body, such as Gas Safe, the Nursing and Midwifery Council and the Chartered Institute of Management Accountants. Alongside the necessity to adhere to professional codes of practice in relation to your teaching it is also important that you adhere to any codes of practice that relate to your subject area and any related professional body.

LEGISLATION AND ORGANISATIONAL POLICIES

The co-operation and support of your organisation is essential in ensuring and maintaining effective classroom and behaviour management, therefore it is important that you spend some time finding out what policies and procedures exist to support you.

Most organisations will have a policy in place relating to behaviour with the aim of providing a safe environment for its staff and learners. These behaviour policies will be informed by a range of legislation including:

o   Equality Act 2010;

o   Children Act 2004;

o   Human Rights Act 1998;

o   Health and Safety at Work Act 1974.

(See Chapter 2 for more information on some of these acts.)

The policy should include guidance and expectations in a number of key areas:

o   Student expectations: this should make it clear what the organisation expects of the learners in terms of behaviour.

o   Staff expectations: this should clearly state what the organisation expects of the staff in terms of their behaviour and how they respond to behaviour.

o   Disciplinary procedures: the disciplinary procedure may be included as part of the policy or it may be a stand-alone procedure and should make it clear what will happen if learners to not adhere to rules. Disciplinary procedures usually follow three stages, with the first being an informal discussion followed by a formal warning and can ultimately lead to exclusion.

o   Rewards: in addition to disciplinary procedures, it is important that an organisational behaviour policy considers how good behaviour will be encouraged. Whilst you can put your own reward systems in place, these need to be applied consistently to ensure effective behaviour management across the organisation (see Chapter 6).

QUALITY ASSURANCE

You need to be familiar with and know your organisation's quality assurance (QA) processes that apply to your area of practice. Talk to your mentor and make sure you are familiar with internal quality procedures as well as external quality assurance. Remember that learners are at the very heart of the quality assurance. Your organisation is likely to have a Head of Quality, who will:

o   oversee internal auditing and validating activities such as course reviews and IQA/EQA moderation procedure and quality improvement plans;

o   provide the QA link with awarding bodies (Quality nominee) including managing annual cross-college quality reviews and co-ordinating award validations, external moderation allocation visits and monitoring of reports;

o   support the managers and staff to prepare for external audit activity such as Ofsted and prepare self-assessment reports;

o   provide baseline information for reviews and reports to both internal and external audiences, including awarding bodies and quality inspectors;

o   develop and implement robust teaching observation processes;

o   lead and report on the learner, employer and parent/carer voice and surveys.

You will be involved in providing information to feed into all of the quality areas mentioned above. Spend time getting to know your quality procedures and focus on the organisation's self-assessment report (SAR) and quality improvement plans (QIPs) to see a whole organisation approach to quality improvement. See *Check your understanding* at the end of the chapter to focus on quality procedures on your organisation.

THE SOCIAL, POLITICAL AND ECONOMIC CONTEXT OF EDUCATION AND TRAINING

To complete your DET qualification you must be aware of some of the drivers of educational policy in this country. See also Chapter 9 for more information on the social, political and economic context of education.

Education plays a huge part in the lives of people and can make significant differences in people's health and well-being (OECD, 2010). Education can bring freedom and a lack of education can be debilitating. An adult attending a course delivered by you may be able to materially alter their life, just by completing a qualification that may subsequently lead to promotion at work. A prisoner can help their job prospects by gaining a qualification. Equality of opportunity is bound up in education being available for all people. In adult education, this may not always be true as location, time, entry qualifications and money may prohibit someone from accessing an adult education course. The government often provides funding to promote learning in a certain area, this drives education in directions that are motivated by external forces.

For example, in 1998 Sir Claus Moser, as head of the Basic Skills Agency, was tasked by the British Government with investigating the level of adult basic skills. Moser's report, *A*

Fresh Start (1999), found that one in five adults in Britain was functionally illiterate and considerably more than that were functionally innumerate. The Moser report stated that these poor basic skills were one of the reasons that Britain was doing so badly in economic productivity compared to other comparator countries. The British Government's response was to set up the Skills for Life agenda in 2001 (DfES, 2001).

From the start of the Skills for Life agenda, the main driver was economic – to get adults ready for work and to be able to fit into the changing economy (Hamilton and Hillier, 2006). This led to a major focus on *practical* skills. In 2006, the Leitch Review (Leitch, 2006) brought these links closer together by reporting that employers did not feel that the mathematics and English skills of school leavers were up to standard for the workplace. This led to the development of *functional skills* qualifications.

SUMMARY

In order to provide an excellent learning environment for your learners it is important that you reflect on what happens outside of the classroom as well as what happens within it. Developing professional links with colleagues, the community and other agencies are important parts of being a teacher. You need to understand your role in your organisation and how it fits with other parts of the organisation. It seems like a tall order but it is all part of what makes you a professional.

 Check your understanding

You will find suggested answers to some of these questions at the back of this book.

Question 1: Are you aware of the ten recommendations made by the CAVTL, and if so how many of these do you integrate into your practice?

Question 2: How many professional bodies can you list that may have some stake in your subject area? Have you thought about becoming a member of any them and if so what benefits would this confer on you? Refer to the organisations' websites for details.

Question 3: Write down three quality procedures that you are involved in and create a diagram of how they feed into quality reports at a higher level. If you are unsure of about any quality processes talk to your mentor or a member of staff involved in quality improvement practices. Reflect on how the quality of your teaching and learning impacts on your organisation.

Question 4: What issues are driving adult education at this moment? Do some research and reflect on how they impact on your practice.

End-of-chapter reflections

○   Think before you speak at work and if you find yourself saying *That is not my responsibility, it has nothing to do with me*, chances are that even in a small way it is your responsibility and it does have something to do with you.

 TAKING IT FURTHER

In addition to the literature already commented upon in this chapter you may find the following of interest.

Lingfield (2012) *Professionalism in Further Education: Final Report of the Independent Review Panel*. [Online]. Available at: www.gov.uk/government/publications/professionalism-in-further-education-final-report-of-the-independent-review-panel (accessed 26 May 2014).

Lingfield (2012) *Professionalism in Further Education: Interim Report of the Independent Review Panel*. London: BIS.

Whitty, G (2008) Twenty years of progress? English education policy 1988 to the present. *Education Management Administration Leadership*, 36(2): 65–184.

Wolf, A (2011) *Review of Vocational Education*. [Online]. Available at: http://dera.ioe.ac.uk/11621/1/DFE-00031-2011.pdf (accessed 26 May 2014).

REFERENCES

CAVTL (2013) *Commission on Adult Vocational Teaching and Learning*. [Online]. Available at: www.excellencegateway.org.uk/cavtl (accessed 26 May 2014).

DfES (2001) *Special Education Needs Code of Practice*. London: DfES, http://webarchive.nationalarchives.gov.uk/20130401151715/https://www.education.gov.uk/publications/eOrderingDownload/DfES%200581%20200mig2228.pdf (accessed April 2014).

ETF (2014) *Professional Standards for Teachers and Trainers in Education and Training*. Education Training Foundation [Online]. Available at: www.et-foundation.co.uk (accessed 26 May 2014).

Hamilton, M and Hillier, Y (2006) *The Changing Face of Adult Literacy, Language and Numeracy 1970–2000: A Critical History*. Stoke-on-Trent: Trentham Books.

IfL (2008) *Code of Professional Practice*. London: Institute for Learning, www.ifl.ac.uk/membership/ifl-code-of-professional-practice/ (accessed April 2014).

Leitch, S (2006) *Leitch Review of Skills: Prosperity for All in the Global Economy – World Class Skills.* London: HMSO.

LSIS (2013) *Teaching and Training Qualifications for the Further Education and Skills Sector in England, Guidance for Higher Education Institutions*. Learning Skills Improvement Services: Coventry.

Moser, C (1999) *A Fresh Start*. London: DfEE.

OECD (2010) *Improving Health and Social Cohesion through Education*. [Online]. Available at: https://community.oecd.org/community/educationtoday/blog/2010/10/13/education-improves-quality-of-life (accessed 26 May 2014).

11 Research and scholarship

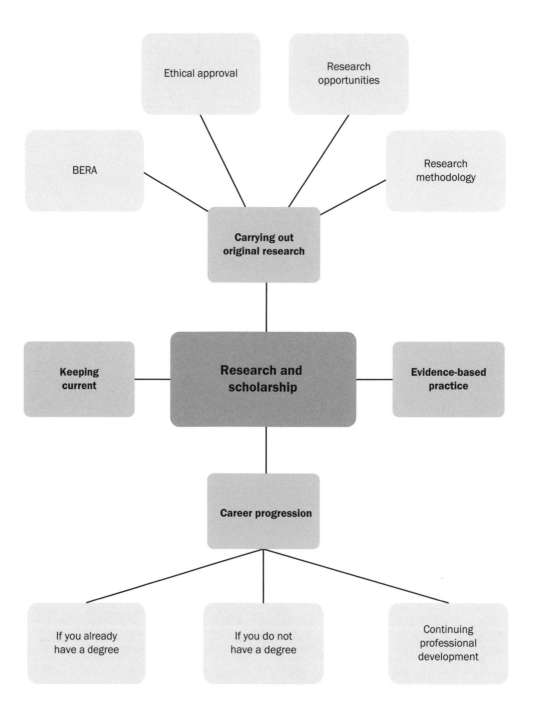

PROFESSIONAL LINKS

This chapter assists with your understanding of the following LSIS (2013, p 28) mandatory content:

○   evidence-based practice;

○   carrying out research.

It also contributes to the following Professional Standards as provided by the ETF (2014):

Professional values and attributes

Develop your own judgement of what works and does not work in your teaching.

2   *Evaluate and challenge your practice, values and beliefs*

Professional knowledge and understanding

Develop deep and critically informed knowledge and understanding in theory and practice.

7   *Maintain and update knowledge of your subject and/or vocational area*

8   *Maintain and update your knowledge of educational research to develop evidence-based practice*

9   *Apply theoretical understanding of effective practice in teaching, learning and assessment drawing on research and other evidence*

A list of all of the Standards can be found at the back of this book (Appendix 7).

   KEY DEFINITIONS

BERA	British Educational Research Authority.
Interpretivist	More subjective way of approaching research.
Meta-study	To analyse results from separate but similar research.
Peer reviewed	Self-regulated evaluation of research by peers.

→

Positivist	More objective way of approaching research.
Qualitative	Observational data to be interpreted.
Quantitative	Numerical data that can then be statistically analysed.
Research paradigm	A framework to guide research.

INTRODUCTION

Carrying out your own research may seem something that is not very relevant to you at the moment, or it could be something you have already engaged in. Whatever the situation, this chapter does apply to you. This chapter is designed to support you in applying evidence-based research to your teaching and learning and developing your own research skills. It therefore aims to support you in:

o   identifying, exploring and critiquing evidence-based practice;

o   developing your use of evidence-based practice;

o   developing research skills;

o   identifying opportunities to carry out research.

STARTING POINT

What do you understand by evidence-based practice and scholarship?

o   What do you currently understand by the term *evidence-based practice*?

o   In terms of you as a teacher, do you read and reflect on educational research and try to apply it?

o   What opportunities for carrying out research are you currently aware of?

o   Are you aware of the ethical guidelines necessary within educational research?

EVIDENCE-BASED PRACTICE: WHAT WORKS AND WHAT DOES NOT

Evidence-based practice can be very empowering as it essentially gives the teacher help and ideas in what works in teaching and learning. These ideas and strategies can then be amalgamated into appropriate teaching strategies of your own. Often we make assumptions about what works best and have no evidence to back it up (Smith, 2013). These assumptions can be seen in the changes in teaching practice at a national level which are often driven by ideology, politics and marketing (Slavin, 2008); for more information about challenging assumptions see Chapter 1.

There are many ideas in education that are taken as truths but have no evidence to support them; this may not mean they are wrong, just untested. Using a medical analogy, if you were taking prescription drugs for an illness, you would probably prefer to know that the drugs had been tried and tested before being given to you and that there was *evidence* that they would help your medical condition. Some of the common beliefs in teaching, that are not evidence based, are:

o   that students have specific learning styles (eg visual, auditory or kinesthetic);

o   that students may be left- or right-brain dominant;

o   that special diets or brain foods (rather than a balanced diet) can improve learning;

o   that brain gyms can improve academic performance.

Critical task

Take one of the common beliefs mentioned above and do some reading (see *Keeping current* overleaf). Find out what research (evidence) there is to back up the claims made.

Evidence-based teaching, according to Petty (2006), can improve your practice by introducing new strategies into your repertoire. However, how do you know if the strategy is any good or will be effective? If you can find research evidence to say that it has been tested properly and has had success it may well be worth trying.

Marzano (2003), cited in (Petty, 2006), conducted a meta-study on strategies to improve behaviour in the classroom. He looked at a variety of studies and then compared them to find out which strategy worked best, given the research conditions. For example, a behavioural strategy that was 100 per cent successful, but only tested on two students, might not be as reliable as a behavioural strategy that was 90 per cent successful but tested on 100 students in a variety of situations.

Ben Goldacre (Smith, 2013) feels that rather than telling teachers what works in a classroom, teachers should do some research to find out what works and then disseminate their findings to other teachers by publishing their research. He cautions though that the research has to be robust and that what works for one teacher in one situation may not necessarily work for another teacher in a different situation, but that it is worth finding out about, attempting and adjusting for your own circumstances. The only way to teach using evidence-based practice is by keeping current so that you are aware of what is being discussed in education.

KEEPING CURRENT

An excellent way of keeping up to date with educational issues and to also become more familiar with academic writing and research methods is to read educational journal articles on a regular basis. Many of these offer online and paper-based issues and are by subscription only. The educational establishment you teach at or are studying at may well have these journals available for staff and learners. If there is something that you think may be worthwhile, that is not available, then suggest it to the librarian. All of the journals in Table 11.1 are generic educational journals, but you may well also want to find journals that relate to your specialist area of teaching. It is good to look for peer-reviewed journals to read. Peer reviewed means that research has been looked at by peers to check the robustness of the research before publishing.

It can be a good idea to keep a list of recent reading, and when completing an application form it may be a good idea to mention recent reading as well as actual continuing professional development events. Remember that reading a journal article does not have to be a purely passive activity. Read, reflect and record any actions or information you are taking from your reading. Then revisit your actions after you have carried them out. Keeping abreast of current research is also an excellent way of identifying gaps and opportunities in order to conduct your own original research. The comments relating to the journals in Table 11.1 are taken from their websites. Additionally, you may want to access journals that are particularly pertinent to your subject area.

Table 11.1 Journals

Name of journal	Comment	Address
Journal of Further and Higher Education	The Journal of Further and Higher Education is an international, peer-reviewed journal containing articles and book reviews representing the field of post-16 education and training.	www.ucu.org.uk/jfhe
Adults Learning	Adults Learning is for adult education practitioners and policy makers, offering an informed mix of news, analysis, expert commentary and feature writing, dedicated to adult learning.	www.niace.org.uk/publications/adults-learning
Journal of Adult and Continuing Education	This journal is for keeping in touch with the field of post-compulsory education. Published twice a year, it provides a forum for rigorous theoretical and practical work in the broad fields of lifelong learning and adult, community and continuing education.	www.manchesteruniversitypress.co.uk/journals/jace

Name of journal	Comment	Address
Research in Post-compulsory Education	Throughout the world, there is a growing awareness of the significance of vocational and post-compulsory education and training systems. This international, fully-refereed journal, reports on research in the increasingly important area of post-compulsory education.	www.tandfonline.com/ action/journalInformation?s how=aimsScope&journalCo de=rpce20#.Uy8IaxuPPIU
British Educational Research Journal	The British Educational Research Journal (BERJ) is the flagship journal of BERA and has gone from strength to strength in recent years. It was ranked 47th of 177 international journals in the area – which is very high for a general education journal.	http://onlinelibrary.wiley. com/journal/10.1002/ (ISSN)1469–3518
British Journal of Learning Disabilities	This is an international, peer-reviewed journal which aims to be the leading inter-disciplinary journal in the learning disability field. It covers debates and developments in research, policy and practice.	http://onlinelibrary.wiley. com/journal/10.1111/ (ISSN)1468–3156

CARRYING OUT ORIGINAL RESEARCH

There are opportunities for carrying out research in education and it is likely that you will need to do some research for your DET qualification and any future qualifications that you take (eg BA in Education or Masters). Alternatively, your organisation may want you to carry out an action research project. Denscombe (2010) believes that the purpose of action research is to solve a particular problem and to produce guidelines for best practice. It may be that you initiate action research within your organisation and then want to share the recommendations or conclusions with your colleagues.

Ethical approval

Cohen et al. (2011) contend that a major ethical dilemma is striking the balance between carrying out research whilst doing no harm. With this in mind, before carrying out any research, make sure you have ethical approval or you have checked that the research is ethical and has the appropriate checks and procedures. All educational research undertaken should have some kind of ethical approval or ethics process. Even if you are not asked for this at the start of the research, you must approach it as if you have and undertake your own ethical approval process.

Within an organisation, such as a university, the process usually relates to what type of ethical process is necessary and whether a short or long ethics form is needed. The short form is for research that does not involve children or vulnerable adults and it is essentially a tick list; however, if you tick yes to certain questions then you are auto-matically directed to completing a long ethics form. The long ethics form is completed in much more detail with extra information and has to be taken to an ethics panel for approval. Approval will either be given or extra information or amendments might be requested.

BERA

Educational research is overseen by the British Educational Research Association (BERA) which was set up in 1974. It is a member-led organisation supporting educa-tional researchers and promoting high quality research in education. Any educational research undertaken in the UK or involving UK education should conform to BERA guide-lines for educational research. In this way you can be sure that the research is ethical and reliable.

The ethical guidelines for educational research (BERA, 2011) are split into four areas:

o   responsibilities to participants;

o   responsibilities to sponsors of the research;

o   responsibilities to the Community of Educational Researchers;

o   responsibilities to educational professionals, policy makers and the general public.

Below is a general overview of each of these areas; however, if you are carrying out research it is better to access the full guidelines from www.bera.ac.uk/.

Critical task

Look at the breakdown of information for each of the following categories and reflect on what these mean in relation to research. Make your own notes and then access the guidelines for the full answers.

Responsibilities to participants

This is the largest area and includes:

o   voluntary informed consent;

o   openness and disclosure;

o   right to withdraw;

o   children, vulnerable young people and vulnerable adults;

o   incentives;

o   detriment arising from participation in research;

○ privacy;

○ disclosure.

Responsibilities to sponsors of research

○ methods;

○ publication.

Responsibilities to the community of educational researchers

○ authorship;

○ misconduct.

Responsibilities to educational professionals, policy makers and the general public

This area does not have any subsections.

Research methodology: a basic introduction to educational research

If you are going to carry out educational research, you will usually have guidelines and supervision on how to carry it out. You must follow the guidelines of what you are being asked to do. The numbered steps below and overleaf are to help guide you if you are not being supported in your research to see how straightforward educational research can be and that fear of research should not be a barrier to progressing to higher level qualifications. If you are carrying out educational research, see the Taking it further section at the end of the chapter.

1. Choose an area of research in which you are interested.

2. Read as much as you can to find out what other research has been carried out in this area; remember international research as well. This forms a review of literature and a starting-off place for your own research. What gaps are there in the research? How has previous research been carried out? This will help you when you come to do your own research.

3. Come up with your own research question, followed by a number of subsidiary questions you would want to answer in your research.

4. Design a robust, ethical and manageable research study. This will involve having to find out about research methodology, which will then help you to design your own research.

   Overleaf are two broad definitions of research that can then lead you either to more statistical/numerical data collection or to more text-based data collection.

Positivist paradigm	Interpretivist paradigm
quantitative methodology;	qualitative methodology;
numerical data;	written data;
statistical analysis;	interpreting thoughts, feelings and opinions;
large samples;	tends towards smaller samples;
achieves breadth of understanding about an issue;	not necessarily generalisable but can give some breadth of understanding;
claims objectivity;	subjective.
claims generalisability.	
Tools commonly associated to collect data: surveys and questionnaires and analysis of existing numerical data.	Tools commonly associated to collect data: interviews, diaries and observations.

5. Collect data using tools decided on in previous step.

6. Analyse data using data analysis chosen in step 4.

7. Create conclusions from analysis. Distribute recommendations.

Research opportunities

Funding for practitioner-based research is often nationally distributed by companies awarded contracts to sort the funding and also oversee the projects. It is worth checking out the organisations in Table 11.2 for funding opportunities.

Table 11.2 Research opportunities

Education and Training Foundation	www.et-foundation.co.uk/bids-tenders/
Skills Funding Agency	www.gov.uk/skills-funding-register-for-opportunities-to-tender
Business and Innovation and Skills	www.dwp.gov.uk/esf/funding-opportunities/
Erasmus+	www.erasmusplus.org.uk./funding-opportunities/education-and-training-funding
Big Lottery Funding	www.biglotteryfund.org.uk/funding

CAREER PROGRESSION

When you have completed your DET qualification you may be given advice from your tutor about other qualifications that you could move on to. It is important to give this some thought before embarking on another qualification and to seek advice about possible progression routes. One starting point could be to consult a line manager at work to find out what progression route your workplace would like you to follow as there may be a difference between your workplace progression and your own preferred professional development. For example, your workplace may want you to complete a qualification so you can be asked to work in a different area of teaching and learning. Although this may not be an area you had thought to move into, it might help to make your position more secure, so it is worth thinking about.

If you already have a degree

If you already have a degree, then you might think about progressing onto a Masters in Education qualification. Each university may have slightly different entry requirements for a Masters qualification, so it is worth checking with individual universities about their specific entry requirements. Generally, the entry requirement is a degree, some will specify that it should be a 2:1 or above, however, if you do not have the required entry qualifications it is always worth having a discussion with someone from the university in case there is any flexibility in the entry requirements. For example, some universities will offer you a place without a degree if you can demonstrate significant prior learning and experience to offset the lack of a degree. A Masters in Education on your curriculum vitae can help to separate you out from other applicants who may have a degree and a teaching qualification. As well as this a Masters qualification provides opportunities for you to undertake research into areas of education that interest you.

If you do not have a degree

You might be interested in using the CAT (Credit Accumulation and Transfer) points (usually 120 points at levels 4 and 5, but check with your educational provider) you have accumulated on your DET to offset them against a degree – such as a BA (Hons) Education. This may help with career progression in an area where progressively more teachers are expected to have a degree. As part of the degree, you will complete a dissertation which will give you the opportunity to carry out educational research.

Continuing professional development

You may well not want to embark on another qualification straight away. That does not mean that you do not need to do anything. Continuing professional development (CPD) is well named, as it is continuous and should be undertaken throughout your teaching career. Watch out for opportunities for CPD in your workplace as well as external CPD events. Finding out what organisations your workplace is a member of can be helpful because there are often significant discounts on events for members, a good bargaining point when requesting your workplace pay for you to attend an external event.

Critical question

Before putting your name down for an event, and both before and after any training, what kind of questions should you ask yourself?

> ## *Comment*
>
> Before the event you should ask yourself: *Is this training at the right level for me? Is it aimed at practitioners? Are there positive reviews for previous training sessions provided by this organisation or individual?*
>
> When you have completed the training you should reflect on: *what am I going to do with this training? How am I going to record this training event?*

Generic and specialist CPD

Generic CPD is professional development that impacts on your generic teaching and learning skills. CPD in your specialist teaching area is becoming increasingly important, to '*confirm occupational competence*' (LLUK, 2007, p 11; see Table 11.3). The Commission on Adult Vocational Teaching and Learning (CAVTL, 2013, p 3) advises: '*Vocational teaching, learning and assessment is a sophisticated professional occupation and demands, therefore, robust initial and continuous development of expertise*' (IfL, 2009).

Table 11.3 Ideas for generic and specialist CPD

Generic CPD ideas	Specialist CPD ideas
Peer coaching (coaching others and being coached in your subject or vocational area)	
Being an active member of a committee, board or steering groups related to teaching and/or your subject area	
Take part in peer reviews	Subject learning coach or advanced learning coach training
Mentoring new colleagues	Peer observation – in own subject/s areas or peer visits to community organisations/partners
Peer observation – in other subject areas or work shadowing	Gaining further qualifications in your subject or industrial expertise through an accredited course
Leading team/department self-assessment	Being a member of a special interest group or another professional body
Carrying out and disseminating action research	Taking on examiner/verifier/assessor responsibilities
Designing innovative feedback mechanisms	Attending briefings by awarding bodies and disseminating to colleagues
Chairing team meetings	Organising trips/residential/work placements
Team teaching	Planning or running a staff development activity or event

Reflecting on your CPD activities

As discussed in Chapter 1, it is important that you reflect on any CPD to see how any new skills and knowledge can be used to improve or to extend your abilities as a teacher.

Critical task

Based on the last time you attended CPD of any kind fill in the reflective template that can be found in Appendix 6. Make sure you think about how you are going to make use of the professional development.

SUMMARY

You have probably all encountered teachers who have been delivering the same materials, in the same way, to very different groups of learners for many years. In order to ensure that you don't become this type of teacher you need to engage in regular professional development, remain current in your specialist areas and, through research, be ready to challenge your practice and any pre-held assumptions (see Chapter 1 for information about reflecting on practice and challenging assumptions).

 # Check your understanding

You will find suggested answers to some of these questions at the back of this book.

Question 1: How do you know if a piece of educational research is robust?

Question 2: What is the difference between qualitative and quantitative research?

Question 3: What is BERA and what does it have to do with you?

Question 4: Why is it important to remain current in your specialist area?

Question 5: Edward is coming to the end of his DET qualification. He is doing an in-service route and already works full time at the local college. As well as his DET, he has a degree in IT, an A Level in mathematics and a GCSE at grade B in English. His line manager has hinted that he may well need to teach functional skills as well as ICT as the cohort numbers for ICT are dwindling. What are his options for moving forward?

End-of-chapter reflections

o   Professional development does not just stop when you get to a certain level.

o   Learning is for life, not just for the young.

o   Unless you make an effort you will get left behind in your specialist area.

o   How do you think you will be able to use your learning from this chapter?

 TAKING IT FURTHER

In addition to the literature already commented upon in this chapter you may find the following of interest.

Basit, T (2010) *Conducting Research in Educational Contexts*. London: Bloomsbury.

REFERENCES

BERA (2011) *Research and Teacher Education*. [Online]. Available at: www.bera.ac.uk/ (accessed 26 May 2014).

CAVTL (2013) *Commission on Adult Vocational Teaching and Learning*. [Online]. Available at: www.excellencegateway.org.uk/cavtl (accessed 26 May 2014).

Cohen, L, Manion, L and Morrison, K (2011) *Research Methods in Education.* New York: Routledge.

Denscombe, M (2010) *The Good Research Guide: For Small-Scale Social Research*. 4th edn. Maidenhead: Open University Press.

Education Training Foundation (2014) *Professional Standards for Teachers and Trainers in Education and Training*. Education Training Foundation. [Online]. Available at: www. et-foundation.co.uk (accessed 26 May 2014).

IfL (2009) *Guidelines for Your Continuing Professional Development*. [Online]. Available at: www.ifl.ac.uk/__data/assets/pdf_file/0011/5501/J11734-IfL-CPD-Guidelines-08.09-web-v3.pdf (accessed 26 May 2014).

LLUK (2007) *New Overarching Professional Standards for Teachers, Tutors and Trainers in the Lifelong Learning Sector*. [Online]. Available at: http://collections.europarchive. org/tna/20110214161207/http:/www.lluk.org/wp-content/uploads/2010/11/new-overarching-standards-for-ttt-in-lifelong-learning-sector.pdf (accessed 26 May 2014).

LSIS (2013) *Teaching and Training Qualifications for the Further Education and Skills Sector in England, Guidance for Higher Education Institutions*. Coventry, Learning Skills Improvement Services.

Petty, G (2006) *Evidence-Based Teaching: A Practical Approach.* Cheltenham: Nelson Thornes, http://geoffpetty.com/geoffs-books/downloads-for-ebt/ (accessed 26 May 2014).

Slavin, R (2008) Perspectives on Evidence-Based Research in Education. *Educational Researcher*, 31(1, January): 5–14.

Smith, M (2013) Evidence-Based Education: Is It Really That Straightforward? *Guardian*, 26 March.

12 Study skills and the requirements of the minimum core for the level 5 Diploma in Education and Training

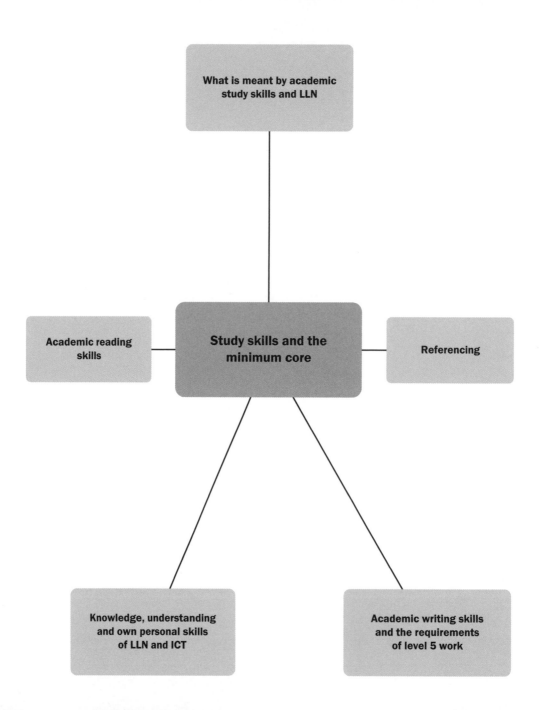

What is meant by academic study skills and LLN

Academic reading skills

Study skills and the minimum core

Referencing

Knowledge, understanding and own personal skills of LLN and ICT

Academic writing skills and the requirements of level 5 work

PROFESSIONAL LINKS

This chapter assists with your understanding of the following LSIS (2013, p 28) mandatory content:

o   knowledge and understanding of literacy, language, numeracy and ICT;

o   own personal skills in literacy, language, numeracy and ICT.

It also contributes to the following Professional Standards available from the ETF (2014):

Professional skills

Maintain and develop expertise and skills to ensure the best outcome for learners.

15   *Promote the benefits of technology and support learners in its use*

16   *Address the mathematics and English needs of learners and work creatively to overcome individual barriers to learning*

A list of all of the Standards can be found at the back of this book (Appendix 7).

KEY DEFINITIONS

Critical reading	Thinking and analysing written text and not accepting it on face value.
Critical thinking	Thinking that is informed by evidence and that has a purpose in mind.
Critical writing	To consider and analyse different arguments included in your written work.
Schema	A framework of current knowledge to help future understanding.

INTRODUCTION

This chapter is designed to support you in your personal study skills and your skills knowledge and understanding in mathematics, literacy and ICT. It therefore aims to support you in:

o   identifying literacy, language, numeracy and ICT skills in your own learners;

o   developing your own personal skills in literacy, language, numeracy (LLN) and ICT.

STARTING POINT

What do you already know about study skills and LLN?

○   In relation to your role as a teacher, what do you understand by LLN?

○   What do you currently understand about the requirements of level 5 and above academic skills?

WHAT IS MEANT BY ACADEMIC STUDY SKILLS AND LLN?

To be able to successfully complete the DET you need to be aware of your own personal skills, both in regard to academic work and the practice of teaching. You need to develop and progress in academic study skills in order to complete written assignments and research. You also need to be able to possess a minimum of literacy, language and numeracy skills to be able to support and develop your learners in their own skills. In this context *language* means supporting learners studying in English who do not have English as a first language.

Critical task

Reflect on what literacy, language and numeracy skills your learners already have and what skills gaps need to be filled in order for them to successfully complete the programme of study. How are you going to support the learners to develop the necessary skills gaps?

ACADEMIC READING SKILLS

You may have been provided with a reading list for each module relating to your DET qualification. This does not mean that this is the only reading that you need to do. If you are looking for a high grade then you really need to read around your module topic in order to develop a depth of knowledge and understanding.

The educational organisation at which you are studying will most likely have a library. Library staff can be very helpful in helping you to find suitable online and paper-based texts. Even if you are familiar with the library system it is worth going on any physical or virtual library tours that are offered. By doing this you will find out about the latest technology they have for searching for texts. Also, many organisations will have a good selection of online resources accessed through their own website, for example, e-journals and e-books which are organised into subject areas. When searching for information online, rather than a normal search engine, try using websites such as Refseek (2013) which makes academic information accessible to all.

Reading critically and analysing what you read

An effective reader is one who can adapt their reading strategies to match the reading tasks. Once you have chosen a text to read, and a suitable time and place to read it, then the next thing you need to do is adopt an appropriate reading strategy to read critically. One of those strategies involves activating your schema (Piaget, 1968; see Table 12.1). Your schema refers to a way of categorising data and activating is a way of retrieving that data. This technique can also be used with adults who are not fluent readers.

Table 12.1 How to activate your schema

Activity	Comment
Previewing	Before you start reading, look at the title, heading and subheadings, the way it is set out, pictures, and you can then start to gauge what the text is going to be about. It also allows us to activate our schema to *recall* everything we know about the topic.
Coding	Once you have previewed the text, list any keywords or terms that you think are relevant to the text.
Predicting	Predict what you think is in the text based on your own knowledge and what you have gleaned from the previewing.
Visualising	When you are reading, try to form pictures in your mind to help to retain the information.
Monitoring	Check to make sure you understand what you are reading.
Recalling	After you have finished reading, recall the information to help to process it with what you already know.

Critical task

Choose one piece of reading from any of the Taking it further sections at the end of the chapters in this book and try out the technique. If the technique does not work for you research different techniques, such as SQ3R (Robinson, 1946), until you find a strategy that does work for you.

ACADEMIC WRITING SKILLS AND THE REQUIREMENTS OF LEVEL 5 WORK

The DET qualification that you are enrolled upon is at least a level 5 qualification, although it can also be delivered at a higher level (for an explanation of the levels, see the Introduction to this book). Taking level 5 as the base line, this is equivalent to the work you would do in the second year of a degree course. In terms of academic study skills, you should already have the basics in place. This section is not supposed to be a complete guide to study skills; it is about improving the study skills you already have and getting you ready for the move to post-graduate study. Even if you already have good academic study skills in place it is always worth brushing up on them.

Structuring essays

Once you have completed your reading and research you need to get your information down on paper. Always remember to read and make sure you understand the requirements of your assignment. If you are writing a standard essay then this structure is an easy one to follow:

Introduction – tell your audience what question you will be answering or what you will be addressing; say how you will go about it and define any specialist terms, if necessary. It can sometimes be easier to write the introduction once you have finished the rest of the assignment.

Main body – there should be one main point within each paragraph. Each paragraph should address the question and group ideas and themes together. A good way is to think of each paragraph as if it were a mini essay on its own. So open with an introductory sentence outlining what the paragraph is going to be about and finish with a sentence that concludes the paragraph by saying what is in the paragraph and linking it to the next paragraph.

Summary and conclusion – summarise what you have written, come to a conclusion, if necessary, and show how it answers the question; never add any new evidence in the conclusion. Your introduction and conclusion together should give the reader a road map of the rest of your essay.

Assessment criteria

When completing your level 5 assignments for the DET qualification you will want to know what a level 5 piece of work looks like. Table 12.2 gives you an overview of some of the skills, knowledge and understanding necessary to complete a level 5 piece of work above a pass, ie in order to gain either a merit or a distinction.

Critical task

Highlight any areas in Table 12.2 that you think you might need to brush up on. Make a plan of how you are going to address these areas.

Table 12.2 Level 5 assessment criteria

	Distinction	**Merit**
Introduction and professional context	Excellent understanding of subject/task. Excellent answer, comprehensive with no important inaccuracies, work of a distinguished quality. Very relevant application to practice or use of examples supported by effective reflection.	Good understanding of the subject/task. Comprehensive answer with few omissions or inaccuracies. Work of a good quality. Relevant application to practice or use of examples supported by reflection.
Literature	Displays an excellent interpretation of the concepts communicating considerable knowledge of the subject area.	Demonstrates a good interpretation of the concepts communicating knowledge of the subject area.
Findings and analysis	Excellent analysis and interpretation of key concepts with an ability to develop an argument making sound judgements. Awareness and use of competing current issues.	Good analysis and interpretation of key concepts with an ability to develop an argument making sound judgements. Some awareness and use of competing current issues.
Conclusions and recommendations	Salient conclusions or key issues identified, substantiated by valid findings.	Conclusions or key issues identified, substantiated by valid findings.
Clarity of reasoning and written style	High standard of Harvard referencing across a wide range of sources. Evidence of extensive wider reading and independent research. High standard of structure/grammar/ punctuation.	Consistent standard of Harvard referencing across a range of sources. Evidence of reading material and some independent research. Good standard of structure/grammar/ punctuation.

Based on Staffordshire University's School of Education (2013) level 5 grading criteria

Critical writing

Critical writing is a way to make sure that your assignments meet the requirements of a higher grade. Table 12.2 outlines the criteria for level 5 assessments which focus on analysis and interpretation, ie not just supplying facts. A narrative piece of work will just display the facts: '*this happened, then that happened, he said this, they said that*'. This leaves no room for a critical appraisal of any topic being discussed.

Critical language

A good approach to making your writing more critical is by having a critical phrase bank, this is a list of phrases that can be introduced into the critical writing and helps with a form of compare and contrast as well as helping you decide on what you believe where there is contrasting evidence. If you type into a search engine *academic phrases* or similar there are many available from university websites. Make sure you are looking at a UK site (in case of differences in acceptable grammatical conventions) and remember to amalgamate them into your own writing, so your *voice* is still there.

The following are a few examples (of many) from a phrase bank on Manchester University's website, which is worth checking out.

Critical phrase bank

Longer phrases

One question that needs to be asked, however, is whether …

A serious weakness with this argument, however, is that …

One of the limitations with this explanation is that it does not explain why …

One criticism of much of the literature on X is that …

The key problem with this explanation is that …

The existing accounts fail to resolve the contradiction between X and Y.

There is an inconsistency with this argument.

There are a number of similarities between X and Y.

This study by Y has been criticised by X.

Some hints and tips for critical writing

○   avoid lots of description;

○   interpret your evidence, show that your understand the research;

○   don't be general, be specific;

○   use counter arguments.

In the Check your understanding section at the end of the chapter there is a critical writing task for you to work on.

Presenting your work

You need to check any conventions laid down by your educational organisation. There might be a specified font type and size, the spacing between the lines may need to be double and print might only be on one side. If no guidelines have been mentioned, set guidelines and stick to those throughout the work. Typical conventions for academic writing include:

○   font size of 12;

○   non-serif font, or a transitional serif such as Times New Roman;

- 1.5 or double line spacing;

- left justify paragraphs;

- insert page numbers and your name, or student number, on each page.

Maximum word count

Check your word count. If you need to save space then look carefully for any sections that are not pertinent to the assignment. Traditionally, academic writing allows you to be 10 per cent under or over the word count but make sure you check this for your institution and do not assume it is the case. Some HEIs have introduced a penalty system for excess length in an attempt to make learners write within suggested parameters. For example:

- 1–10% excess no penalty;

- 11–20% excess 10% reduction in the mark;

- 21–30% excess 20% reduction in the mark;

- 31%+ excess the work will be capped at a pass.

You will notice that there is not a penalty for being under the minimum word count on this scale. The reasoning behind this is that you are automatically limiting your grade by not using all of the words available to you to cover the task given.

REFERENCING

Why and where to reference

As part of your academic writing, you are going to read literature by other people and will want to use their theories and ideas to support your own. In academic writing, you must reference what you have written so that you are giving credit to the person who has done the hard work. This is so you cannot be accused of plagiarism and it shows you have researched your work and it has academic veracity.

The educational establishment at which you are studying will tell you what method of referencing they want you to use and you must use this method. A common form of referencing used, at the moment, is Harvard Referencing. This form uses brackets containing basic information for references in the main body of the text followed by a list at the end of your work that provides fuller details about the sources of any texts cited. This system does not use footnotes.

Bibliography versus reference list

At this level you are probably not going to be asked to provide a bibliography, just a reference list. However, it is still good to know what the difference is. A bibliography is where you list all of the books, journals, websites that you have read but may not have used in your assignment, as well as those that you have actually used in your assignment. A reference list is where you just provide the books, journals, websites and any other materials that you have actually used in your assignment.

Harvard referencing

There are two places in an assignment where you need to complete your referencing:

○ In the main body of your assignment – called in-text referencing or citing. This is where you will refer to theories and ideas to support your writing. With in-text referencing, generally you should only include the authors' surname/s (no initials) and the date.

○ At the end of the assignment is the reference list. This is where you list in detail all of the references that you have used in your assignment so that any reader can easily locate where you have got your references from. You must refer to the author/s in the reference list in exactly the same way as you have referred to them in the text.

In-text referencing

Citations

Citations are where you have read someone else's work and then you have put it into your own words. Citations are better than direct quotations because it shows to your tutor that you have thought about and have understood what you have read.

Example

Maslow (1943) proposed that, as humans, we are driven by certain needs. A pyramid structure is frequently used to represent these needs, with the most basic needs being represented at the bottom (see Chapter 6 for more information about Maslow's hierarchy of needs).

As well as texts and literature, you must include a reference when you refer to reports, government acts or legislation. A date alone is not enough; you need to include the sources as well as the date.

Example

The Tomlinson Report (FEFC, 1996) was a key contributor to the development of inclusive practice in the further education and skills sector.

Direct quotes

Try to use any direct quotes sparingly. If you do use them, they should be placed in quotation marks, with the author's name, date and page number.

Example

The Tomlinson Report (FEFC, 1996, p 12) suggested the 'redesign of the very process of learning, assessment and organisation so as to fit the objectives and learning styles of the learners'.

Longer quotes that are more than two lines of text should be separated from the main text and indented, followed by the reference and page number.

Example

The report emphasised:

That learners with learning difficulties or disabilities should be considered first and foremost as learners suggesting the redesign [of] the very process of learning, assessment and organisation so as to fit the objectives and learning styles of the learners.

(FEFC, 1996, p 12)

Secondary referencing

Secondary referencing occurs when you are reading a book or journal article whose author uses facts or information from research done by someone else, and you want to use this to support your own assignment. Try to avoid secondary referencing as much as possible by going back to the original source. If that is not possible, here is an example of how to reference a secondary source:

Example

Maslow (1943), as cited in Hillier (2007).

The reference list at the end of the text only needs to give the details of the source/s that you have read for the assignment. Using the above example, you would simply refer to the main text (Hillier, 2007) as follows: Hillier, Y (2007) *Reflective Teaching in Further and Adult Education*, 2nd edn. London: Continuum International Publishing Group.

Internet referencing

You may use references from the internet but the rule is *if you cannot find an author, try not to use it*. In this sense an author does not have to be a named person or persons, it could be an organisation or national body. There is a lot of unreliable material on the internet. Wikipedia should be regarded as a research starting point, not the end point. For in-text citation of an internet source, simply cite the author/organisation and date, never put the website address.

Example

The Leitch Review of Skills (HMSO, 2006) was an attempt to undertake an independent review of the UK's long-term skills needs.

It is when you come to put an online source into the reference list that you treat it differently. In the reference list, whatever you have used for the author in the text must be used as the author's name in the reference list. The extra information that you are adding is that the reference is [online] – always use square brackets; where it is available – giving the full web address; then when you last opened the web page – (accessed 26 May 2014). The accessed information is very important as websites change all of the time. See *reference list* below for an example of an online source referenced.

Reference list

A complete list of all of the references you have included within the main body of your assignment must be provided at the end of the assignment, under the heading *References*. Double check to ensure there are no references in your text that are not included in your list, and nothing in your list that is not in your text. A reference list is a vital part of your assignment and is not an *add-on extra*. Take time to prepare it and, remember, it generally takes longer to prepare than you think. References must be listed in alphabetical order by surname or organisation. You do not need to separate the reference list into categories or sections, for example, *books*, *legislation* and *websites*, unless you are asked to do so. Remember that you do not need to provide a separate bibliography of material that you have read but not used (unless it is specifically asked for).

Example

Berne, E (1964) *Games People Play*: The Psychology of Human Relationships. London: Penguin Books.

Education Training Foundation (2014) *Professional Standards for Teachers and Trainers in Education and Training*. [Online]. Available at: www.et-foundation.co.uk (accessed 26 May 2014).

Hargie, O (2004) *Skilled Interpersonal Communication – Research, Theory and Practice*. Hove: Routledge.

Hartley, P (1999) *Interpersonal Communication.* 2nd edn. London: Routledge.

Hasson, G (2012) *Brilliant Communication Skills: What the Best Communicators Know, Do and Say.* Harlow: Pearson Education.

Note that the internet reference is just alphabetically included in the reference list. In the earlier days of the internet, online sources were often separated from book lists. Harvard referencing no longer does this.

KNOWLEDGE, UNDERSTANDING AND OWN PERSONAL SKILLS OF LLN AND ICT

As part of the entry requirements for the DET qualification you may be expected to already have level 2 literacy and numeracy qualifications, or you may be expected to be able to demonstrate by the end of the qualification that you have those skills. You may well have had to undertake an initial assessment of skills in English, mathematics and ICT, unless you have already completed a level 3 Award in Education and Training or a level 4 Certificate in Education and Training. Your record of development needs and any previous actions taken to address them should inform opportunities to continue the development of these skills as required by the appropriate minimum core elements.

Whatever the situation, the minimum core of literacy, language, numeracy and ICT details the knowledge, understanding and personal skills in English, mathematics and ICT expected of all teachers in the sector.

The minimum core document comprises three sections:

○ language and literacy;

○ numeracy;

○ ICT.

Each of these sections comprises two parts:

○ Part A: knowledge and understanding;

○ Part B: personal skills.

Knowledge, understanding and personal skills requirements for literacy, language, numeracy and ICT are included in the DET qualification. If you would like to view these documents, see Taking it further on page 204.

Elements of the minimum core should be delivered and assessed across the following units:

○ *Teaching, learning and assessment in education and training* (level 4);

○ *Developing teaching, learning and assessment in education and training* (level 5).

If you know that there are areas of literacy and numeracy on which you need to brush up, try visiting some of the websites in Table 12.3, a mixture of diagnostic and self-help sites.

Table 12.3 Self-help websites for improving literacy and numeracy skills

Website	Address	Comment
DfE numeracy skills tests – practice materials	www.education.gov.uk/sta/ professional/b00211213/numeracy/ practice-numeracy	These are the tests that school teachers need to pass, a mixture of online marked tests and non-interactive practice papers.
DfE literacy skills tests – practice materials	www.education.gov.uk/schools/ careers/traininganddevelopment/ professional/b00211208/literacy/ practice	
DfE literacy and numeracy glossaries	www.education.gov.uk/schools/ careers/traininganddevelopment/ professional/b00211208/literacy/ glossary www.education.gov.uk/schools/ careers/traininganddevelopment/ professional/b00211213/numeracy/ glossary	Glossaries of key literacy and numeracy terms.
Youtube video for literacy skills	www.youtube.com/ watch?v=VzOCaEALrUE	Revision video for literacy tests.
DfE numeracy refresher	www.education.gov.uk/schools/ careers/traininganddevelopment/ professional/b00211213/numeracy/ areas	Numeracy split into sections to help refresh skills.
BBC Skillswise	www.bbc.co.uk/skillswise/english www.bbc.co.uk/skillswise/maths	Practical literacy and numeracy skills for adults – choose level 2 when searching for resources.
NCETM: National Centre for Excellence in Teaching Mathematics	www.ncetm.org.uk/self-evaluation/	Mathematics self-evaluation tools for teachers to check understanding. You will need to register on this site. It is a free, well-regarded site and just asks for basic details.
DCSF: Grammar for writing	http://webarchive.nationalarchives. gov.uk/20100612050234/ nationalstrategies.standards.dcsf. gov.uk/node/153924	Downloadable KS2 teaching ideas and resources to help with the basics.
Keyed-in magazine	www.netagency.co.uk/keyedin2/ mental.html	Mental mathematics help.

The *language* in LLN

Supporting the language skills of learners can be problematic for teachers who have never dealt with learners who do not have English as a first language in their classrooms before. Here are a few ideas to get you thinking about the needs of these learners:

○ create an environment in which learners are not afraid to risk making mistakes in front of speakers of English as a first language. Encourage peer support;

○ every subject has its own key words. For each lesson you can teach these at the start of the lesson or make sure you explain them as they arise. The words can be displayed in a word chart on the wall where learners can see it easily. Learners could be encouraged to keep their own personal diary and add to it after every lesson;

○ do not just rely on verbal explanations, try to incorporate as many practical demonstrations, images, real objects and diagrams as possible;

○ teach skim and scan techniques so that learners do not stop reading if they do not understand one word;

○ activate the schema before giving learners a piece of literature to read (see how to activate the schema earlier in this chapter);

○ give learners, who may be translating from one language to another, time to answer;

○ use collaborative group activities in which each learner has a role or where learners have to work together to present their information or results;

○ if a learner has not understood, think how to rephrase the question or statement, do not just repeat it a little more loudly than the last time!

With thanks to Lynn Evans at Stafford College

Information and communication technology

Table 12.4 A summary of the minimum core elements for ICT (continued overleaf)

Personal, social and cultural factors influencing ICT learning and development	Need to brush up on
The different factors affecting the acquisition and development of ICT skills	
The importance of ICT in enabling users to participate in and gain access to society and the modern economy	
Understanding of the range of learners' technological and educational backgrounds	
The main learning disabilities and difficulties relating to ICT learning and skills development	
Potential barriers that inhibit ICT skills development	

Explicit knowledge about ICT	Need to brush up on
Making and using decisions about understanding	
Communicating processes and understanding	
Purposeful use of ICT	
Essential characteristics of ICT	
How learners develop ICT skills	
Communicate with others with/about ICT in an open and supportive manner	
Assess own, and other people's, understanding	
Express yourself clearly and accurately	
Communicate about/with ICT in a variety of ways that suit and support the intended audience, and recognise such use by others	
Use appropriate techniques to reinforce oral communication, check how well the information is received and support understanding of those listening	
Using ICT systems	
Finding, selecting and exchanging information	
Developing and presenting information	

Taken from Minimum Core for ICT (LLUK, 2011)

Critical task

Look through Table 12.4 and identify any areas that you need to research or brush up on.

It could be a good idea to buddy up with someone else on your DET course so you can support and help each other to develop these core skills. For example, if you have good mathematics skills but need to brush up on ICT, you could ask someone in the group who is proficient in ICT but might need to brush up on mathematics.

SUMMARY

In order to achieve the DET qualification you need to have good academic skills and also be able to help your learners to develop their own skills to be able to succeed at their qualifications. These skills include the development of your and your learners' LLN skills which are essential for achieving within a learning environment and for employability.

Check your understanding

You will find suggested answers to these questions at the back of the book.

Question 1:   What questions might you ask when searching for suitable text for any research that you are doing?

Question 2:   Read through the two paragraphs below and highlight where you think critical writing occurs.

Links between entry qualifications and achievement

There is some existing literature on student retention in HE based on entry qualifications in certain subjects that is relevant to this research because it suggests a clear correlation between levels of achievement on entry to HE, and retention and achievement in certain subjects. For example, the National Audit Office (NAO) (2007) found that full-time university students with three A grades at A-level (3A students) were more likely to continue to the second year of a medical degree course than those with two D grades at A-level (2D students) with an odds ratio of 2.2. The odds ratio is a comparison of the chances of 3A students proceeding to the second year of their degree course, compared with 2D students. On this basis 3A students were 2.2 times more likely to proceed to the second year of their course than 2D students. This corroborates the findings of Arulampalam et al. (2004) which stated a direct correlation between the A-level entry profile of medical students and the drop-out rate, ie the higher the A-level profile, the less likely a student was to drop out. An attrition rate of 2.9 per cent of those with more than 340 UCAS points was contrasted with 5.2 per cent in those with less than 200 UCAS points. This was endorsed by the findings of Jeffreys (2007), who undertook a retrospective evaluation study in the US to assess (inter alia) the entry characteristics of associate degree nursing students from a sample of students entering the first clinical nursing course in 1997–98. Jeffreys found that graduates had higher grade point averages in their pre-nursing qualifications than non-graduates.

The literature thus far suggests a link between entry qualifications, retention and achievement, however, its limitations in relation to the current topic must be noted. Firstly, the timespan covered by Arulampalam et al. (2004) ended 19 years ago, when BTEC Nationals did not actually exist, and the profile of threshold qualifications was different to that which exists today. Secondly, the environmental context of Jeffreys' study is in a different educational jurisdiction and involves entry-level qualifications that are a specific pre-nursing qualification requirement. Furthermore, both Jeffreys and Arulampalam et al. were investigating medical courses which carry a more vocational and practical component than the business courses that are the subject of this research. Their findings may not therefore be generalisable to other disciplines, and so further investigation is warranted.

Thanks to Sharon Inglis, Staffordshire University

End-of-chapter reflections

o   At each level of academic study you will develop your academic skills. Be prepared to do this.

o   For every cohort of learners you face, you must consider their LLN skills and then adapt your delivery accordingly.

o   How do you think you will be able to use your learning from this chapter to develop your practice?

 TAKING IT FURTHER

In addition to the literature already commented upon in this chapter you may find the following of interest.

Casey, H, Cara, O, Eldred, J, Grief, S, Hodge, R, Ivanič, R, Jupp, T, Lopez, D and McNeil, B (2006) *You Wouldn't Expect a Maths Teacher to Teach Plastering*. London: NRDC.

This is an excellent read if someone wants to know the value of embedding.

This LLUK document will help you to understand the depth and breadth of the skills needed for teaching.

Machin, L (2009) *The Minimum Core for Language and Literacy: Audit and Test (Achieving QTLS Series)*. Exeter: Learning Matters.

An excellent, in-depth guide to the literacy minimum core and how to achieve it.

Ontario Education (2005) *Many Roots, Many Voices*. Toronto: Ministry of Education.

An international perspective on how to make learners without English as a first language comfortable in the classroom.

REFERENCES

ETF (2014) *Professional Standards for Teachers and Trainers in Education and Training*. Education Training Foundation [Online]. Available at: www.et-foundation.co.uk (accessed 26 May 2014).

LLUK (2011) *Addressing Literacy, Language, Numeracy and ICT Needs in Education and Training: Defining the Teacher Education Programmes*. [Online]. Available at: http://repository.excellencegateway.org.uk/fedora/objects/import-pdf:93/datastreams/PDF/coccccntent (accessed 26 May 2014).

LSIS (2013) *Teaching and Training Qualifications for the Further Education and Skills Sector in England, Guidance for Higher Education Institutions*. Coventry, Learning Skills Improvement Services.

Piaget, J (1968) *Six Psychological Studies*. New York: Vintage.

Refseek (2013) *Refseek*. [Online]. Available at: www.refseek.com (accessed 26 May 2014).

Robinson, F (1946) *Effective Study*. New York: Harper and Row.

Staffordshire University (2013) *Level 5 Grading Criteria*. [Online]. Available at: www.staffs. ac.uk (accessed 26 May 2014).

Appendix 1: Optional units available for the level 5 DET qualification

As noted in the Introduction at the beginning of this book, in order to be awarded a level 5 DET qualification you need to achieve:

o   120 credits – this is the total credit value of the DET qualification.

These 120 credits are made up from:

o   75 credits from the mandatory units in Group A;

o   45 credits from the optional units in Group B.

Of these 120 credits:

o   a minimum of 20 credits needs to be at level 4 and a maximum (according to the guidance for HEIs) of 60 credits at level 4 (LSIS, 2013a, p 7).

Optional units are selected from a range of units that are available in Group B. Your tutor will be able to advise you about the choice that is available to you as, often, this choice may be dependent on what has been approved by the awarding body or institution accrediting the DET qualification for which you are enrolled.

The table below provides a list of the units that are available at levels 4 and 5. Some of the optional units are taken from the Learning and Development qualification and require practice beyond the mandatory 100 hours. This additional practice needs to be in a real-work environment, with groups or with individual learners (LSIS, 2013b, p 8). Your tutor will be able to advise you about these optional units. You will find information about these and also about other optional units (those that do not require additional practice evidence) from reading the *Optional Units for QCF Education and Training Qualifications* (LSIS, 2013b) document. You will also find up-to-date information about them by accessing the Excellence Gateway website (see Taking it further at the end of this appendix).

Optional units for the level 5 DET qualification

Unit title	Credit value	Level
Effective partnership working in the teaching and learning context	15	4
Inclusive practice	15	4
Teaching in a specialist area	15	4
Principles and practice of lip-reading teaching	12	4
Specialist delivery techniques and activities	9	4
Quality procedures within education and training	6	4

Unit title	Credit value	Level
Understanding and managing behaviours in a learning environment	6	4
Understanding the principles and practices of externally assuring the quality of assessment *(Learning and development unit)*	6	4
Understanding the principles and practices of internally assuring the quality of assessment *(Learning and development unit)*	6	4
Delivering employability skills	6	4
Develop and prepare resources for learning and development *(Learning and development unit)*	6	4
Develop learning and development programmes *(Learning and development unit)*	6	4
Engage with employers to facilitate workforce development *(Learning and development unit)*	6	4
Equality and diversity	6	4
Identify the learning needs of organisations *(Learning and development unit)*	6	4
Internally assure the quality of assessment *(Learning and development unit)*	6	4
Manage learning and development in groups *(Learning and development unit)*	6	4
Evaluating learning programmes	3	4
Preparing for the coaching role	3	4
Preparing for the mentoring role	3	4
Understanding and managing behaviours in a learning environment	15	5
Action learning to support development of specialist pedagogy	15	5
Action research	15	5
Developing, using and organising resources within the lifelong learning sector	15	5
Action learning to support development of specialist pedagogy	15	5
Action research	15	5

Source: LSIS (2013b, pp 14–15)

TAKING IT FURTHER

Excellence Gateway, *Addressing Literacy, Language, Numeracy and ICT Needs in Education and Training. Defining the Minimum Core of Teachers' Knowledge, Understanding and Personal Skills.* [Online]. Available at: www.excellencegateway. org.uk/node/12019 (accessed May 2014).

LSIS (2013) *Qualifications Guidance for Awarding Organisations: Level Four Certificate in Education and Training (QCF).* Coventry: Learning Skills Improvement Services.

Machin L (2009) *Language and Literacy, Minimum Core, Audit and Test.* Exeter: Learning Matters.

Machin L, Hindmarch D, Richardson T and Murray S (2013) *A Complete Guide to the Level 4 Certificate in Education and Training.* Northwich: Critical Publishing.

Murray S (2009) *Information, Communication, Technology, Minimum Core, Audit and Test.* Exeter: Learning Matters.

REFERENCES

LSIS (2013a) *Qualifications Guidance for Awarding Organisations: Level Five Diploma in Education and Training, Including Level Five Specialist Pathway (QCF).* [Online] Available at: www.excellencegateway.org.uk/node/65 (accessed May 2014).

LSIS (2013b) *Qualifications Guidance for Awarding Organisations: Optional Units for QCF Education and Training qualifications (QCF).* [Online]. Available at: www. excellencegateway.org.uk/node/65 (accessed May 2014).

Appendix 2: Glossary of acronyms and terms

AO	Awarding organisation
ASCL	Association of School and College Leaders
ATL	Association of Teachers and Lecturers
ATLS	Associate Teacher Learning and Skills
BDA	British Dyslexia Association
BIS	Business Innovation and Skills (Department)
BKSB	Basic and Key Skills Builder
CAT	Credit Accumulation and Transfer
CAVTL	Commission on Adult Vocational Teaching and Learning
CET	Certificate in Education and Training
CfBT	Centre for British Teachers
CIF	Common Inspection Framework
CPD	Continuing Professional Development
CPPD	Continuing Professional and Personal Development
CRB	Criminal Records Bureau
Credit	One credit equals 10 notional hours of learning (QCF)
CTLLS	Certificate in Teaching in the Lifelong Learning Sector
DBS	Disclosure and Barring Service
DCSF	Department for Children, Schools and Families
DET	Diploma in Education and Training
DfES	Department for Education and Skills
DIUS	Department for Industry, University and Skills
DTLLS	Diploma in Teaching in the Lifelong Learning Sector
EFA	Education funding agency
EHRC	Equality and Human Rights Committee
EQF	European Qualifications Framework
ESOL	English for speakers of other languages
ETF	Education and Training Foundation
FE	Further Education

FEDA	Further Education Development Agency
FENTO	Further Education National Training Organisation
FESS	Further Education and Skills Sector
FHEQ	Further and Higher Education Qualifications
FOG	Frequency of gobbledegook
GCSE	General certificate of secondary education
GLH	Guided learning hours
HE	Higher Education
HEI	Higher Education Institute
HSE	Health and Safety Executive
ICT	Information and Communication Technology
IfL	Institute for Learning
ILP	Individual learning plan
In-service	Employed in a teacher role
ISA	Independent Safeguarding Authority
ITE	Initial Teacher Education
ITT	Initial Teacher Training
JRF	Joseph Rowntree Foundation
LLN	Literacy, language and numeracy
LLS	Lifelong Learning Sector
LLUK	Lifelong Learning UK
LRC	Learning resource centre
LSA	Learning Support Assistant
LSIS	Learning Skills Improvement Services
NAO	National Audit Office
NARIC	National recognition information centre
NIACE	National Institute of Adult and Continuing Education
NQF	National Qualifications Framework
Ofqual	Office of Qualifications and Examinations Regulation
Ofsted	Office for Standards in Education
PCET	Post Compulsory Education and Training
PESTLE	Political, Economic, Social, Technological, Legislative and Environmental
PGCE	Post Graduate Certificate in Education
PISA	Programme for International Student Assessment
Pre-service	Not yet employed in a teaching role

PTLLS	Preparing to Teach in the Lifelong Learning Sector
QCF	Qualification Credit Framework
QTLS	Qualified Teacher Learning and Skills
RARPA	Recognising and recording progress and achievement
RNIB	Royal National Institute for the Blind
ROC	Rules of combination
RPL	Recognition of prior learning
SEN	Special Educational Needs
SFA	Skills Funding Agency
SMART	Specific, measurable, attainable, relevant, time bound
SoW	Scheme of Work
SQ3R	Survey, question, read, recite, review
SSC	Sector Skills Council
SWOT	Strengths, weaknesses, opportunities and threats
TA	Transactional analysis
TALENT	Training adult literacy ESOL and numeracy teachers
TES	*Times Educational Supplement*
UCU	University and College Union
VARK	Visual, auditory, read/write, kinaesthetic
WBL	Work-based learning

Appendix 3: Teaching and learning plan template

Teaching and learning plan

Teacher:	Course title:	Awarding body:
Location:	Date:	Time:
Number of learners:	Resources:	

Lesson aims:	Objectives – by the end of the lesson:
	• all learners must...
Equality and diversity/inclusivity:	• some learners will...
Development of Functional Skills:	• a few learners may...

Time	Teacher activity	Learner activity	Assessment	Resources		

Appendix 4: Individual learning plan

Individual Learning Plan

Learner name:		Course:	

Prior knowledge, experience and qualifications

Additional support requirements

Initial assessment results	Mathematics	English	Other

Long-term goal

Initial targets	Targets		Date to be achieved
	Stretch target		

1st review	Progress towards targets		
	Learner comments/self-assessment on progress		
	Revised targets		Date to be achieved
	Stretch target		

Appendix 5: Scheme of work template

Scheme of work

Teacher:		Course title:		Awarding body:			
Course aims:				Level:			
				Course length:		Lesson length:	
				Day(s):			
				Time:			

Week	Learning outcomes	Teaching / learning methods	Assessment methods	Resources

Appendix 6: CPD reflective template

Critical task

Based on the last time you attended CPD of any kind, fill in the reflective template. Make sure you think about how you are going to make use of the professional development (see Chapter 1 for further information about reflection).

CPD Reflective Template
Date:
CPD event Brief details (length of course, who delivered it, internal or external):
Participants Were other people from your workplace on the course? Where were the majority of people from?
Key learning outcomes* What did you learn/discover?
Reflections How can this be used in your teaching and learning?
Action points What actions do you need to take to use what you have learned in your job? (Do you need further training on this, do you need to speak to a line manager, can what you have learned be cascaded to other members of staff?)

* If you did not learn/discover anything useful, please use the boxes above to explain why this was. Perhaps the training was not at the right level for you or it was not appropriate for your job? Outline what training would be more suitable for you and discuss with your line manager.

Appendix 7: Chapter links to the Professional Standards

STANDARD	CHAPTER
Professional values and attributes	
Develop your own judgement of what works and does not work in your teaching and training.	
1 Reflect on what works best in your teaching and learning to meet the diverse needs of learners	Chapter 1
	Chapter 8
2 Evaluate and challenge your practice, values and beliefs	Chapter 1
	Chapter 8
	Chapter 11
3 Inspire, motivate and raise aspirations of learners through your enthusiasm and knowledge	Chapter 2
	Chapter 6
4 Be creative and innovative in selecting and adapting strategies to help learners to learn	Chapter 8
5 Value and promote social and cultural diversity, equality of opportunity and inclusion	Chapter 3
	Chapter 6
	Chapter 8
	Chapter 10
6 Build positive and collaborative relationships with colleagues and learners	Chapter 2
	Chapter 3
	Chapter 5
	Chapter 6
Professional knowledge and understanding	
Develop deep and critically informed knowledge and understanding in theory and practice.	
7 Maintain and update knowledge of your subject and/or vocational area	Chapter 2
	Chapter 10
	Chapter 11
8 Maintain and update your knowledge of educational research to develop evidence-based practice	Chapter 2
	Chapter 11

STANDARD	CHAPTER
9 Apply theoretical understanding of effective practice in teaching, learning and assessment drawing on research and other evidence	Chapter 4
	Chapter 5
	Chapter 6
	Chapter 9
	Chapter 11
10 Evaluate your practice with others and assess its impact on learning	Chapter 1
	Chapter 6
	Chapter 8
	Chapter 9
11 Manage and promote positive learner behaviour	Chapter 3
	Chapter 8
12 Understand the teaching and professional role and your responsibilities	Chapter 2
	Chapter 10
Professional skills	
Develop your expertise and skills to ensure the best outcomes for learners.	
13 Motivate and inspire learners to promote achievement and develop their skills to enable progression	Chapter 3
	Chapter 7
14 Plan and deliver effective learning programmes for diverse groups or individuals in a safe and inclusive environment	Chapter 6
	Chapter 7
	Chapter 8
	Chapter 9
	Chapter 10
15 Promote the benefits of technology and support learners in its use	Chapter 5
	Chapter 8
	Chapter 12
16 Address the mathematics and English needs of learners and work creatively to overcome individual barriers to learning	Chapter 7
	Chapter 8
	Chapter 12
17 Enable learners to share responsibility for their own learning and assessment, setting goals that stretch and challenge	Chapter 4
	Chapter 8
18 Apply appropriate and fair methods of assessment and provide constructive and timely feedback to support progression and achievement	Chapter 4
	Chapter 5

STANDARD	CHAPTER
19 Maintain and update your teaching and training expertise and vocational skills through collaboration with employers	Chapter 2 Chapter 10
20 Contribute to organisational development and quality improvement through collaboration with others	Chapter 10

Source: ETF (2014) *Professional Standards for Teachers and Trainers in Education and Training: England.* [Online]. Available at: www.et-foundation.co.uk (accessed May 2014).

Appendix 8: Abbreviations and acronyms quiz

How many of the following abbreviations and acronyms from the further education sector do you know?

ATLS...

BIS...

CAT..

CET..

CPD..

DBS..

DET..

ETF...

GLH..

HEI...

IfL..

ITE...

ITT...

LLN..

LSIS...

NIACE..

Ofsted..

PCET..

QCF..

QTLS..

RARPA...

SWOT...

VARK..

WBL...

You will find the answers to these in the glossary (Appendix 2) or in the content within this book.

Appendix 9: Reflections and actions from CPD event

CPD session topic: ....

Key points noted:

Relevance to my teaching and learning:

Implications for my area of work and for my role:

Response to these issues/actions I should take:
(eg discussion with a critical friend, line manager, colleagues; reading relevant newspapers, reports, etc.)

Answers

Below you will find answers to some of the questions within the Check your understanding section of each chapter.

CHAPTER 1

Question 1: Critical reflection and evaluation require you to develop and to use your meta-cognition (thinking about thinking) skills and to make a judgement about an issue or situation based on your reflections in order to improve your practice.

Question 2: Reflection can be through the identification and challenging of your assumptions and engaging in new or different ways of thinking. Reflection of practice can also be through the consideration of others' views, for example asking learners to complete end-of-module evaluation forms and speaking with peers and colleagues about your practice and to learners about their experiences.

Question 3: Effective reflection needs the involvement of another person (or persons) who is (or are) able to ask you appropriate questions so that you are able to consider and challenge any pre-held assumptions. Reading a broad range of literature can also help you to develop your skills of reflection as doing this can improve your understanding of a range of issues and topics.

Question 4: Answers could include:

○ Brookfield's four lens approach;

○ Kolb's experiential learning approach;

○ Schön's in and on action approach;

○ Argyris and Schön's single and double loop learning.

Question 6: Answers could include:

○ asking more questions;

○ making reflection of practice part of your daily routine;

○ listening to the views of others in order to change/build on your current thinking.

Question 7: Answers could include: keeping a diary or journal of your practice to see what, if any, the recurring issues are and then reflecting on possible reasons for this; engaging in CPD to remain current in your understanding of practice; recording yourself in practice and using this to critically reflect and evaluate your practice.

Question 10: Den could reflect about his reasons for wanting to be a teacher; why it is that the learners don't seem to be motivated – what can he, as their teacher, do about this (eg the quality of teaching and learning encounters) and what responsibility should the learners take for this? He may also want to reflect about how to manage his time more effectively.

These issues are impacting upon the learners' experiences and also on Den's experience as a trainee teacher. Den could continue to seek information from his peers and could also ask them for advice. He could ask the learners for more detailed feedback on the lessons and seek approaches that give the learners more responsibility for their own learning. He could make some changes to his lessons and management of time and he should reflect on and evaluate what difference the changes make to the previous issues encountered.

CHAPTER 2

Question 1: Answers could include:

○ promoting safe, supportive and inclusive environments for all learners;

○ adherence to key legislation, regulatory requirements and codes of practice;

○ modelling professional behaviour at all times to inspire your learners;

○ updating subject/industry expertise and requirements;

○ developing employer links;

○ contributing to a team of professionals;

○ contributing to curriculum development;

○ planning learning activities based on the needs of your group and specific individual needs within the group;

○ developing learning resources which are appropriate to the award aims, varied, accessible and intellectually challenging for your learners;

○ keeping accurate records to contribute to your organisation's quality improvement strategy, including accurate records of recruitment, retention, achievement and progression of learners;

○ providing learners with appropriate points of referral as required.

Question 2: Answers could include:

Equality Act 2010, Education Act 2011, Public Sector Equality Duty 2011, Equality and Human Rights Commission key concepts (2010).

CHAPTER 3

Question 1: Answers could include:

Enrolling learners without an IA: without an IA it is unlikely that you will know whether your teaching is excluding learners by not providing the right levels and types of learning strategies for them or (unless specified on the learners' application form) if reasonable adjustments for learners with SEN are necessary.

IA at the beginning of your course: any adjustments to your delivery will need to be made after you have already planned the course – adding extra work.

IA during your course: some courses work on a *roll-on, roll-off* basis, where learners join at any point of the year. While there are advantages to this you need to be mindful of possible barriers to learning, for example:

○   support systems must be able to be activated quickly to enable new learners immediate and appropriate access;

○   the need to plan your teaching to meet the changing needs of your learners;

○   the need to nurture a constantly changing group of learners;

○   if you teach on a *roll-on, roll-off* course, ensure that any new learners to your group settle in as soon as possible and with minimum disruption to the learners who are already on the course. This can be done through one-to-one tutorials, through group activities and by using a buddy system.

'Deficit model' IA: the DfES (2006) argue that a 'deficit model' regarding IA focuses only on what a learner cannot do and this demotivates learners as well as giving them a sense of failure right at the beginning of the course. Any IA should be a *'positive experience for learners'* (DfES, 2006, p 10).

'Box ticking' IA: the DfES (2006, p 10) found *box ticking* to be a common aspect of poor quality providers, eg not considering a broad range of learners' skills and needs.

IA to define and label learners with learning styles: during IA, you may use *learning styles* assessments or inventories which purport to identify specific ways in which learners learn. Findings may claim to inform the planning process to enable learning to take place in the most efficient learning style for the individual. However, there are inconsistencies in their usage and application (Coffield et al., 2004). Therefore, consider how information about your learners' learning styles can help engage them in their own learning process.

Question 2: Answers could include:

○   learners bring their ILP to the tutorial. An ILP kept in the staffroom is of no use to the learner;

○   learners outline discussion topics, including achievements, goals and study skills before the tutorial;

○   learners self-assess progress against targets regularly and bring their assessment to the tutorial. Ask the learners to write the ILP.

CHAPTER 4

Question 1: Answers could include:

○   splitting up practice assessments into small sections related to the topic that you're covering at the time. This gives vital assessment practice integrated into your normal learning routine;

o providing mock assessments towards the end of the course (although these can be time consuming);

o turning your objectives at the beginning of the lesson into questions at the end of the lesson/as a review at the beginning of the next lesson;

o asking learners to form questions based on the lesson and get them to test each other (QIA, 2008).

Question 2: Answers could include:

o What grade do you think should be given to the work you have handed in and why?

o What did you do best in the assessment and why?

o What did you do least well in this assessment and why?

o What was the hardest part of this assessment and why?

o What was the most important thing you learned in doing this assessment and why?

Question 5: Answers could include:

Examinations

Advantages: with robust ID checks this is an authentic assessment of the learner's own work. Rigorous piloting of questions and standardisation procedures should make results reliable and fairly easy to organise standard exam times and marking periods. Generally quite practical as scripts can be allocated between a team of markers and multiple-choice tests can be computer marked, but may have questionable validity in terms of assessing higher level affective or cognitive skills.

Challenges: examinations may focus on Bloom's (1956) lower cognitive levels of knowledge and understanding although Rust (2002) advocates exam tasks which focus on application rather than rote memorisation of facts. Not all learners respond well to examinations and they are not a particularly valid reflection of realistic work scenarios. Their time-limited nature means that they are testing learners' ability to work quickly as well as their ability in the subject, and this also reduces curriculum coverage, meaning it may lack sufficiency. Also, literary eloquence may be rewarded more than the actual substance of work (Rust, 2002). Multiple-choice tests can cover the curriculum very quickly, but this might be superficial as it is difficult to assess higher level skills of analysis and evaluation using such an approach.

Written essay/report

Advantages: Dunn (2002) argues that essays can promote higher level skills such as organisational capability, including ability to meet deadlines, critical thinking and analysis.

Challenges: it may be difficult to verify the authenticity of work submitted. Anti-plagiarism software is adept at spotting published materials, but the opportunity for others to do the work remains. While written assessments promote useful work-based higher level thinking skills, they do not assess the ability to practically apply them, so may lack validity. As with open answer exams, rigorous standardisation is required to agree on how the criteria are applied.

Observation of practice

Advantages: this approach scores highly in terms of validity by directly testing higher level affective skills. They can represent a real demonstration of learners' ability within their work environment, or at least a realistic simulation of one.

Challenges: workplace observations tend to be very expensive and time consuming in terms of staff time required. Observations need to be carefully standardised through joint observations on interpretation of criteria. Observed practice might not be a realistic representation of actual practice but a show put on for the assessor and they lack sufficiency as they will only cover a very small part of the syllabus, so must therefore target the most important aspects of work.

Project work

Advantages: project work combines knowledge and evidence of practical application and is generally a very valid approach to assessments. It can develop learner autonomy by giving learners' freedom to develop their own ideas.

Challenges: the autonomy associated with project work means that very clear criteria need to be set and understood by learners and assessors for reliable assessment – though subjectivity is to some extent inevitable. With extended projects there is a danger of external support (such as from parents) which can question the authenticity of the work. In terms of practicality resources might be expensive as well as difficulty finding storage space.

Work-based portfolios

Advantages: portfolios encourage personal development through enabling learners to demonstrate their application of knowledge in practice (Dunn, 2002). Professional development portfolios are useful for the learner to take to job interviews to evidence their achievement and ability to meet deadlines.

Challenges: portfolios can provide a tick-box approach based on meeting criteria rather than genuine in-depth engagement with the learners' professional development. Unless submitted online, these can become very unwieldy and also can struggle to evidence authenticity. Portfolios should therefore be focused in terms of what is required with learners graded on the quality rather than quantity of work submitted – after all, the ability to sift and sort information is a key employment skill.

Presentations/posters

Advantages: useful for demonstrating knowledge and understanding skills, these can also develop broader employability skills relating to self-confidence, communication and ICT.

Challenges: they can be time consuming to assess and have the same reliability issues of observation.

CHAPTER 5

Question 1: Communication is the exchange of information in a range of forms between two or more people and will involve a range of elements including verbal communication, non-verbal communication and para-language.

Question 2: The rules of communication indicate the accepted behaviours in communication given a certain set of circumstances.

Question 3: Shannon and Weaver's model comprises sender, receiver and the notion of interference or noise.

Question 4: Both Berlo's and Shannon and Weaver's models comprise sender, receiver and interference. However, Berlo's model recognises that communication skills, attitudes, knowledge, social systems and cultural factors also influence communication.

Question 6: Providing feedback using a range of methods can help to engage learners with different feedback preferences, however, it may be confusing to learners who prefer a consistent approach and mean that the feedback is not conveyed effectively.

Question 7: Kinesics is the study of body and facial movements whereas para-language involves the study of elements of speech, including pitch, tone and speed.

CHAPTER 6

Question 1: An inclusive learning environment is one in which the teacher ensures that learners are not excluded for any reason and meets the needs of a diverse range of learners.

Question 2: A motivating learning environment will make learners feel welcomed and valued and will help them to achieve. It will also reduce the possibility of behavioural problems occurring.

Question 3: Extrinsic motivation is provided by a source external to the learner, whereas intrinsic motivation comes from within the learners themselves.

Question 4: You might have suggested a pay rise or other financial incentives, a qualification, a trophy or career progression.

Question 5: Maslow's hierarchy suggests that if lower stages are not met learners will not be motivated to meet higher level needs.

Question 7: Resources should be evaluated to ensure that they meet the varied needs of learners and are effective in supporting learning.

CHAPTER 7

Question 1: You probably recognised that the *purpose* of initial assessment was overlooked in this example. Whilst appropriate records should of course be maintained, any auditors and inspectors would expect to not only see the records but how the teacher has taken those into account when planning for both the group as a whole and the individual learners.

Question 2: All courses will have elements of the teaching of skills, knowledge and attitudes and by exploring these you will gain a better understanding of the individual elements and will be able to tailor your planning accordingly.

Question 3: Clear aims and objectives not only enable you to identify what you want the learners to learn during a lesson, but they provide the learner with an opportunity to self-assess their progress towards those aims and objectives.

Question 4: A scheme of work is a long-term planning document and there will be one scheme of work for a course that you deliver. A teaching and learning plan is a short-term planning document and you will have one of these for every lesson that you teach.

Question 5: An ILP evidences the learner journey through the course and allows the learner to take responsibility for their own learning.

Question 6: Learners need to learn more than just course content in order to put them in the best position to secure employment when they have completed their course.

Question 7: As a teacher in FE you need to be able to support learners in developing their own skills in each of the areas. Additionally, you need to be aware of issues that may hinder the development of those skills in order to effectively overcome them.

CHAPTER 8

Question 1: Answers could include:

Before the lesson

○   Do you have a scheme of work and teaching and learning plan that is appropriate for the needs of the learners (individuals and group) and the subject?

○   Do you have access to all of the resources needed for that lesson, including any extension activities?

○   Is any technical equipment needed working, do you have a back-up plan for any failure of technical equipment?

○   Does the room layout need changing?

At the beginning of the lesson

○   take the register and remember to record any latecomers as they arrive;

○   challenge latecomers, as appropriate;

○   recap the topic from the previous lesson;

○   make sure learners understand what the learning outcomes are for that lesson.

In the lesson

○   use activities that are interesting and suit learners' needs in terms of ability;

○   get the learners actively engaged in the learning;

○   make sure that the learners understand how what you are teaching them fits into their vocational or academic area and how it can be used in their everyday lives;

○   give the learners clear instructions about what they should be doing in each part of the lesson, including assessment strategies;

○   vary assessment strategies including self-assessment and peer assessment, where appropriate;

○   make sure the learners' individual needs, equality and diversity are catered for and all learners are engaged in the learning;

○   support literacy, numeracy and language where appropriate;

○   use age-appropriate, inclusive resources, including ICT;

○   give feedback within the lesson (written and verbal);

○   be aware of and address any inappropriate behaviour or language.

Towards the end of the lesson

○   check if learning outcomes have been met;

○   ask or get the learners to write down what they have learned;

○   check to see if any elements are still outstanding and need to be carried over to the next lesson;

○   make sure that any homework is clearly set;

○   explain to the learners what you are going to cover in the next lesson and how it fits in with what has been done in the current lesson.

At the end of the lesson

○   gain verbal feedback as soon as possible from your observer;

○   reflect on the lesson, using your own feedback as well as your observer's feedback;

○   write a reflective account of the lesson;

○   discuss the lesson, feedback and reflection with your mentor;

○   build on any developmental aspects for your next lesson and your next observation.

Question 2: Answers could include:

Why do we differentiate?: To ensure that nobody gets left behind or demotivated due to not being sufficiently challenged.

Benefits to the learner: Provides opportunities to discover personal strengths and intelligences. There is likely to be less frustration due to confusion or boredom.

Benefits to the teacher: A greater understanding of each learner's ability to learn. It allows equal opportunity for success for all learners. Perhaps less behavioural issues as all learners can access the learning.

Question 3: Answers could include:

Case study 1: the protected characteristic that is potentially being discriminated against is disability. This could be unlawful discrimination as it could be considered a failure by the school to make a reasonable adjustment. The person could complain to the college. If the college didn't do anything about it, then they could speak to a lawyer and make a claim under the Equality Act 2010.

Case study 2: the protected characteristic that is potentially being discriminated against is religion and belief. This could be unlawful discrimination, although it could be objectively justified as a proportionate means of achieving a legitimate aim – ie it could be considered reasonable. The person could complain to the hairdressers. If the hairdressers didn't do anything about it, then they could speak to a solicitor and make a claim under the Equality Act 2010.

Case study 3: the protected characteristic that is potentially being discriminated against is race. This could be unlawful discrimination because of treating a person less favourably because of their race. They could complain to another teacher who should do something about it. If they didn't then they could speak to a solicitor and make a claim under the Equality Act 2010.

Case study 4: the protected characteristic that is potentially being discriminated against is pregnancy and maternity. This could be unlawful discrimination and the person could complain to the college. If the college didn't do anything about it, then they could speak to a solicitor and make a claim under the Equality Act 2010.

CHAPTER 9

Question 1: Answers could include:

○ a course of study;

○ all of the courses in an organisation;

○ the content that you teach;

○ knowledge or skills;

○ a teacher's plan or timetabled lessons.

Question 2: Answers could include:

○ curriculum levels (Porter, 2002) – intended, enacted, assessed, learned;

○ dimensions (Nasta, 1994) – quality, accessibility and validity.

Question 4: Answers could include:

○   in order to develop your own practice;

○   to meet organisational requirements;

○   to ensure that the course is as effective as possible;

○   to ensure that the course still meets the needs of its intended audience.

Question 5: The quality of a course is not judged only by the quality of teaching. Quality also includes retention and achievement rates and these are always an organisational priority because they provide statistics on which they themselves are judged.

Question 6: Analysis of curriculum requires that you examine in detail the multiple aspects and influences, whereas evaluation requires that you identify the strengths and areas for development. The two are inextricably linked, with analysis informing every stage of evaluation.

CHAPTER 10

Question 1: In order to build on the excellent examples of practice the CAVTL had observed, they make ten recommendations – these can be located from the Excellence Gateway: www.excellencegateway.org.uk/ (accessed 26 May 2014).

Question 3: Answers could include:

○   internal and external verification processes;

○   college observations;

○   safeguarding.

Question 4: Answers could include:

○   numeracy and mathematics and the need for functional skills;

○   learners who are not in education, employment or training (NEETS);

○   raising the school leaving age;

○   GCSE mathematics and English.

CHAPTER 11

Question 1: Answers could include:

○   checking if the research appears in a peer-reviewed journal;

○   if the research methodology is reliable;

○   if researchers are conforming to the ethical guidelines produced by BERA.

Question 2: Answers could include:

○   qualitative research is based on people's thoughts, ideas, beliefs and observations for you to then interpret;

- quantitative research is based on numerical data that can be statistically analysed and is less open to interpretation;

- mnemonic for remembering the difference: qualitative has an 'l' in the middle of the word = literature; whereas quantitative has an 'n' in the middle of the word = numbers.

Question 3: BERA is the organisation that has responsibility for the ethical guidelines that should be employed in any educational research. You might be carrying out research and using the guidelines yourself or checking the validity and reliability of research using the guidelines.

Question 4: An example could include to be recognised as a specialist, you need up-to-date information. This gives you credibility both with your learners and with your peers. Why would you want to deliver out-of-date information? As part of the Professional Standards, it is your responsibility, as a teacher, to remain current.

Question 5: Edward has quite a few options open to him. He could progress on to a Masters in Education. Or he could complete a level 5 subject specialist qualification in mathematics. This would make him more employable. Edward may opt to keep up to date with his specialist area through non-accredited forms of CPD.

CHAPTER 12

Question 1: Answers could include:

Q	Does it need to be a current text?	A	Yes, it does need to be relatively recent – within the last few years, unless there is nothing more recent to use or you are going back to an original source, of a theory, for example. Always check to see if you are using the most up-to-date edition of a book.
Q	How do you know if a text is academically reliable?	A	If it is contained within an academic library then chances are it is worth reading. Look on the internet for reviews and also look at the publisher to see what else they have published.
Q	Are internet sites worth visiting?	A	Yes, but look at them in the same way as a book, ask questions and make a judgement to see if it is more anecdotal than academic.
Q	Can I reference Wikipedia?	A	There is nothing wrong with Wikipedia as a starting point for research but it should then lead you to other places from which to get your information.
Q	Are search engines, for example Google, the only way to make an academic search?	A	No, there are others that can be tried and used. The organisation that you are studying at may have links to various academic databases and search engines, you can also use websites such as Refseek (2013) which makes academic information accessible to all.

Question 2: Examples of critical writing are underlined in the text below.

Links between entry qualifications and achievement

There is some existing literature on student retention in HE based on entry qualifications in certain subjects <u>that is relevant to this research because it suggests a clear correlation between levels of achievement on entry to HE, and retention and achievement in certain subjects</u>. For example, the National Audit Office (NAO) (2007) found that full-time university students with three A grades at A-level (3A students) were more likely to continue to the second year of a medical degree course than those with two D grades at A-level (2D students) with an odds ratio of 2.2. The odds ratio is a comparison of the chances of 3A students proceeding to the second year of their degree course, compared with the 2D students. On this basis 3A students were 2.2 times more likely to proceed to the second year of their course than 2D students. <u>This corroborates the finding of Arulampalam et al. (2004) which stated a direct correlation between the A-level entry profile of medical students and the drop-out rate, ie the higher the A-level profile, the less likely a student was to drop out</u>. An attrition rate of 2.9 per cent of those with more than 340 UCAS points was contrasted with 5.2 per cent in those with less than 200 UCAS points. This was endorsed by the findings of Jeffreys (2007), who undertook a retrospective evaluation study in the US to assess (inter alia) the entry characteristics of associate degree nursing students from a sample of students entering the first clinical nursing course in 1997–98. Jeffreys found that the graduates had higher grade point averages in their pre-nursing qualifications than non-graduates.

The literature thus far suggests a link between entry qualifications, retention and achievement, <u>however, its limitations in relation to the current topic must be noted. Firstly, the timespan covered by Arulampalam et al. (2004) ended 19 years ago, when BTEC Nationals did not actually exist, and the profile of threshold qualifications was different to that which exists today</u>. Secondly, the environmental context of Jeffreys' study is in a <u>different educational jurisdiction</u> and involves entry-level qualifications that are a specific pre-nursing qualification requirement. Furthermore, both Jeffreys and Arulampalam et al. were <u>investigating medical courses which carry a more vocational and practical component than the business courses that are the subject of this research</u>. Their <u>findings may not therefore be generalisable to other disciplines, and so further investigation is warranted</u>.

Index